A Final Accounting

A Final Accounting

Philosophical and Empirical Issues in Freudian Psychology

Edward Erwin

A Bradford Book
The MIT Press
Cambridge, Massachusetts
London, England

This book was set in New Baskerville by Wellington Graphics and was printed and bound in the United States of America.

Library of Congress Cataloging-inPublication Data

Erwin, Edward, 1937–
A final accounting : philosophical and empirical issues in Freudian psychology / Edward Erwin.
   p. cm.
"A Bradford book."
Includes bibliographical references and index.
ISBN 0-262-05050-1 (alk. paper)
1. Psychoanalysis. 2. Freud, Sigmund, 1856–1939. I. Title.
BF173.E658 1995
150.19′52—dc20   95-8338
                                                                    CIP

To Patricia

Contents

Acknowledgments

I would like to thank the following colleagues who read parts of the manuscript or made useful suggestions: Alan Goldman, Howard Pospesel, Susan Haack, Ramon Lemos, Harvey Siegel, Risto Hilpinen, Leonard Carrier, Eddy Zemach, Reed Richter, Morris Eagle, Fred Crews, Sidney Gendin, Lowell Kleiman, and Shiela Fox. I would also like to thank three anonymous referees for the MIT Press for their helpful comments.

I am grateful as well to Maria Reynardus for typing most of the manuscript, and to Bertha Danon and Lianne Dookie for their help in preparing the manuscript.

Most of all, I would like to thank two people. The first is my wife Patricia, to whom the book is dedicated, who made a number of useful critical suggestions. The second is my good friend Adolf Grünbaum. His seminal work on psychoanalysis has set the highest of standards for rigorous scholarship in this area. His suggestions for improving the text were extremely useful and are too numerous to itemize.

Some of the chapters originated in earlier published work of mine including the following: "Establishing Causal Connections: Meta-Analysis and Psychotherapy," *Midwest Studies in Philosophy* IX (1984); "Is Confirmation Differential?" (co-author, H. Siegel), *British Journal for the Philosophy of Science* 40 (1989); "Philosophers on Freudianism: An Examination of Replies to Grünbaum's Foundations," in J. Earman, A. Janis, G. Massey, and N. Rescher (eds.) *Philosophical Problems of the Internal and External Worlds: Essays Concerning the Philosophy of Adolf Grünbaum,* Pittsburgh: University of Pittsburgh Press (1993); "The Effectiveness of Psychotherapy: Epistemological Issues" in G. Graham and G. Stephens (eds.) *Philosophical Psychopathology,* Cambridge, Mass.: MIT Press (1994); "On the Logic of Psychoanalytic Explanations: A Reply to Nussbaum," *Philosophy and Social Criticism* 20 (1994); and "The Effectiveness of Psychoanalytic Therapy: A Question of Standards" in W. O'Donahue and R. Kitchener (eds.) *Psychology and Philosophy: Interdisciplinary Problems and Responses;* Boston: Allyn and Bacon, in press.

Introduction

More than 100 years have elapsed since Sigmund Freud and his collaborator Joseph Breuer published their "Preliminary Communication." Is that not enough time for the development of a consensus concerning Freud's legacy? With some hard work and sober reflection, should it not have been possible to sift the evidence and to determine with some measure of finality what is valuable in his work? It should have been, but such a "final accounting" has not yet been given, or if it has, no consensus exists about what it shows.

Most scholars agree that Freud was a genius and that his theories and therapy have had a profound impact on Western culture. Once we go beyond these two points, however, we are likely to encounter wildly conflicting evaluations. On one side, there is the judgment of the Nobel prize–winning biologist Peter Medawar (1975, 17), that Freud was the creator of "the most stupendous intellectual confidence trick of the twentieth century," and the verdict of a leading British psychologist, Hans Eysenck (1985), that what is true in Freud's work is not new and what is new is not true. On the pro-Freudian side, there is the assessment of Ernest Jones that Freud was the Darwin of the Mind, and the judgment of the philosopher of science Arthur Pap, that psychoanalysis competes with relativity theory and quantum theory for the title of the most dramatic intellectual revolution of this century. Many commentators avoid these extreme characterizations of Freud's contribution, and are content to argue that some of his ideas are profoundly important, original, and right, but others are quite wrong. Yet, many of these same writers will radically disagree with one another if asked the further question: Exactly which Freudian propositions are true and which are false?

Even if we disagree about the truth of Freud's claims, can we at least agree about how his research program is faring? Here are some recent assessments. One writer claims that his program is clearly on the wane (Kitcher 1992); another notes that the clinical psychology of today is closer to psychoanalysis than it was a decade ago and is rapidly converging on it (Erdelyi 1985); a third says that Freud's reputation and place in the history of the modern world have never stood higher or enjoyed a firmer security than they do today (Marcus 1984).

Disagreements of this sort are not rare in the social sciences, but the Freudian case may be unique. It is difficult to think of another scientific theory that has been assessed by so many reputable scholars, over such a long period of time, without a consensus developing concerning its merit. Whether the case is unique or not, the persistent disagreement invites speculation about its cause. One possibility is that Freudian theory is not scientific at all; it is a grand piece of metaphysics or a prime example of pseudoscience. Consequently, it cannot be assessed empirically in the manner that scientific theories generally are. This account, if true, would explain why pro-Freudians and their antagonists have been unable to find evidence cogent enough to convince the other side, but it fails to explain why so many participants in the debate believe that we possess firm evidence either for or against central parts of Freudian theory.

A second possibility is one that Freud himself favored. If his theory is true, it is not surprising that many people will feel so threatened by what it says that they will be motivated to dismiss supporting evidence. This explanation, of course, will not appeal to those who doubt the theory's truth, but there is a problem even if the theory is true. Many supporters of Freudian theory and therapy have never been psychoanalyzed. Why, as a class, are they not threatened by the theory's content to roughly the same degree that anti-Freudians are?

There are many other possible causes of why Freudians and anti-Freudians disagree, and probably no single factor explains all of the disagreements. There is one factor, however, that I believe is of major importance, both causally and philosophically. It causes much of the disagreement, but it would be of philosophical interest even if its causal role were minor. I am referring to disagreement about the proper standards to be used in evaluating Freud's theory and therapy. Two competent commentators, with seemingly healthy psyches, will often look at the same body of evidence and reach widely divergent conclusions because they use different criteria of assessment. Sometimes the disagreement about standards is hidden in the conflicting arguments, but often it is openly acknowledged.

Questions about standards surface in the Freudian debates in several forms. Perhaps the most abstract issue concerns scientific realism. Should Freudian theory be evaluated "realistically," that is, should we judge it on the basis of whether its postulated entities and processes really do exist, and whether what the theory says about them is true? One alternative, recommended by some analysts and philosophers of science, is that we be content to determine whether the observable data are "as if" the theory is true; another is that we judge the theory solely by its utility in generating and guiding clinical research. I do not object to the use of such pragmatic criteria, but I assume, partly for reasons given in Erwin (1992), that it is also of value to ask of Freud's hypotheses: Are they true?

A second basic question about standards is whether Freudian theory should be assessed by *scientific* standards as opposed to those commonly employed in the humanities. If we answer affirmatively, a third question naturally arises. Should the theory be judged by the standards used in physics, or should some other science, say biology or medicine, serve as a model for evaluation? Or should Freud's theory be judged by criteria that are, to some degree, unique to a psychoanalytic paradigm?

If one argues, as I intend to, that the appropriate criteria for judging Freudian theory are, with some qualifications, the same as are proper for judging any scientific theory, then another question arises, which is probably the hardest question of all. What *are* the proper standards for assessing a scientific theory? Finally, there is the much debated question about the *kind* of evidence needed to confirm Freudian causal claims. Is experimental evidence needed? Always? Most of the time? Or, as Freud himself held, can nonexperimental clinical case studies often yield satisfactory, confirming evidence?

If we ask about the effectiveness of psychoanalytic therapy, some of the issues about standards will be the same as those concerning the evaluation of Freudian theory. For example, there is an ongoing debate about whether an experimental standard must be met or whether case studies can be confirmatory under certain conditions. However, some important issues arise only for the therapy. One concerns the idea of a therapeutic benefit. What are the proper criteria for deciding whether an outcome is beneficial to the client? Should we be guided primarily by the therapeutic goals of psychoanalysis or by criteria external to a psychoanalytic paradigm? If the latter, what are the "right" criteria? Do they even exist? Or is the choice of outcome criteria ultimately subjective?

A second outcome question concerns the standard to be used in judging effectiveness *after* determining criteria for a beneficial outcome. Is it sufficient that a therapy do better than no treatment, or must it also have the capacity to outperform a credible placebo? The answer one gives to this question will have a crucial impact on how one evaluates experimental studies of psychoanalytic effectiveness. Although it is arguable that there are no experimental studies of orthodox, long term psychoanalysis, there have been such studies of short term psychoanalytically oriented psychotherapy. These studies are of uneven quality and to some extent their results conflict. This raises one more issue about standards. In evaluating the outcome evidence, should we proceed along the lines of the traditional "qualitative review"—impeach the studies that fall below a certain epistemic standard, throw them out, and somehow make sense of the remaining data? Or, as many reviewers and statisticians now argue, should we employ the methods of data integration developed by proponents of meta-analysis?

I can now state the two main goals of this book: first, to fix the proper standards for evaluating the Freudian evidence and, second, to use them in determining exactly which Freudian hypotheses are true and which are false. I develop standards primarily in part I. In part II, I use them to reach conclusions about what the evidence shows.

Evaluating the best current evidence is important, but can we do more? Are we now in a position to give a "final accounting" of Freud's work? Before answering, I should say what this means, or rather what *I* mean.

If we mean a verdict that is certain, in the sense that it could not possibly be overturned by new evidence, then no assessment of Freud's work can be final in this sense. A more modest goal would be to give a final accounting in the same sense that we have given one for, say, the hypothesis that penicillin is effective in treating syphilis, or that Laetrile is not effective in treating cancer, or, to take a case more analogous to Freud's, Darwin's theory. We have enough evidence in such cases to warrant belief in the respective propositions, even if new evidence could conceivably make a difference. In this sense, we can render a "final" verdict, one not likely to be nullified by new discoveries. Can we do something analogous for Freud's hypotheses?

One practical problem is that the body of existing evidence is quite large. There are well over 1500 experimental studies of the theory, and a large mass of clinical data, as well as evidence from everyday life. I try to deal with this difficulty by focussing on the best evidence that we now possess. Another problem is the myriad of Freudian hypotheses—too many to deal with in a medium–sized book. I propose to handle this problem by concentrating primarily on Freud's central hypotheses, especially those that are now claimed to have some empirical support. Freudian hypotheses that are clearly speculative, such as his conjecture about the origin of theism, are rarely claimed to be supported by evidence, and will not be discussed here.

Concerning the remainder of Freud's hypotheses, I believe that once we fix the proper standards of evaluation, we are in a position to say of *some* of them: There is now enough evidence to judge that this one is true and that one is false. In most cases, alas, the evidence is not so strong in either direction. Consequently, our judgments must be much more tentative. The most we can reasonably say is: This hypothesis has very little empirical support (or no support at all, or is even disconfirmed to some degree); or the hypothesis has more than a little support, but not enough to warrant our believing it.

For most parts of Freudian theory, then, I do not believe that the evidence warrants either acceptance or rejection. Yet, in another sense, I think that a final accounting is possible. If one uses the right standards of evaluation, and gives a correct reading of the current overall evidence, then, except in a few areas where new research is likely to change the picture, a final verdict can be rendered, not because the evidence is definitive, but because it is not likely to get any better. Whether this is so or not depends on several factors, including the kind of evidence that is required for confirmation. The issue of a final accounting is taken up in the last chapter.

This book is intended for philosophers, psychiatrists, psychologists, and others who are interested in either the fate of Freudian theory or therapy, or in philosophical issues about criteria of theory evaluation. The philosophical issues most relevant to assessing the Freudian evidence are the epistemological and philosophy of science issues talked about in part I, but some conceptual, philosophy of mind, and evaluative issues are also discussed in part II.

Part I

Chapter 1

Non-Natural Science Standards

Before turning to evidential issues, it will be useful to say something about the hypotheses to be evaluated.

It is extremely difficult to lay out all of Freudian theory, and it is doubtful that anyone has done this in a perspicuous way (see, e.g., Holt 1989, 327, on the difficulty of separating the clinical theory from the metapsychology). Here, I will be content to specify important parts of Freud's theory, relying heavily on the formulations of writers sympathetic to Freud, such as Brenner (1973), Fisher and Greenberg (1977, 1985), and Kline (1981).

As several commentators have pointed out, it can be misleading to talk as if there were a single item that is "Freudian theory." What often goes by that name is a collection of minitheories that are in varying degrees independent of one another. The epistemological significance of this fact is that they are not all likely to be felled by the same blow. Some may be true; others may be false.

The Hypotheses

The Mental Apparatus

Perhaps the most widely known part of Freudian theory is the division of the human mind into consciousness, the preconscious, and the unconscious. In addition, there is a threefold division of a different sort: an id, ego, and superego. The id is present at birth, is unconscious, and is the source of all instinctual energy. The ego develops out of the id, is partly conscious, and protects against the id's unacceptable impulses by the operation of defense mechanisms, especially repression. As the child develops, he or she internalizes certain characteristics and demands of the parents; thus, the super-ego or conscience is formed.

The Theory of Dreams

In *The Interpretation of Dreams* (1900, *S.E.*, 4, 5), Freud held that all dreams are wish fulfillments. Furthermore, the operative wishes are repressed wishes originating from the infantile period. They affect dream content in the following way. Dreams serve a sleep-preserving function, but that function is interfered with by wishes emanating from the unconscious that are unacceptable to the ego. Because a person's usual defenses are weakened during sleep, the ego is forced to compromise: sleep continues, and the repressed wishes are allowed into consciousness as the person dreams, but only in a disguised form. So there is something akin to censorship: the dreamer is allowed to become aware of something that reflects a repressed infantile wish, but not in a recognizable form.

Freud thus distinguishes between the manifest and latent content of a dream, that is, the collection of dream images experienced by the dreamer and their underlying meaning. Many of the items that appear as part of the manifest content are symbols, most of which are sexual in nature. In addition to interpreting the dream symbols, an important technique for deciphering the dream is to have the dreamer free–associate about its manifest content. At least in theory, an analyst can thus figure out the latent content and ultimately learn about the dream's unconscious determinants.

The foregoing, simplified account needs to be modified in more than one way. In his later writings (1925, *S.E.*, 20), Freud concedes that not every dream represents a wish fulfillment. Sometimes, as in anxiety dreams, the attempt to represent a repressed wish fails. A better formulation, then, is that every dream constitutes an *attempt* at wish fulfillment. Furthermore, Freud later agrees, in his *An Outline of Psychoanalysis* (1940, *S.E.*, 23), that a residue of preconscious activity in adult waking life can also affect the content of a dream.

Personality Types and Stages of Sexual Development

According to orthodox Freudian theory, each of us goes through four stages of sexual development. In the first year of life, the child passes through the oral stage, during which the mouth is its primary source of pleasure. During the next 3 years, the anal stage, the child's interest shifts to the anus. How it responds to such things as toilet training, defecating, and, in general, the use of its bowels, can have an important effect on personality development. Roughly, from age 3 to 5 years, the child passes through the phallic period, and its genitals become of major concern. There is then a latency period until puberty when an interest in sexual things re-emerges.

How the child reacts during the various stages of sexual development may play a crucial role in the development of the adult personality. A child may become fixated at one stage, or because of later problems may regress to it. In his "Character and Anal Erotism" (1908, *S.E.*, 9), Freud describes the constellation of traits causally linked to the anal stage. The anal character consists essentially of three traits: obstinacy, parsimony, and orderliness. Other Freudians, most notably Abraham ([1924] 1965), have also delineated an oral character. Which traits are likely to be present, however, will vary depending on whether their etiology is linked to the early oral (sucking) or later oral (biting) stage. Kline (1981, 10), following Abraham, connects such items as optimism, impatience, hostility, and cruelty to the sucking stage, and envy, hostility, and jealousy to the biting stage.

The Oedipal Phase and the Castration Complex

Approximately, between the ages of 3 to 5 years, the male child develops a desire to possess his mother sexually, and sees his father as his chief rival. Soon, however, partly because of threats he receives in reaction to his masturbation, the boy comes to fear that his father will cut off his penis. If he can recall seeing genitals of females, he will infer that these females have been castrated and this will enhance his fear that he will be the next victim. Thus, the child develops castration anxiety. As a consequence, the oedipal period comes to an end. The boy ceases his sexual advances to his mother, and begins to identify with his father.

When the female child discovers that men have a penis and she does not, she concludes that she has been castrated. She turns against her mother, whom she blames for this state of affairs, and develops a desire for a penis, or "penis envy." She then shifts her affection toward the father, whom she fantasizes as impregnating her. The oedipal phase comes to an end for the female, not because of fear of castration, but because of fear of loss of love.

There has long been controversy about the centrality of the oedipal theory to Freudian theory, but it clearly was of great importance to Freud. Kline (1981, 131) quotes Freud as saying " . . . if psychoanalysis could boast of no other achievement than the discovery of the repressed Oedipus complex, that alone would give it a claim to be counted among the precious new acquisitions of mankind."

The Defense Mechanisms

In his early writings, Freud sometimes uses "repression" as a synonym for "defense." In later works, repression counts as but one kind of defense: the keeping of something out of consciousness. (Whether this is all there is to the Freudian idea of repression is controversial; see the discussion of repression in chapter 6, pp. 220–224.) Still, repression is of far more importance in Freudian theory than any of the other defense mechanisms. It plays a crucial role in Freudian explanations of the etiology of the psychoneuroses, dreams, and parapraxes. Indeed, as Grünbaum points out (1984, 3), Freud saw the idea of repression as the "cornerstone" of the whole structure of psychoanalysis (1914, *S.E.* 14:16).

Other Freudian defense mechanisms include denial, reaction formation, projection, and displacement. In denial, the ego wards off something from the external world which it feels as painful; it does this by denying some perception that brings knowledge of such a demand on the part of reality. When engaging in reaction formation, the subject develops an attitude or behavior that is the opposite of the one being defended against. In projection, one attributes to someone else characteristics of oneself that one unconsciously rejects. Displacement involves the ego's protecting against instinctual demands of the id by redirecting aggression originally aimed at someone or some thing, and redirecting it toward someone else or some other thing.

The Etiology of Psychoneuroses and Slips

Freud distinguishes between "actual neuroses," such as anxiety neurosis and neurasthenia, and "psychoneuroses," such as obsessional neurosis, hysteria, and depression. The former are caused by events in adult life and are not explainable by Freudian theory. The psychoneuroses, in contrast, arise from the repression of erotic wishes; their symptoms are compromise formations. In fact, neurotic symptoms represent the most economical expression of unconscious conflicts. If they are eliminated without changing the underlying psychic conflict, new and less advantageous symptoms are likely to arise.

Slips of the tongue and other parapraxes, insofar as Freudian theory purports to explain them, are analogous to neuroses. They are caused by repressed wishes, and also constitute compromise formations.

Paranoia

In the Freudian account, the delusions of the paranoid represent a defense against repressed, unacceptable homosexual urges. Through reaction formation, the proposition "I love him" is transformed in his psyche into "I hate him." That proposition, in turn, is transformed, through projection, into "He hates me." It is thus "a remarkable fact," Freud writes, "that the familiar principal forms of paranoia can all be represented as contradictions of the single proposition 'I (a man) *love him* (a man)'" (Freud's emphasis, 1911, *S.E.*, 12:63).

The above highly schematic and incomplete account is intended to identify some of the major sections of Freudian theory to be evaluated; it clearly is not intended to be a substitute for a detailed presentation of Freud's views. One thing that should be clear, however, is that the subject is Freudian theory and therapy (see chapter 6), not later psychoanalytic theories such as ego psychology, object relations theory, or self-psychology. Many of the epistemological arguments of part 1 are relevant to these theories as well, but they are not my topic (for an excellent discussion of the evidence for these theories, see Eagle 1993).

The topic is also not Freud himself. There has been much discussion recently of arguments that Freud was guilty of self-deception or even calculated fraud in his handling of some of his evidence (Esterson 1993; Crews 1993; Masson 1984). These arguments are clearly relevant to the history of psychoanalysis and to the assessment of Freud's scientific integrity, but they bear on only some of Freud's arguments, and they are clearly insufficient to undermine all of the evidence that others have tried to amass in support of Freudian theory and therapy. I turn next to issues about evidential standards.

Evidential Standards

What are the proper standards for evaluating Freudian hypotheses? One tradition holds that we should use non-natural science criteria, a second that we use the same standards that are employed in the natural sciences. I take up the first tradition in this chapter and the other in the next.

Intuitive Credibility

Some who argue for the use of special evidential standards in Freudian psychology employ such concepts as *self-evidence, insight,* or *intuitive credibility.* The philosopher and psychiatrist Karl Jaspers was one of the first to defend such a standard, although in one crucial respect his view was different from contemporary Freudians. In his *General Psychopathology* (1963), Jaspers refers to the 1922 edition of the same work, where he argues for a psychology of "meaningful connections." He claims that the proper standard for determining meaningful connections is self-evidence, but he does not apply this standard directly to Freud's theory, which he takes to be causal in nature. Instead, he recommends its use in judging the theory that is to replace Freudian theory. In fact, he rejects Freud's theory precisely because of its causal character: "The falseness of the Freudian claim lies in the mistaking of meaningful connections for causal connections" (Jaspers, 1963, 539).

Some contemporary Freudians in the Jaspers tradition liken psychoanalytic interpretations to judgments about works of art. Just as an art critic might have the insight that the elements in a painting have a harmonious relationship to one another, an experienced analyst, at some point in the analysis, can intuit that a certain interpretation of the patient's problem is correct.

The philosopher Charles Taylor has developed a view of this sort. He points out (Taylor 1985) that there are two rival epistemologies that divide American psychologists: the classical and the hermeneutical. The "classical" view, he claims, is dominant among experimentalists. It includes at least two principles. The first requires that hypotheses be "intersubjectively univocal," by which Taylor means that they be based on what he calls "brute data" (117, 121). The second requires that the auxiliary assumptions that link data to a hypothesis be interpretation-free (118).

The first requirement of the classical model, Taylor claims, rules out the use of certain data that we encounter in everyday life, such as the judgment that a painting reflects a powerful harmony between certain elements, or judgments about peoples' characters and motives (118). Taylor's other examples include psychoanalytic interpretations of verbal slips, and the application of the concepts of resistance and repression. These psychoanalytic examples show, Taylor argues, that psychoanalysis cannot meet the demands of the classical epistemological model, nor need they. Psychoanalysis, he claims, is an example—"the most obvious case" (122)—of a hermeneutical science.

What sort of evidential standards does the hermeneutical view presuppose? In his 1985 paper, Taylor does not say, but in an earlier influential paper (1979, 66), he claims that the sciences of man, insofar as they are hermeneutical, have to rely on intuition. In this respect, they differ from the physical sciences, whose theories can be judged by their predictive capacities. Theories in the hermeneutical sciences, in contrast, "are founded on intuitions" (Taylor 1979, 71).

Let us see how the appeal to intuition might work in an example where a Freudian interpretation is offered. Consider an actual case of a 54 year old schizophrenic woman who dragged a broom around a hospital ward for approximately 1 year. Allyon, Haughton, and Hughes (1965) asked two psychiatrists to observe her through a one-way window and to interpret the meaning of her bizarre "symptom." The first said that the broom represented to the patient some essential perceptual element in her field of consciousness and that her behavior was analogous to that of a small child who refuses to be parted from some favorite toy, or piece of rag, etc. The second psychiatrist gave a more Freudian-like interpretation. Her pacing and broom dragging, he pointed out, could be seen as a ritualistic procedure, a magical action. Her broom would then be, he said: "(1) a child that gives her love and she gives in return her devotion, (2) a phallic symbol, (3) the scepter of an omnipotent queen . . . " (43).

An immediate problem is that we have competing intuitions as to why the woman was dragging the broom around. How do we tell which intuition is correct? Taylor is hardly unaware of this problem. He comments that, in at least some cases where our intuition is challenged, a valid response is to tell the other person to change himself or herself:

Thus, in the sciences of man insofar as they are hermeneutical there can be a valid response to "I don't understand" which takes the form, not only "develop your intuitions," but more radically "change yourself." This puts an end to any aspiration to a value-free or "ideology-free" science of man (Taylor, 1979, p.68)

I fail to see how a Taylor-type response helps. In the case of the broom-dragger, each psychiatrist can tell the other to change, but who is right: the Freudian or the non-Freudian? Intuition alone does not tell us.

The truth is that neither psychiatrist was right. The woman dragged the broom around because she was reinforced for doing this by the hospital attendants. Allyon, et al. (1965) instructed the attendants to give both a cigarette and a broom to the woman, and to reward her with cigarettes every 15 minutes if she continued to hold the broom. By gradually shaping her behavior in this manner, they induced her to drag the broom around the hospital ward approximately 40% of her waking time. She continued to do this for about a year, at the end of which the investigators deliberately extinguished the so-called symptomatic behavior. Why did the investigators instigate the broom dragging behavior? They apparently wished to expose the baselessness of many psychiatric interpretations.

The case of the schizophrenic woman is only one case, but conflicting intuitions are likely to be a recurring problem in interpreting psychoanalytic data. In cases where a Freudian interpretation might seem appropriate, non-Freudian, psychoanalytic theorists, such as those who embrace ego psychology, self-psychology, or object relations theory, are likely to have intuitions that conflict with those of the Freudian. Cognitivists, operant conditioning theorists, and proponents of either commonsense or physiological hypotheses will also have intuitions in competition with the Freudian's.

Consider Taylor's example of a verbal slip allegedly revealing repression and displacement (1985, 123). If it can be established that this is what the slip reveals, then the revelation might be used as evidence to support some other Freudian hypothesis. One can agree to this without accepting a hermeneutical epistemology. If, however, there are rival and equally plausible interpretations of the slip, then, in the absence of further evidence, we are not warranted in taking the Freudian interpretation to be a datum. Intuition alone is not sufficient for choosing between equally plausible rival interpretations. Suppose, however, that the Freudian interpretation of a patient's behavior is the only one accepted by the analyst? Does such an endorsement enhance the plausibility of the Freudian interpretation, as Taylor appears to suggest? (123) That depends on our empirical evidence. Do we have independent empirical evidence that analysts are usually right in making certain sorts of interpretations of peoples' slips or of other events? If we do not, then the analyst's intuition in favor of a particular interpretation will fail to confirm its correctness.

Taylor's intuitionist criterion, moreover, fares poorly even where we can think of no other interpretation of a neurotic symptom, dream, or slip but a Freudian one. I say that my client cannot remember his friend's name not merely because he forgot it, but because he is harboring some repressed wish. You agree. You have the same intuition. Even if we cannot think of any other explanation, how would our shared intuitions provide any evidence at all for our hypothesis? If I say that my intuitions tell me that repression caused my client's forgetting, how is that different from saying that I *think* that this is what occurred? If there is no difference, then it can be asked: "Yes, this is what you think, but what is the evidence that your belief is correct?"

Am I saying that intuition can never count as reason for belief? No. Perhaps my intuition that one proposition logically entails another can be a good reason for believing that the entailment holds, but this is a different sort of case. We are talking in the Freudian case about a causal hypothesis (see below), not an obvious necessary truth.

One could reply that there is no need in such a case to appeal to intuition. If the Freudian explanation is the only one available, then we can rely on what philosophers call "an inference to the best explanation." Assume that the repressed wish hypothesis, if true, would satisfactorily explain the client's forgetting, and that it is consistent with what we know about him or her. We might then reason as follows: The repression hypothesis provides the best available explanation of the client's forgetfulness; so, we have some rational grounds for believing it to be correct.

If the above form of inference were valid, it would be valid when applied in the natural sciences. It does not qualify, then, as a nonnatural science standard, which is what Taylor (1979, 66) is trying to provide. I discuss the issue of its validity in chapter 2.

I conclude that Taylor's version of a "hermeneutical epistemology," insofar as it relies on intuitive support, yields an inadequate standard for evaluating Freudian hypotheses. I do not intend, however, to rely on his alternative, the "classical model." That model demands that we have "brute data" for confirmation. As Taylor defines this notion (1985, 121), this requires that confirmatory data be *beyond dispute* arising from personal interpretation or discernment. I agree with Taylor that this would impose too high an evidential standard on Freud's hypotheses. If a case can be made for requiring experimental evidence for confirmation, the argument has to be more subtle than saying simply that we need "brute data," and that this, in turn, requires experiments.

There are other hermeneutical standards besides Taylor's, but before turning to them, I want to look at a more powerful attempt to provide an evidential role for intuition.

In two recent brief papers, Thomas Nagel (1994a, 1994b) argues for a nonexperimental approach to the justification of Freudian hypotheses. He argues, first, that most psychoanalytic hypotheses cannot be tested by experiment or statistical analysis, and, second, that such testing is unnecessary for confirmation (1994a, 35). Although both claims are important, the first is of marginal interest to the present topic: the question of the adequacy of non-natural science standards of confirmation. Even if Freudian theory could not be tested experimentally, experimental evidence might still be required to confirm its claims. To say that meeting a certain standard is necessary for confirmation is not to imply the feasibility of doing what is needed to meet the standard. I will be brief, then, in discussing Nagel's first claim.

Nagel argues that testing Freudian hypotheses experimentally is not logically impossible but is generally impractical. If his argument is cogent, we can save time when examining the evidence from the 1500 plus Freudian experiments that have already been done. We can know in advance that most of the evidence is defective. However, the only reason Nagel gives for thinking Freudian experiments to be impractical is that much of mental life (including, presumably, that part talked about by Freudian theory) consists of multiple causes and background conditions that will never precisely recur (Nagel, 1994a p. 35). The same situation arises, however, when the causes are conscious mental events, but the problem has not prevented cognitive psychologists from doing convincing experimental tests of cognitive hypotheses. Nor has it prevented Freudians from doing numerous experimental studies of repression, to take but one example. What these latter experiments show is controversial (see Holmes, 1990 for a skeptical review), but they cannot be discredited for Nagel's reason *unless* it can be shown that their capacity to provide genuine tests presupposes that the phenomena do not consist of multiple causes and background conditions that will not precisely recur. I see no reason to think that this can be shown.

Nagel's point would have more force if it were restricted to singular causal judgments, as in his example of Freud's explanation of why a certain young man forgot the word *aliquis* in a Latin quotation. However, he does not do that; he says (1994a, 35) that the "same problem" (about nonrecurring conditions) also arises for more general Freudian principles.

Even in the case of singular causal judgments, experimental evidence might be indirectly supportive. Suppose that experiments confirmed both that repression does occur and that its occurrence tends to cause the forgetting of certain types of words. That evidence might provide indirect support for Freud's conjecture concerning the young man's forgetting of the Latin word.

Nagel bases his second claim, that experimentation is generally unnecessary for the justification of Freudian hypotheses, on a view about the justification of commonsense psychological explanations *and* about Freudian theory being an extension of commonsense psychology.

In speaking of an extension of commonsense psychology, one might mean that Freudian theory gains credibility from the empirical evidence supporting commonsense claims. An obvious problem for this view is that many Freudian hypotheses, about the oedipal phase of sexual development, the latent meaning of dreams, the sexual etiology of psychoneuroses, etc., go far beyond common sense; in many cases, common sense and Freudian psychology are at war with each other. Nagel, however, is not defending what might be called "an empirical extension" of common sense. He points out (1994a, 34) that Freud took the familiar idea that people are often unaware of their true motives, but carried it so far that he could not defend it just by appealing to common sense.

What Nagel has in mind is a methodological extension of common sense. Commonsense explanations, he contends, provide a distinctive form of understanding from within (1994a, 34), and they are evaluated by a distinctive standard, one not appropriate for particle physics, cancer research, or the study of reflexes (35). Nagel's further point (35) is that Freudian explanations provide the same sort of understanding "from within" and should be judged by the same standard we use in commonsense psychology.

An understanding from within works like this. To understand someone else's thoughts, feelings, or behavior requires that we make sense of the phenomena, even if only "irrational sense," from his or her point of view, by using our own point of view as an imaginative resource (1994a, 34). In providing Freudian explanations, we do pretty much the same thing, Nagel claims. We put ourselves, so to speak, "in the shoes" of other people, and make sense of their symptoms and responses by attributing to them beliefs, desires, feelings, and perceptions—with the difference that these are aspects of their point of view of which they are not consciously aware (p.34.).

Suppose that Nagel is right about what we typically do when we offer Freudian explanations. What is the distinctive standard of commonsense psychology that we use to evaluate them? First, we need observational data about the subject, something to which we apply our understanding from within. After we figure out how to make sense of someone's behavior, however, how do we tell if our explanation is correct? Suppose, for example, that we know a good deal about a friend's personal problems and we try to understand it in Freudian terms, but his or her analyst has a conflicting interpretation. How do we tell which one is correct? The analyst may have more extensive data, but suppose that another analyst looks at the same data, and reaches a different conclusion. By what criterion do we judge who is right?

Nagel's answer to my question initially appears to be that we judge Freudian explanations by their intuitive credibility. Thus, he says (1940,. 35), that in evaluating Freud's conjecture about the forgetting of part of the Latin quotation, we simply have to decide whether it is an "intuitively credible" extension of a general structure of explanation that we find well supported elsewhere, and whether it is more plausible than its alternatives. He also says (36), although here he is making a different point, that to many of us, it certainly *feels* (his italics) as if, much of the time, consciousness reveals only the surface of our minds. For many, he notes, this feeling is confirmed by their dreams.

Nagel's special evidential standard, then, seems, at first, to be exactly the same as Taylor's: judge Freudian explanatory hypotheses by appealing to intuition. In that case, his proposal would be open to the same objections as Taylor's.

Grünbaum (1994) rightly asks of this proposal, Whose intuition is to decide which of the rival explanations "makes sense" of the phenomena correctly? He adds that Nagel's recipe degenerates into subjectivity. Nagel's response (1994b) is to explain "intuitive credibility" in a way that distinguishes his evidential standard from Taylor's:

The fundamental causal principle of commonsense psychology is that in most cases, you can discover causally relevant conditions (conditions that make a *difference* in precisely Grünbaum's sense) for a human action or thought or emotion by fitting it into a rationally coherent interpretation of the whole of the person as an intentional subject of this type—by seeing how from the person's point of view it is in some way *justified*. Interpretation reveals causation, because that's the kind of system a human being is. (Nagel's italics, 56)

Referring to the above principle, Nagel says "That's what I mean by intuitive plausibility, and it necessarily applies in the first instance to specific explanations, rather than to general principles" (56).

What reason do we have for thinking that Nagel's principle is correct? An a priori justification is not likely to suffice. It is not an obvious necessary truth that a reason that justifies an action from an agent's point of view was also a cause of it. Nagel's grounds, however, are not a priori but empirical. The principle is well supported, he claims (56), in endless simple cases where it can be independently corroborated by prediction and control. The support from these simple cases, he contends, warrants our application of the same principle in identifying psychological causes in unique and unrepeatable cases: by trying to make intentional and purposive sense of them.

As an example of a simple case, Nagel refers to a man who puts on a sweater because he feels cold. The man, let us assume, desires to be warmer and believes that putting on extra clothing will help him to achieve that goal. He thus has a reason to act, one that justifies his behavior. We reasonably infer that this justificatory reason made a difference in the way he acted, and, therefore, was a cause of his behavior. If we had reason to doubt that this was the man's reason (perhaps someone paid him to model the sweater), there would be ways to check the accuracy of our explanation. Nagel's principle appears to work in this simple case, but what is the warrant for extending it to non-simple cases?

Nagel's answer (1994a, 35) is that we simply have to decide whether an application is an "intuitively credible" extension of a general structure of explanation that we find well supported elsewhere. I disagree. The justification requires empirical support. The reason is that Nagel's principle can be justifiably applied in simple cases precisely because certain empirical presuppositions hold. We need empirical evidence to know that these conditions are met in a new case; without such evidence, Nagel's principle fails to support a causal inference.

One presupposition of applying Nagel's principle in the case of the man putting on a sweater is that he does this intentionally. Suppose that I trip at a political luncheon, and spill a glass of wine on a rival. I might well want to embarrass him, but without evidence that the act was deliberate, it would be rash to infer that this reason, because it would make sense of the act, was in fact the reason I acted.

A second empirical presupposition is that the cited reason, the desire to become warmer, typically does make a difference in the sort of circumstances under discussion. As Grünbaum puts it in his (1994) reply to Nagel, we need evidence that in a reference class, C, the incidence of Y's (say, putting on one's coat) in the class of X's (say, desiring to be warm) is different from its incidence in the class of non-X's. We have such background evidence to draw on in the case of the man putting on his coat, but not, for example, in the case of an academic who feels fully justified in doing something to hasten the death of a hated colleague. If I am such a person and I ignore the colleague's threat of suicide, it would be premature to conclude that my desire to see him out of the picture was what caused my inaction, unless one had evidence that such a desire would typically move me or someone like me to do something so extreme.

A third presupposition is that there be no competing cause, be it a reason or something else, that is just as likely to have been the cause of the action. If it is equally likely that I gave a homeless man $10 for either of two reasons (but not both), either to help him or to impress my girlfriend, then Nagel's principle does not support one explanation rather than another.

There is, finally, a fourth presupposition in Nagel's simple case. We are taking for granted that the man had a desire to get warmer. If we had no reason to believe that, we would not be warranted in moving from "This reason would justify the action" to "This reason caused, or was a partial cause, of the action." In general, we are obviously not entitled to infer that X caused Y without having some good reason for thinking that X occurred or was present.

If even one of the above empirical presuppositions is missing, the use of Nagel's principle to warrant a causal inference is problematic. Yet, in typical cases in which Freudian theory is potentially applicable, one or more of these presuppositions does not hold. When people have a particular sort of dream, or commit a slip of the tongue, or develop neurotic symptoms, do we have evidence that they are *intentionally* doing these things? We might if we had prior evidence for Freud's theory of repression, but Nagel is not assuming that we do; if he were, he would not need to appeal to his principle to support Freudian theory. A second crucial presupposition also generally fails in the Freudian cases. Even if we had evidence that slips, dreams, etc. are generally intentional (something that I deny), is there good evidence that they are typically preceded by repressed wishes? The history of attempts to demonstrate the existence of repression (see Holmes 1990) strongly suggests otherwise. Without such evidence, a third presupposition of commonsense psychology is not met: We have no good reason, in applying Freudian theory to a particular case, for believing that repressed wishes generally make a difference to the occurrence of dreams, slips, or neuroses. Finally, quite often, when we try to explain something in Freudian terms, there are competing explanations of equal or greater plausibility.

I conclude, then, that Nagel's principle is generally insufficient to justify singular Freudian causal inferences. The reason is that one or more of the required empirical presuppositions are generally unmet. Of course, we will often encounter similar problems if we try to warrant commonsense explanations by using Nagel's principle. Nagel cites Gorbachev's dismantling of the Soviet empire as a case where experimental evidence is unlikely to be of much help. But is this not a case where Nagel's principle also fails to provide a justification for a causal inference? It fails precisely because certain empirical presuppositions do not hold. Most of us do not know enough about Gorbachev to say what reasons he had, let alone which ones made the primary difference. Consequently, it is not enough to say: Reason X, given his overall views, would have justified his doing what he did. We would still need evidence that this reason was one of *his* reasons *and,* if it were, that it played a part in his decision. Similar problems arise in "endless" cases, to use Nagel's term, where people unjustifiably draw a causal conclusion when all they are warranted in saying is that their explanation makes sense of the agent's behavior.

Is it surprising that Nagel's principle works in simple cases but not in more complex cases? There should be no surprise at all once we realize that the justificatory work it appears to be doing in the simple cases is really being done by the empirical presuppositions that permit its application. Suppose that I have the following empirical evidence concerning the man with the sweater: (*a*) he intended to put it on; (*b*) he had a certain reason to put it on; (*c*) people often put on their sweater for that very reason; and (*d*) we know of no credible alternative explanation. To justify my causal inference, I can appeal directly to this empirical evidence. There is no need to add: his desire to get warm justified his behavior from his point of view. Nagel might agree with this; he does not say that his principle is a basic epistemological principle that by itself supplies warrant. Rather, we trust the principle because of its successful application in simple case.

If Nagel agrees that even in simple cases the warrant for a causal inference is provided by certain empirical presuppositions, then our disagreement lies elsewhere. He holds that intuitive credibility can decide if it is legitimate to extend his principle to Freudian cases. I have argued, in opposition, that this is not enough: We need empirical evidence to decide if the required empirical presuppositions are met, and that evidence is lacking.

Nagel's view of Freudian psychology as an extension of common-sense psychology is shared by other philosophers (e.g., Cavell 1993). I discuss this position further in chapter 3 (pp. 106–124).

Noncausal Readings of Freudian Theory

Although some advocates of a hermeneutical epistemology (e.g., Taylor 1985, 123) agree that Freudian theory makes causal claims, others (e.g., Ricoeur, at least in his early writings, e.g., 1970; Klein 1976, 26) are skeptical about this reading of Freud. They see his theory as being essentially about meanings rather than causes. This position does not by itself entail the appropriateness of special evidential standards. However, its proponents also argue that if a theory is about meanings rather than causes, then natural science standards do not apply. The position must face two powerful objections.

The first is that many of the central hypotheses of Freudian theory, including many defended by such Freudians as Kline (1981) and Fisher and Greenberg (1985), are patently causal in nature. For example, when Freudians claim that repressed wishes engender slips of the tongue, or bring about neuroses, or instigate certain types of dreams, they are obviously making causal claims. Even Ricoeur apparently now concedes this fact (see Grünbaum 1984, 48).

The second problem is that even when Freudian theory does make claims about the meaning of such items as neurotic symptoms, dreams, and slips of the tongue and pen, and these claims are not obviously causal, they typically presuppose causal hypotheses, or their confirmation requires confirmation of related causal claims. To illustrate, suppose that an analyst says that the latent meaning of a dream about watching a girl riding horseback on a desolate beach is as follows: the dreamer has a repressed wish to sleep with his sister who is represented in the dream by the horseback rider. This interpretation presupposes a causal hypothesis: that the repressed wish made a difference to the manifest content of the dream. The dreamer dreamt what he did at least partly because of that wish. In this example, talk about the meaning of the dream presupposes a causal claim. If there were no repressed wish, or none that made a difference to what was dreamt, the meaning hypothesis would be false. In other cases, Freudian meaning hypotheses may not logically imply or presuppose any causal hypotheses, but *proving* them is likely to require confirmation of one or more causal claims.

For example, Freudian theory holds that objects that commonly appear in dreams, such as trees, poles, and other elongated items, symbolize the penis and curved, rounded items represent female sexual organs. Some Freudians have tried to establish the hypothesis in the following way. First, they reason that if such items represent sexual organs outside of dreams, then they probably do so in dreams as well. They then argue as follows: males tend to prefer the sexual organs of females, and females, the sexual organs of males. So we can find indirect evidence for Freudian symbolism in dreams by doing experiments and seeing if male subjects prefer rounded shapes and females, elongated shapes (Jahoda 1956). This argument clearly requires answers to causal questions. In particular, if male subjects express a preference for rounded shapes, is that *because* they associate, perhaps unconsciously, such shapes with female sex organs? Perhaps some other argument could be given for the Freudian view about the meaning of dream symbols, but it is hard to see how such an argument could work without relying on any causal hypotheses at all.

Either of the two points made above about dreams and dream symbols applies to typical (not necessarily all) Freudian hypotheses about the meanings of neurotic symptoms, dreams, and slips of various sorts. Either the hypothesis or its proof will presuppose some causal hypothesis.

Rather than argue that Freudian theory is essentially about meanings, one could argue that the unconscious motives that it postulates are not said to be causally sufficient so even if the theory is true, these motives do not causally necessitate behavior (Radnitzky 1985, 201). The point is correct, but it fails to show that Freudian theory is not a causal theory. The theory does postulate factors that are causally relevant, that is, they make a difference as to what human beings do. If they do, then they are causes.

Radnitzky could reply that unconscious motives, reasons, intentions, and the like never even make a difference to how people act, but then his position would become incoherent. He believes that psychoanalytic theory can be used to explain an individual's conduct, experience, or emotions (206), but it could not do that if unconscious motives and reasons never made any difference. I may have had an unconscious reason for marrying my wife, but citing it does not explain what I did if I acted solely because of a different reason. In general, it is inconsistent to say that I did X because of reason or motive Y, and yet Y made no difference at all to what I did.

Instead of arguing that Freudian theory is entirely or *essentially* noncausal, one might also argue that it is partly causal and partly not. Charles Nussbaum (1991) defends a mixed account of this sort. He argues (193) that confirmation and disconfirmation of the repression hypothesis require an explanatory model that makes use of reasons or intentions that are not causes, but he also holds that causal explanations cannot be dispensed with altogether. Nussbaum (94–95) acknowledges the problem just mentioned—of saying that reasons are noncausal and yet explanatory—but makes no direct attempt to deal with it. Perhaps his discussion of Freud's "redescription" of his patient's behavior (200, 204) was intended to resolve the problem. However, as I will argue shortly, it does not.

The connection between intention and action cannot be causal, according to Nussbaum (196), because in order to explain an action, the connection *must* be described by an analytic statement. It must be so described, Nussbaum argues (195–196), because to explain an event, we must first identify it, and that requires that we construct a practical syllogism of the following form:

P intends to bring about b.
P believes (considers, thinks) he cannot bring about b unless he does a.
P does a.

The above "syllogism," Nussbaum contends (195), is best understood as a hypothetical statement, which, he claims, is analytically true.

To illustrate, Nussbaum considers the behavior of a man looking around in a field: "When we explain (by reasons) that the man in the field is looking for his lost watch, we construct a practical syllogism which states that he intends to find his watch, that he believes that he will not find it unless he looks about the field, and that he therefore looks about the field" (195). However, the corresponding hypothesis—if P intends to find his watch, and believes he cannot do so unless he looks about the field, then he looks about the field—is analytic, according to Nussbaum (195–196). Consequently, the connection between intention and action is not causal.

Nussbaum's argument has at least two serious problems. The trouble begins with one of the first steps: Why believe that to identify an action we need to construct a practical syllogism? If I see a man apparently looking about a field, to identify his action, it is enough to know that he intends to be looking about a field. To know what he is doing, I need not construct a syllogism specifying a belief and further intention (say, to find his watch). Nussbaum concedes (198), in fact, for certain types of behavior, such as that of neurotics, it is not even possible to identify them by constructing a practical syllogism. Yet, in his example (200) of Freud's analysis of an obsessional woman, the patient performed various actions (such as ringing a bell for her housemaid) and Freud was able to ascertain what they were. He had to do that in order to accomplish what he next attempted: to explain the woman's behavior in terms of her preconscious desire to mitigate her husband's embarrassment at being impotent on their wedding night. Nussbaum says of this case (201) that Freud's explanation consists of offering a redescription: What the patient was "really doing," according to Freud, was restoring her husband's honor, or protecting his pride. I shall return to Nussbaum's contention shortly, but even if it is accepted without objection, my point remains: Freud was trying to explain the woman's obsessional actions, but to do that, he first had to identify them, and he did that without the help of a practical syllogism.

Without support for this crucial premise—that identification of an action always requires construction of a practical syllogism—Nussbaum's entire argument collapses, for his conclusion that intentions are not causes depends on the assumption (196) that the connection between intention and action *must* be described by an analytic statement, which in turn is dependent on his initial assumption about the need to invoke a practical syllogism to identify an action.

Even if the initial assumption were granted, however, Nussbaum would need support for a second controversial claim: that the hypothetical proposition that expresses the practical syllogism is analytic. To see the problematic nature of this claim, consider an example given by G.H. von Wright (1971, 116): "We have the premises of a practical argument: an agent intends to bring about something and considers the doing of something else necessary for this end. It is time for him to act. He thinks so himself. Perhaps he has resolved to shoot the tyrant. He stands in front of the beast, aiming at him with his loaded revolver. But nothing happens." Nussbaum allows (1991, 195) that an intended action may not occur because of interfering conditions so he might respond that there must be such conditions in von Wright's case that prevent the man from acting. Why, however, *must* there be such conditions? It might turn out that determinism is not true at the level of human action, and that the causation of action is irreducibly stochastic. Even if determinism is true, at least at the macro level, it is not analytically true: we have no logical or conceptual guarantees that when an action fails to follow, when someone has an appropriate intention and belief, that there will always be interfering conditions or a competing intention.

Nussbaum (195) cites von Wright as a supporter of the logical connection argument, but von Wright, at least in his later writings, does not argue that it is logically or conceptually impossible for the premises of a practical syllogism to be true and the conclusion false. He argues the opposite. Thus, in discussing the man intending to shoot the tyrant, he denies that there is a logical compulsion to say that either he gave up his intention or there were interfering conditions (such as his being paralyzed). On the contrary, he says that we can just as well say, If the case can be imagined, it shows that the conclusion of a practical inference does not follow with logical necessity from the premises. To insist otherwise, he contends, would constitute dogmatism. He adds: "Thus, despite the truth of the Logical Connection Argument, the premises of a practical inference do *not* with logical necessity entail behavior" (von Wright, 1971, 117).

Nussbaum (195) concedes that the issue of the logic of the practical syllogism is difficult, so he is somewhat hesitant in expressing his view. However, for his argument about intentions not being causes to work, he needs to defend his hardly self-evident claim that the hypothetical proposition corresponding to the practical syllogism is analytic. He does not do that, nor does he answer opposing arguments.

I conclude that Nussbaum fails to show that intentions (and reasons) are not causes. The failure of his argument prevents him from reaching his stated goal (194–195) that of showing, contrary to Grünbaum's view, that some Freudian explanations make use of reasons that are not causes.

Nussbaum also contends (200, 204) that psychoanalytic explanation involves a *redescription* of a patient's behavior. In support of this general claim, he cites but one case, the one mentioned earlier in which Freud attempts to explain a woman's obsessional behavior. It would be risky to rest much on this single case given that, as Nussbaum realizes, Freud did not invoke his repression theory to explain the woman's behavior; rather, he appealed to a noninfantile wish in the woman's preconscious. Furthermore, the woman herself discovered the wish; it was not uncovered through the use of psychoanalysis. Putting aside doubts about how representative the case is, does Freud attempt to explain by offering a redescription? Does he say, as Nussbaum puts it (201), that what the woman was "really doing" was restoring her husband's honor or pride? He does not; the "really doing" locution is Nussbaum's. Instead, Freud explains the obsessional behavior by referring to the woman's preconscious wish to mitigate her husband's embarrassment. In doing so, Freud is giving a causal explanation. He is not saying merely that the wish was present when the action was performed; he is also implying that it made a difference to what the woman did. Furthermore, if it had made no difference, then what would be the point of saying that what she was "really doing" was trying to restore her husband's pride? There are many ways to describe her actions. Why deem Nussbaum's description privileged unless the woman's desire to restore her husband's pride made a difference to what she did?

I am not objecting to the use of the phrase, "what the woman was really doing." My point is that redescribing the woman's action by means of Nussbaum's locution is compatible with also giving a causal explanation of her behavior, which is what Freud was attempting. If he were not attempting to do that, it is unclear how he would be explaining her actions even if he were right about her motive. I conclude that Nussbaum's attempt to show (202) that some psychoanalytic explanations are noncausal does not succeed.

Thematic Affinity

Instead of interpreting Freud noncausally, some philosophers make a case for special evidential standards by arguing that meaning connections (or so-called thematic affinities) are evidential signs of causal connections. Thus, Donald Levy (1988, 212) claims that to speak of an affinity of any kind (including a thematic affinity) between things signifies generally a causal relation between them. Stated in this bold fashion, Levy's thesis has obvious counter examples. If I speak of an affinity of meaning between two words, I need not signify a causal connection between them; an affinity of content between two wishes in two different people is not evidence, I think even Levy would grant, that one wish caused the other. Last night's dream may have a manifest content very similar to that of a dream I had last year, but that is not reason to think that one dream caused the other. What Levy means, I think, is that generally a thematic affinity between certain *kinds* of items, such as one person's motive and action, or wish and verbal slip, or desire and dream image, is some evidence of a causal connection between the two. However, even this less general thesis seem wrong.

Consider some examples that Grünbaum (1988, 1990) discusses. In the first case, I have a dream that includes the image of a house. There is a thematic affinity between my seeing a house the previous day and my now dreaming about a house, but there may be no warrant for thinking that the first event caused the second. I see at least one house almost everyday (e.g., my own) regardless of whether I then dream about a house. That is true of many other people as well. So, in the absence of additional evidence, I am not warranted in believing that seeing a house the previous day made any *difference* to what I dreamt—despite the presence of a thematic affinity.

In contrast, consider a woman who sees for the first time Frank Lloyd Wright's house Falling Water and then dreams about a house containing the same details. Here we have a strong thematic affinity and a warrant for believing in a causal connection, but what supplies that warrant is specific background information rather than thematic affinity. For example, Grünbaum stipulates that the woman had, until her visit, never heard of Falling Water or seen a picture or description of it. Another crucial piece of information is that the woman's dream occurred the night of the day she visited Wright's house. Without such background information, the causal inference is unwarranted. Finally, consider a case where a student writes a term paper by copying from an old encyclopedia article. Here we have an extremely high degree of meaning affinity—the two texts are exactly the same—and yet our background evidence about, for example, the very low probability of two papers written by different people being identical if there is no copying supports the charge of plagiarism. These and other cases (Grünbaum, 1990) support the following contentions.

First, thematic affinity *by itself* is not generally evidence of a causal connection. Second, it is not generally evidence of such a connection even when the degree of meaning kinship is very high. If we accept these two points, however, a problem arises, as several philosophers have pointed out (Levy 1988, 212–213; Sachs 1989, 374–377; Hopkins 1988). How do we account for our knowledge of a causal connection in cases of commonsense psychology where there is a meaning affinity between *A* and *B* but no *experimental* evidence that the first caused the second? Consider, for example, Freud's inference that a repressed wish caused a certain young man to forget the Latin word *aliquis* when quoting a line from Virgil's *Aeneid*. As Levy (213) points out, Grünbaum (1984, 258–259) grants, for the sake of the argument, that the man later remembered the word as a result of free-associating, but challenges Freud's conclusion that a repressed wish caused the original forgetting. If thematic affinities are not counted as indicators of a causal connection, Levy asks (213), how do we warrant the claim that free-associating restored the forgotten word to the young man's consciousness? He suggests (213) that to insist on re-creating the situation Freud encountered in controlled experiments seems "far-fetched." If we grant, however, that thematic affinity warrants the causal inference here, then why cannot it not also warrant Freud's inference about the cause of the forgetting?

Sachs (1989, 444) makes the same point when he discusses a certain slip of the tongue. A man turns from the view of a woman's exposed bosom and mutters "Excuse me, I have got to get a *breast* of *flesh* air. Sachs assumes that the slip was prompted by a wish to caress, although he concedes that the motive is not obvious. His point is that if we do not allow that the meaning affinity between the wish and the slip is evidence that the first caused the second, then we are unable to account for our knowledge of the causal connection. If we do allow it, then the way is open for Freud to appeal to meaning connections to warrant his causal inferences about repressed wishes in what Sachs calls (374) cases of "opaque" parapraxes.

Both Sachs and Levy assume that we have but two choices in the cases they discuss: either insist on experimental evidence to support our belief in a causal connection *or* concede that thematic affinities (or perhaps, thematic affinities of high strength) are generally evidence of causal connections. There is, however, a third choice (assuming that a causal inference is warranted): we support the inference by appeal to empirical evidence of a nonexperimental kind. Putting aside skeptical doubts about all causal inferences or about knowledge of other minds, there are noncontroversial cases where we reasonably infer that a certain mental event made a difference. Hopkin's case (1988, 38) of watching someone move a glass toward a tap and inferring a desire to get a drink clearly illustrates the phenomenon. In this sort of case we do not need experimental evidence, but that is because there are an abundance of empirical details available, gleaned from what people tell us about their intention, observations of their subsequent behavior, etc., that support the inference. There is no need, then, to look to thematic affinities or to require experimental confirmation.

In the cases cited by Sachs and Levy, it is not clear that the available empirical details are supportive. But it is also not clear that the causal inferences are warranted. The case of the man who witnessed the exposed breast is not an actual case; it was made up by Grünbaum (1984, 200) to illustrate a point about causal fallacies. Sachs provides no grounds whatsoever for concluding that if such a case were to occur, the slip of the tongue would likely be caused by a wish to caress. If such a slip were to occur, there might well be other equally plausible alternatives (see Erwin, 1993, 440–441). Questions have also been raised about whether Freud's *aliquis* case was not also made up. If it is an actual case, did Freud have evidence that the free associating restored the memory of the forgotten word? If he did, he does not tell us what it was. The young man did remember the word after free associating, but he, presumably, was also trying to remember the word. Perhaps it was the striving and not the free associating that caused him to remember.

I am not suggesting that we cannot find evidence to make it plausible that the free associating helped restore the memory. My point is that *if* there is no such evidence, it does not follow that we must concede the legitimacy of appealing to thematic affinities. Another obvious alternative is to say that the causal inference, in the absence of any sort of empirical evidence, is unjustified.

Levy (1988, 214) asks for an argument for denying all evidentiary weight to thematic affinity. I would reply that the burden of proof lies with those who appeal to such affinities to support causal hypotheses. Suppose I were to say, *B* followed *A;* so there is evidence that *A* caused *B*. One could reply as follows. It is not necessarily true that temporal succession is evidence of a causal connection. The proof of this is that there are known cases where *B* follows *A* but there is no evidence that *A* caused it. So, it is unlikely that we can know *a priori* that *B*'s following *A* is generally evidence that *A* caused *B*. Still, we might have empirical evidence that it is generally (but not universally) true that the perception of one event following another is evidence of a causal connection. I say we might have, but in fact we do not. So the burden of proof is on those who would appeal to temporal sequence as a reliable indicator of causation.

An exactly parallel reply can be made to those who say, as James Hopkins does, "So quite generally, connection in psychological content is a mark of causal, and so potentially of explanatory, connection" (1988, 39), Hopkins makes it clear that by "connection in psychological content" he means a meaning connection. As the cases cited earlier show, it is not a necessary truth that where there is a meaning similarity, even one of very high degree, the items being compared are causally connected. If it is not necessarily true, then how can *a priori* considerations show, as claimed by Gardner (1993, 243), that it is *generally true* that psychological proximity, and effectively charged connections of content, signify causal influence? If there is some *a priori* argument to show this connection, then what is it? The only reason that Gardner gives (1993, 243) is that the alternative is to view the mind as an "atomized jumble of ideas," which would contradict its identification *as* a mind. But why is this the only alternative? It might be that the mind is not an atomized jumble of ideas and yet sometimes where there is a connection of content, a causal connection is present, but often it is missing.

It might be missing, for example, in Freud's example (1901, *S.E.*, 6:9) of the young man who tried unsuccessfully to quote a line from the *Aeneid*. A chain of associations, according to Freud, later led from a reflection on the missing word *aliquis* to the miracle of St. Januarias' clotted blood and eventually to the man's expressing anxiety about his girlfriend missing her period and possibly being pregnant. Yet what caused the man to forget the word *aliquis* might have had nothing to do with his anxiety about his girlfriend. Rather, his preoccupation with her problem might have caused him to free-associate to the thought of blood, and might have done so even if he had begun the chain of associations by reflecting on a different word, even one he had not forgotten.

As Hopkins points out (1991, 87), there is also a connection in content between a certain experience of Breuer's patient Anna O and some of her symptoms. Yet, for all we know, the cause of her symptoms may have been physiological. In the case discussed by Sachs (1989, 444), where a man slips and says "breast of flesh air," even if free-associating revealed a desire to caress, that desire might not have caused the slip. In these cases, where a meaning connection is not correlated with a causal connection, are the minds of the people involved necessarily an "atomized jumble of ideas?" That is hardly obvious. Gardner's argument, then, lacks cogency: It depends on the dubious premise that if it were not generally true that thematic affinities signified causal connections, the mind would be an atomized jumble of ideas. Perhaps all that Gardner means is that where there is a meaning similarity between two items, there is likely to be a causal explanation of this fact, not that the similarity is evidence of those two items being causally connected to each other. If that is all Gardner is saying, then his point is too weak to be of help to those who take the meaning similarity between X and Y to be evidence that X caused Y, or that Y caused X.

Instead of searching for an a priori argument, we might try to develop an empirical argument for the thematic affinity thesis, but it is up to those who place evidentiary weight on such connections to provide the argument. Perhaps Levy did try to do this by arguing that in cases of commonsense psychology, we are warranted in drawing a causal inference, but do not have, and perhaps could not have, experimental confirmation. However, I have already answered that argument. Neither Levy nor Sachs (1988) provides any other argument. Sachs simply asserts (1988, 374) that certain parapraxes *show* that a wish or effect that preceded them also caused them. That seems very close to saying that the causal connection is self-evident in such cases. As I argued in the exposed breast and the *aliquis* cases, however, if there is a causal connection, it is hardly self-evident.

Hopkins, in contrast, to Sachs and Levy, does try to show, in an interesting series of papers, but especially (1991), that under certain conditions, meaning affinities are signs of causal connections. What Hopkins argues is pertinent not only to Freudian psychology but also to the philosophy of mind and the philosophy of psychology generally (e.g., it is relevant to the traditional problem of other minds and to the defense of folk psychology against criticisms of eliminative materialists).

As Hopkins (123, *n*.5) uses the term "motive," it applies to a variety of types of psychological causes including beliefs, wishes, or desires and affects such as love, hatred, greed, and lust. A close connection holds between language and motives, Hopkins contends, in the sense that motives characteristically have, or can be given, what he calls a "linguistic articulation" (88). For example, if we say that John believes (hopes, fears, or whatever) that Freud worked in Vienna, we can articulate John's motive by using the sentence "Freud worked in Vienna." The motive, then, can be said to have a *content,* which is given by the sentence used to articulate it (89). Hopkins claims (incorrectly, I believe) that such a sentence states what he alternatively calls a "truth-condition" or a "satisfaction condition": "As I shall be using these terms, the truth condition of 'Snow is white' is that snow is white, of 'Grass is green' that grass is green and so on, ad infinitum. The notion is used for motives by the way of the sentences that articulate them. Thus the sentence that articulates the motive of belief in 'John believes that snow is white' is 'Snow is white.' The truth-condition of this sentence, and hence of the belief itself, is that snow is white" (124, *n*. 9).

As further examples, Hopkins claims that the satisfaction condition of the *hope* that snow is white is that snow is white, and of the *desire* that snow be white is that snow is white (or be white). Finally, Hopkins claims that a logical or conceptual connection lies between a motive and its satisfaction condition: "The condition of satisfaction, realization, or whatever, of a given motive stands in a relation to that motive that is logical or conceptual. It is a norm or rule, given in language, that having a drink of water satisfies a desire to have a drink of water, or that a belief that grass is green is true if grass is green" (124, *n*. 9).

Given this truth-condition relationship, Hopkins claims that the linguistic articulation of a desire serves to describe it as a cause, and in grasping that articulation, we already know a central feature of its causal role, that is, what it is supposed to do (p. 92). Furthermore, the way we interpret one another, according to Hopkins, is by assigning sentences to motives (sentences specifying their content). In doing this we also understand one another in terms of causes: "The finding of sense or meaning, the articulation of object- and satisfaction-directedness, and the establishing of commonsense causal orders, are one and the same" (95). And so our natural criteria for sound interpretation, which are based on content, are at the same time, Hopkins contends, criteria for good causal explanation. Thus, the better a desire and action match in content, the better we take the former to explain the latter. For example, singing the national anthem and a desire to sing the national anthem overlap in content (there is what Grünbaum calls "a thematic affinity") and this makes the desire particularly well suited to explain the action (95–96).

I will not explore here the prospects for using Hopkins's analysis, *if* it were correct, to support the more contentious of Freud's dream interpretations or in warranting his hypotheses about the origin of neurotic symptoms (97, 116). Instead, I want to challenge the analysis itself.

To begin with, I deny Hopkins's (124, *n*. 9) claim that there is the stated logical or conceptual connection of being a truth condition between the assertion of the existence of a motive and its condition of satisfaction. That snow is white is, of course, a truth condition for "snow is white," but it is not a truth condition for "John believes that snow is white." Clearly, John may *not* believe that snow is white, although it actually is. Similarly, it is not a truth condition for "John desires to have a drink of water" that John actually has a drink of water. Hopkins does realize that John may desire to drink and yet not drink, but the point is that John may drink water without having desired to do so. What might have misled him is the logical or conceptual connection between the following: 1. "John has a desire to have a drink of water," and 2. "Having a drink of water satisfies that desire." Given what Hopkins means by "satisfies," (1) implies (2), but that lends no support to his claim that the motive and its satisfaction condition (desiring the drink and having a drink) are logically or conceptually connected by way of the action being a "truth condition" for the assertion of the existence of the motive. They are not so connected.

Hopkins claims that a connection between a motive and its satisfaction condition enables the articulation of the content of the motive to establish its causal role. Thus, in his view, when we specify the satisfaction condition of a desire (i.e., articulate its content), we thereby "describe it as a cause" (92). But suppose I articulate John's desire to act always in a purely selfless manner. The satisfaction condition is that John always acts in that manner. I state this condition, but it does not follow that I have described John's desire as a cause. I would not contradict myself if I said, for example, that John has such a desire, and that the aforementioned condition would satisfy it, and yet the desire has no effect on his actual behavior: whenever he thinks he acts selflessly, he deceives himself. Nor would understanding the content of John's desire guarantee that I know whether the desire plays any causal role in explaining his behavior. Hopkins speaks of knowing what a desire is "supposed to do" (92). This means what a desire *should* do if acted on intentionally. For example, he claims that a desire to get a drink, if someone acts on it intentionally, *should* produce an action of getting a drink. The basis for this claim, or even what it means is unclear. However, even if Hopkins is right about what desires should do, knowing what a desire is "supposed to do" is not sufficient for knowing its actual causal role. Do people ever act on the desire to get a drink? Does such a desire ever make any difference at all to the way people behave? These are empirical questions, even if they have obvious answers: they cannot be answered merely by articulating the content of the desire. The overlap in content between the desire to get a drink and the action of getting a drink may be grounds, then, for believing that the desire is, in Hopkins's words, "supposed to" bring about that action, but it is not grounds for believing that it actually does so.

Even if Hopkins's claim were only about what a desire is supposed to do, it does not follow that "hermeneutic understanding, and a grasp of the causes of behavior, form a unity" (92). At most, what follows is a unity between the understanding of the content of a desire and knowing what it is *supposed to do*. Knowing the actual causes of behavior requires empirical information, not merely hermeneutical understanding.

It also does not follow from Hopkins's argument that the finding of motivational "sense" or "meaning" and the establishment of commonsense causal order are one and the same. It is one thing to make sense of what people do by postulating motives; it is another thing *to establish* that a motive featuring content overlap with an action really did cause it. The desire to sing the national anthem may be "particularly well suited" to explain someone's singing the national anthem, if this means that if the desire is actually present, then singing the anthem would satisfy it, but noticing this overlap in content between the desire and the action is no evidence that the desire did cause the action. Perhaps the action was performed to curry favor with someone who is very patriotic or because failure to sing would incur penalties. Or perhaps the singer did act voluntarily, but had no desire to sing the anthem sincerely, and sang it only to mock the audience. In brief, unless I have seriously misunderstood him, Hopkins's claims about the articulation of the content of motives fail to support his thesis that an overlap in content between a motive and action or motive and alleged manifest dream symbol is conceptual evidence of a causal link between them.

Besides appealing to linguistic articulation, Hopkins presents examples in which overlap in content purportedly provides grounds for a causal hypothesis. However, in all of his cases, either there is no evidence of causality or if there is, the warrant is provided by other background evidence and not thematic affinity.

Hopkins's first example is that of Josef Breuer's patient, Anna O, who suffered from an aversion to drinking. Under hypnosis, she traced this symptom to an episode in which she watched a dog drink water from a glass. Hopkins claims that the causal link between episode and symptom seems marked in the content of the symptom itself since both were concerned with such topics as drinking water, disgust, anger, and refusal (87). Indeed we have an overlap in content, but why is that grounds for thinking that the episode caused the symptoms to appear? As Grünbaum (1990, 572–573; see also 562–663) notes, Breuer's treatment of Anna O's aversion to drinking water was a failure; that is reason to doubt that he had identified and removed the cause of her phobic reaction.

Another example Hopkins uses concerns Freud's Irma dream. In his preamble to his dream analysis, Freud tells us that his treatment of his patient Irma was only partly successful: some of her somatic symptoms remained. On the day preceding the dream, a junior colleague, Otto, made a remark about her condition, one that Freud interpreted as a reproof. The next morning Freud had a dream about Irma in which the cause of her problems is attributed to an injection given by Otto, who probably, it is suggested in the dream, used an unclean syringe. Later, when reflecting on his dream, he writes, "It occurred to me, in fact, that I was actually *wishing* that there had been a wrong diagnosis; for if so, the blame for my lack of success would have been got rid of" (1900, *S.E.* 4: 109). This hypothesis may have occurred to Freud, but he nowhere gives any evidence that it is true. He was not aware prior to the onset of the dream that he ever had such a wish. Even if he had, he gives no reason to think it had any effect on the content of his dream.

Hopkins says that the hypothesis "fits with" (1991, 101) material in the rest of the dream, in particular with Freud's dreaming that the illness was caused by Otto's injection. If "fits with" means "coheres with," that is true of indefinitely many rival hypotheses and is not evidence for Freud's particular hypothesis. Hopkins, however, presumably means that Freud's conjecture *explains* the dream segment involving Otto. But how satisfactory is the explanation? Freud would not have been responsible for Irma's pain if it were due to Otto's injection, but he would then have been responsible for a misdiagnosis and the ensuing consequences; for his treatment plan was based on his contention that her pains had a psychological origin. So one has to assume not only that Freud did not want to be blamed for Irma's continued problems but also, and implausibly, that he did not mind being blamed for a gross misdiagnosis. A more plausible explanation of the Otto dream segment is that Freud had no wish for a misdiagnosis, but merely wished to shift the blame for Irma's problems to the thoughtless Otto. (He does report remembering that Otto was thoughtless, or something like that, the previous afternoon (*S.E.,* 4: 117.) In short, without some supporting evidence or argument, the hypothesis that Freud puts forth (rather tentatively) concerning the causal relevance of his alleged wish for a misdiagnosis is unsupported. Other things that Freud says about his Irma dream are more plausible, but as Grünbaum (1984, 229) notes, they are supported by grounds from commonsense psychology, as opposed to thematic affinities.

In contrast to the two cases just discussed, it is plausible that Freud's dreaming of drinking cool water (another case Hopkins cites) was caused by his being thirsty. At the very least, there is reason to believe that he was thirsty while dreaming. He reports having eaten anchovies before going to bed and waking up thirsty. A clear alternative, however, to mere thematic affinity can be given as to what makes the hypothesis plausible. We have background evidence of a Millian kind (see Grünbaum 1993, 154), that events or conditions such as being thirsty or having a desire to urinate often make a difference as to what people dream.

To take another of Hopkins's examples, when we see someone moving toward a tap with glass in hand, we are often in a position to infer that he or she wants a drink. However, that is not always true. I often perform the same action in order to wash a glass and there is no reason to think that I desire a drink. Where the inference is warranted, it is so because we have background evidence that the act is not intended to serve some other purpose, that it is voluntary (I am, e.g., not hypnotized), that the agent is thirsty, that people often drink water to satisfy their thirst, and so on. This background information, not mere thematic affinity, provides the warrant. That is also true of someone singing the national anthem. If we did not have grounds for thinking that a particular rendition of the anthem was voluntary, or that people generally sing the anthem because they want to, we might very well have no reason to believe that the desire to sing caused the action.

Hopkins does have some additional examples, but they, too, fail to help his case. In each example, either it is not clear that the inference to a causal hypothesis is warranted *or* it is very questionable that thematic affinity rather than background evidence supplies the warrant.

A proponent of thematic affinities' evidential value could try another tack. Instead of trying to find convincing examples, we could try to formulate a cogent general rule that allows us to separate cases where thematic affinities are signs of causation from those where they are not. It is clearly insufficient, however, to say merely: Thematic affinities are evidence of causation *given* the proper background evidence. We can also say: If *B* followed *A*, that is evidence that *A* caused *B* *given the proper background evidence*. Such "rules" are too trivial to be of any use to the Freudian cause.

Hopkins does try to state more informative general conditions than the above (for thematic affinities being evidence of causation). He writes: "These conditions include, at the outset, the accurate ascription of base motives, and also a degree of connection between motive and dream that is significant enough effectively to rule out coincidence" (1991, 106). By "degree of connection," Hopkins means degree of *meaning* as opposed to *causal* connection. At least two problems arise with his conditions. The first, and minor, one is that, on at least one natural reading of "coincidence," we may rule out a coincidental relationship between events *A* and *B*, but be unable to discount the operation of some third factor causing *B*, or causing both *A* and *B*. We can avoid this problem by stipulating that ruling out a "coincidental" relationship between a motive and dream (or action) requires guaranteeing that the relationship is causal. The major problem concerns the applicability of Hopkins's conditions. In the light of Grünbaum's arguments that even a strong meaning connection is not by itself evidence of causation, it is question begging to assume without argument that cases exist in which the degree of (meaning) connection between motive and dreams is significant enough to rule out coincidence. In addition, to apply the rule to Freudian cases of dream interpretation or purported explanation of neuroses, we would have to obtain evidence both that: (a) the postulated motive did exist; and (b) the degree of meaning connection is significant enough to rule out coincidence.

There is no reason to think that we can obtain such evidence without using Millian methods. Hopkins (1991, 128) claims that Mills's methods are inapplicable to a psychology of motives because motives are unobserved. However, in employing Mills's methods, one need not claim to use them to demonstrate that a putative cause *exists*, but rather to argue that a hypothesized event makes a difference. (For a discussion of this point, see Grünbaum 1993, 154.)

Before leaving thematic affinities, we might consider an attempt to weave them into an abductive type of inference. Mathias Kettner (1991, 174) argues that an analyst need not base causal inferences on the strength of meaning affinities alone so long as an extra premise is available: that meanings and their affinities are causally embedded in interpretive processes belonging to a single causally connected mental life, namely, that of the person analyzed. I have no doubt that this extra premise can be confirmed, but what is left unclear is how this premise will help warrant Freudian hypotheses. Anna O, for example, may well have seen an affinity between her watching a dog drink water from a glass and her hydrophobia. Assume that her drawing of this connection was "causally embedded in interpretative processes" belonging to a single causally connected mental life (174). Yet, we are still left without rational grounds for inferring that the remembered episode caused her symptom to either appear or persist (see my discussion in the previous section).

Kettner (175–176) does give an example of an analyst's causal inference allegedly involving meaning affinities, which he claims is valid. A patient, who is a teacher, is said to understand the means by which she can assert her authority over her pupils, but she is unable to do so. After speaking of the necessity of self-discipline, she remembers being a rebellious child. From these facts alone, the analyst infers, "Her difficulty now is particularly related to her unconscious identification with her pupils" (quoted in Kettner, 177). Kettner claims that the analyst's argument can be represented by a pattern of abductive inference based on thematic affinity. He presents two versions of that pattern and claims that both are valid. His second version, however, does not contain a premise and conclusion (it consists of a single statement). For that reason, I will examine only the first (176):

Abductive premise: It is surprising that S's (= the woman's) behavior manifests features F1, F2. . . *Fn.*

Abductive premise: It is unlikely (= not to be expected) that S's behavior should show so many features F1, F2. . .*Fn* that could derive from M without being so derived.

Abductive conclusion: That M is causally relevant for S's behavior is a reasonable hypothesis.

This pattern of reasoning makes no mention of thematic affinity, so even if it were valid, it is unclear how it would serve Kettner's stated purpose of rebutting Grünbaum's charge of a "thematic affinity fallacy." Whether the pattern is valid depends on the interpretation of "could derive" in the second premise. If Kettner means "could possibly derive," then the conclusion fails to follow. The features of the woman's behavior could possibly have derived from (i.e., resulted from) her unconscious identification with her pupils, but the features may also have resulted from her *conscious* sympathy for the students. Indeed, many causes are logically possible. Kettner's premises fail to guarantee that it is reasonable to believe that any particular one was causally relevant. What Kettner may mean, however, is that the features could *plausibly* be said to derive from M (see Kettner, 1991, 165, his discussion of the role of background conditions in sifting out unreasonably "abduced" explanations). On this second interpretation, the schema is trivial. Suppose that we first establish that the teacher's unassertiveness is unlikely if it is not caused by her unconscious identification with her pupils *and* that it is reasonable to think that it was so caused; then, of course, the hypothesis that this factor was causally relevant is reasonable. It is hard to see how such trivial arguments could be of use in defending Freudian theory, or in showing how thematic affinities warrant causal claims.

Conclusion

Should psychoanalysis, then, be judged by non-natural science standards? Before answering, several points should be stressed. First, there are many different types of standards for evaluating scientific theories; some might be peculiar to a particular science or to a small group of them, but be irrelevant to the present discussion. For example, physicists might not take seriously any theory in physics that is nonquantitative. Such a standard for deciding "what to take seriously," however, is not an evidential standard. It does not say that for data to be confirmatory, it is either necessary or sufficient that they possess such and such characteristics.

Second, within the class of evidential standards, it is important to distinguish between fundamental and nonfundamental standards. We might, for example, have empirical evidence that experimental data are unlikely to confirm the efficacy of a certain drug unless a double blind procedure is used. It might not be necessary to meet this standard, in contrast, in confirming the efficacy of certain surgical procedures when expectations of cure are known to be causally impotent. These cases do not show that different fundamental epistemic standards are to be used in judging the effects of drugs and surgery. Rather, there is simply a difference in what the empirical evidence shows as to what rival hypotheses need to be ruled out in the two cases. This point is relevant to Hopkins's contention (1988, 37) that psychoanalytic theory is an extension of common-sense psychology. In some respects, this is true. For example, both appeal to motives in explaining behavior. Yet experimental evidence might be needed to confirm certain Freudian causal claims and not certain commonsense causal claims, not because fundamentally different epistemic standards apply but because empirical evidence mandates that confirmation of Freudian hypotheses be experimental. (For a further discussion of the connection between commonsense psychology and Freudian psychology, see chapter 3, pp. 106–124.)

A third point concerns the appropriateness of using certain rigorous standards that, for practical or moral reasons, cannot be satisfied in certain areas of inquiry. For example, many analysts would consider it inappropriate to demand experimental evidence for confirming the interpretation of a single dream of a single patient. It would be inappropriate, so the argument runs, because it is simply not feasible to do such an experiment. The lack of feasibility, however, is no guarantee that an experimental standard is inappropriate. Suppose that the effects of capital punishment on the homicide rate can only be gauged by doing a controlled experiment. If it is not feasible to do such a study, what follows is not that experimental evidence is unneeded, but rather that hypotheses about the deterrence value of capital punishment cannot be warranted.

So, should psychoanalysis be judged by special evidential standards? Based on an examination of the proposals made in the literature so far, there is no reason to think that the basic evidential standards for judging psychoanalytic causal claims are different from those appropriate for judging causal claims in the natural sciences.

I turn next to some natural science standards that are relevant to debates about Freudian theory. It might be misleading, however, to call them "natural science standards." They are in one respect like principles of deductive logic. They are applicable to the natural sciences, but they are also "content-neutral" and therefore relevant to conjectures of the social sciences and folk psychology as well.

Chapter 2
Natural Science Standards

There exist today powerful considerations driving many philosophers and psychologists to deny the possibility of establishing interesting, objective, nonrelativistic evidential standards for appraising scientific theories. These include the total failure of the logical empiricists' program for developing a logic of confirmation, or even any agreed upon theory of confirmation; the alleged failure of all foundationalist and coherence theories of knowledge (for an interesting third alternative, see Haack 1993); the widespread influence of Kuhnian relativism; and the development of certain types of naturalist and feminist epistemologies. Fine and Forbes (1986) allude to one piece of this overall picture, the lack of an agreed upon theory of confirmation, and make the following suggestion: that psychoanalysis be judged by whatever standards are employed in somatic medicine. This is an interesting possibility, but there are certain obstacles. There is a growing minority within medicine who contribute to what is sometimes called "holistic medicine" or "alternative medicine" (see the critical papers in Stalker and Glymour 1985). Some of the standards employed by, for example, those who advocate the use of holistic psychotherapies or the use of mental imagery in treating cancer or homeopathic medicine are very low indeed. The problem, then, arises: which standards in somatic medicine are to be used in judging psychoanalysis—the relatively low standards of holistic medicine or the higher standards of more traditional medicine?

If one abandons all normative judgments about standards, and limits one's approach to an empirical description of standards that are in fact used (this may not be what Fine and Forbes have in mind), there appears to be no satisfactory basis for choosing. Even if this problem were solved, some analysts might complain that medical standards are the wrong ones for judging Freudian theory, which after all is a psychological theory. The proper standards, it might be said, are those employed generally in the field of psychology. Again, however, which are these? Should we use the standards of those behaviorists who rule out *a priori* any psychological theory that talks about unobservables? Or should we use the standards embraced by those cognitivists who insist on experimental evidence for the confirmation of all causal hypotheses, thus begging the question against analysts not accepting this requirement? Because I see no way around the obstacles confronting a purely descriptive tack, I intend to adopt a more traditional approach, that of philosophy of science and epistemology, to try to articulate and defend certain standards that ought to be employed if we care about the confirmation of Freudian theory. I shall not directly discuss the arguments of those who say that such objective standards cannot be found, but if I am right, there must be something wrong with their arguments. The proof will be the standards that are articulated and the arguments that are made on their behalf.

The standards that I do defend are relatively modest; even taken together, they hardly constitute a general theory of theory appraisal. Even if they are correct, they do not hang together in the right sort of way. My primary reason for discussing them is their relevance to disagreements about the Freudian evidence, although they also have application outside of Freudian psychology.

Evidential Standards

Differentialness

One evidentiary issue in the Freudian debate concerns the need to rule out all plausible rivals to a Freudian hypothesis. Some defenders of Freud deny the need to do this.

One such Freudian, Calvin Hall, is the author of experimental studies of Freudian hypotheses about dreaming. Although his arguments have been criticized on the grounds that he fails to consider rival interpretations of his data, Hall anticipates and tries to block the criticism. Hall argues (1963) that there is no need to consider empirical findings from the point of view of other theories so long as the theory being tested meets three conditions that maintain: (1) its heuristic value; (2) its capacity for making sense out of a wide variety of phenomena; and (3) its ability to generate correct predictions.

Some analysts also object to the requirement that all rival hypotheses be discredited on the grounds that there are, in principle, an infinite number of them. If we do an experiment that eliminates two or three, there remain an infinite number of other rivals. Consequently, the argument continues, the tested hypothesis will still have a zero degree of probability. Assuming that some scientific hypotheses have empirical support, but none would if we had to rule out all competitors, then there is something wrong with the requirement that all rivals need to be ruled out. It sets the standards for confirmation at too high a level.

Two philosophers of science, Arthur Fine and Mickey Forbes (1986), also reject the need to rule out all plausible competitors to a Freudian hypothesis. They write: " . . . the availability of alternative explanatory hypotheses for a given body of data is a well-known feature of every reasonably complex scientific investigation. Moreover, one is generally not able to eliminate all the plausible rivals to a particular hypothesis. It follows from the fact that science goes on in this situation that for data to count as supporting a hypothesis it is not necessary to first rule out all competitors" (238).

Another philosopher, Kathleen Wilkes (1990, 248–249), responds to a paper of mine (Erwin 1988) by criticizing what she alleges to be my argument: that experimental evidence in support of Freudian hypotheses is weakened because one could always find an alternative explanation. She comments that this is not a good argument, that the ingenious mind can always dream up a rival explanation. She concludes (249) that hypotheses can win support even when there are rivals.

The aforementioned views would seem to receive intuitive support from the following consideration. Suppose that there are a number of hypotheses that purport to explain certain data and we narrow down the list to two or three. Have we not, then, increased the probability for each surviving hypothesis? For example, suppose that there are exactly five rival hypotheses, and experiments rule out all but two. If prior to the experiments the probability of each of the five was .20, then later the probability of the remaining two has been increased to .50. Assuming that confirmation is an increase in probability, then each of the surviving hypotheses has been confirmed to some degree.

Consider the following case. Dozens of hypotheses have been proposed to explain why graduate record examination (GRE) scores fell in America over a decade. One commentator claims to have found 50 rival explanations. Let us assume that he did and that all are roughly equal in plausibility, but we begin a process of looking for data to rule out some of them. Suppose that through ingenious experiments, we rule out most of them. Do we not now have more reason to believe each of the remaining hypotheses? If the answer is yes, have we not then found at least some supporting evidence for these? Granted, decisive evidence has not yet been uncovered: we still do not know which of the remaining hypotheses are true. Nevertheless, has not the epistemic standing of the survivors improved?

Despite the above arguments, Erwin and Siegel (1989) take the position that *all* confirmation is "differential." What this means is the following: For any body of evidence *E* and any hypothesis *H*, *E* confirms *H* differentially exactly if *E* provides at least some reason for believing *H* to be true and does not provide equal (or better) reason for believing some incompatible rival hypothesis that is at least as plausible. Saying that all confirmation is "differential" in this sense implies a high standard for evidential support. Suppose that in my example of falling GRE scores, a long series of experiments rules out 48 rival hypotheses, but two remain and are equally plausible. On the differential standard, both hypotheses have zero empirical support—despite all the work that has been done. What we have confirmed is the disjunction of the two remaining hypotheses:

either H_1 or H_2 is true. Neither disjunct by itself, however, has been confirmed to any degree.

One argument that might be given for a differential view of confirmation is that it gives a better account than a nondifferential view of actual scientific practice. In cases where scientists deem experimentation necessary, the main epistemic reason becomes obvious on a differential view. We do experiments to rule out plausible competitors to the hypothesis being tested, and the reason this is required is that confirmation cannot take place without the discounting of competitors. The trouble with this argument, however, is that it begs the question against Freudians who do not agree that experimentation is necessary precisely because they reject a differential standard of confirmation. We could say that they are not being *scientific,* or are not being *good scientists,* but without some independent argument, such charges would be unfounded.

A better argument is given in Erwin and Siegel (1989, 116–117). It concerns the epistemic nature of confirmation. Suppose that we run 50 equally good experiments, and find 25 positive and 25 negative results. The overall results support neither the hypothesis being tested nor its negation. The obvious reason is that there is a canceling effect: the data provide just as much reason to believe not-H as H and, consequently, no (good) reason to believe either. However, this same canceling effect occurs in a single experiment when the results are nondifferential. Suppose that evidence E is consistent with both T_1 and its logically incompatible and equally plausible rival T_2. Assume for a moment that E confirms both. If they are logically incompatible (when combined with suitable auxiliary assumptions), and E confirms T_2, then from T_2 (and the auxiliary assumptions) we can infer *not* T_1. So, if E were to confirm T_1, it would equally well confirm its negation.

In saying this, we are not saying that the warrant for T_2 automatically transfers to the denial of T_1. We are not, that is, committed to the following principle: If E is evidence for H_1, and H_1 entails H_2, then E will necessarily be evidence for H_2. One may not realize that H_1 entails H_2. However, in the example being discussed, it is assumed that we are aware of the incompatibility of T_1 and T_2. Consequently, if we had evidence that T_2 were true, then we would have some reason to believe not-T_1.

So, assuming that we are aware of the incompatibility, if E gives us some reason to believe that T_1 is true, it gives us just as much reason to believe that T_1 is not true. There is a canceling effect exactly analogous to that in the case where a series of experiments provide flatly inconsistent results. In both sorts of cases, the evidence is not confirmatory to any degree because it provides just as much reason to believe the negation of a hypothesis as the hypothesis itself. Such a reason is not a good reason to think that the tested hypothesis is true, or that it is false.

The above argument appears to beg the question against someone who holds that increasing the probability of a hypothesis is to confirm it to some degree. In this view, if we were to eliminate several plausible rivals to T_1 and T_2, we would increase the probability of both, and thereby confirm both, despite their incompatibility and their equal plausibility. So a separate argument is needed against the idea that any increase in the probability of a hypothesis necessarily confirms it to some degree. Erwin and Siegel (1989) provide such an argument, as does Achinstein (1983). There are many cases where the probability of H increases and yet there is no supporting evidence. If I buy a lottery ticket, I have increased the probability of winning compared to my not buying a ticket. I can also say: I have more reason than I did before to think that I will win. Yet, there may still be no good reason to think that I will win; I have no good evidence, even a weak amount, that my ticket will be the winning ticket. So, too, if a man on death row has his death sentence commuted, he has increased his chances of surviving until the 22nd century, but he has no confirmation for that proposition. He has no evidence that he will live that long. In brief, not every increase in probability constitutes a reason for believing a proposition to be true (for further counter-examples, see Erwin and Siegel 1989; Achinstein 1983).

Someone who holds an increase in probability view of confirmation could reply that a small increase may yield no reason for belief, but still provide some degree of confirmation. However, our disagreement, then, is only verbal. Siegel and I are using "confirmation" in an *epistemic* sense: We are stipulating that to say that a hypothesis is confirmed by certain evidence means, in part, that the evidence provides an epistemic reason for believing that the hypothesis is true.

It could also be replied that even though a small increase in probability is not necessarily sufficient for confirmation, an increase in probability to more than .50 always is enough. On this point, however, Siegel and I agree, but we note that this claim is compatible with a differential standard. In any case where the probability of *H* being true is greater than .50, *H* will have no incompatible competitor that is just as likely to be true. (For a discussion of additional issues, see Erwin and Siegel 1989; for a reader who remains unconvinced about a differential standard, see the conclusion of the next section.)

I return now to the reasons for rejecting a differential view. As noted earlier, Calvin Hall (1963) claims that we can ignore the fact that some theory besides the one we are using could have predicted our findings, provided that his three conditions are met. However, he gives no argument for thinking that these conditions are sufficient.

Suppose that a behaviorist claims that a wide range of human behavior can be explained by an operant conditioning hypothesis (roughly, current environmental stimuli plus a subject's history of rewards and punishments explain the behavior). This hypothesis might meet all three of Hall's conditions, but if a cognitive explanation were equally plausible, we could still ask: what argument is there for believing that the operant conditioning hypothesis is correct? Hall does nothing to meet this challenge; he gives no reason to believe that satisfying his three conditions will always be sufficient for confirmation. In fact, the absence of an argument is not the only problem.

Suppose that we run a series of experiments using a so-called disassociative design, in which the experimenter attempts to separate awareness from the alleged conditioning process, to determine which of these is causally responsible for the responses. Such experiments have been carried out and the data clearly support a cognitivist explanation, as shown by Brewer's (1974) extensive review.

Suppose, then, that we do new experiments without using a disassociative design and the findings are neutral between a behaviorist and conditioning hypothesis. If Hall were right, the satisfaction of his three conditions for the behaviorist hypothesis would secure confirmation for it—despite the fact that a *more* plausible explanation exists, that is, the cognitivist explanation would have the edge given the data from the disassociative experiments.

In response to the objection about the sheer number of rivals, it is true than even if we discredit all known rivals to a hypothesis, an infinite number of unformulated rivals remain. However, this fact does not show that the differential standard cannot be met. What this standard requires is that we discredit all rivals of equal or greater plausibility. Unformulated hypotheses have no empirical plausibility; consequently, they do not need to be ruled out. I should also note that on a differential standard, an experiment can yield confirmation without ruling out even all of the *known* competitors to the hypothesis being tested. In many cases, an experiment will be designed to rule out only one or two competitors, but that will suffice if our background evidence renders implausible the remaining known hypotheses (except for the hypothesis that survives the experimental test).

As to Fine and Forbes's (1986) comment that "science goes on" in situations where one is not able to eliminate all plausible rivals to a hypothesis, Erwin and Siegel reply (1989, 107) that it fails to follow that the tested hypothesis is supported. Many Freudians have gone on for quite a long time believing that central parts of Freudian theory are warranted by clinical data. They may be right, but they may also be mistaken. The fact that they continue to believe in clinical confirmation is no guarantee that their hypotheses are supported. However, this reply may misconstrue what Fine and Forbes meant. They might have meant by "science goes on" that confirmation occurs even without ruling out all plausible competitors. If that is what is meant, however, then they are merely asserting—and not arguing—that confirmation occurs even in the absence of meeting a differential standard. On the contrary, I have argued that it does not.

When Wilkes (1990, 249) claims that hypotheses can win support even where there are rivals, I assume she means *plausible* rivals. If she does not, then her criticism of my paper (Erwin 1988a) is totally irrelevant. I nowhere claim that a putative confirmation for a Freudian hypothesis can be undercut by pointing to a rival but implausible explanation, or even one that has some degree of plausibility but not as much as the Freudian one. If 3 years of analysis are followed by the elimination of a patient's phobia, it would hardly undercut the analyst's claim of a cure to point out that a change in the weather or a change in government or excessive sunlight *might* have caused the result. Suppose, however, that the rival explanation holds that spontaneous remission occurred, and suppose that we have solid evidence that this type of phobia usually disappears without formal treatment within 3 years. Would not the failure to rule out this quite plausible explanation undercut the analyst's evidence for a cure? More generally, the issue raised in my (1988a) paper, and the issue raised by a differential standard, is this: Can confirmation of a Freudian hypothesis occur even when a rival hypothesis explains the same data *and* is at least as plausible as the Freudian one? If Wilkes is answering yes, which she must do if her comments are to be relevant to my paper, she needs to argue for that position. She does do that, but her argument is not a good one. After commenting about the desirability of having alternative theories, she writes:

What is intellectually dishonest, however (given that we are discussing a theory that purports to be comprehensive), is to argue that Freudian psychoanalysis is unsupported because: for Smith's neurosis we can offer X as an alternative explanation, for Brown's neurosis we can offer Y, for Jones' z, . . . and so forth. This is *ad hoc* and more of a spoiling operation than an attempt to supply a real alternative; Kline [reference omitted] is entirely right to stamp on it. Hypotheses can win support even where there are rivals. (249)

Suppose that Smith is depressed, Brown suffers from extreme anxiety, Jones has an obsessive-compulsive disorder, and a Freudian explains all three problems in terms of repressed infantile wishes. Would it be "intellectually dishonest"—or even unreasonable—to offer three separate explanations? Not necessarily. For example, someone might explain Smith's depression by pointing to the recent death of his wife, Brown's anxiety in terms of operant conditioning (Ullmann and Krasner 1969) and Jones' disorder in terms of Eysenck's modified classical conditioning theory. Surely, it is conceivable that the problems have three separate causes and the empirical evidence indicates that this is so. If that is what the evidence shows, why would it be unreasonable to accept the three separate explanations? The answer is obvious: it would not.

It might be complained that in the above example there are three different types of "neurotic" problems. (One reason for deleting the category "neurosis" from the *Diagnostic and Statistical Manual of the Mental Disorders [DSM-III]* of the *American Psychiatric Association [APA]* is that it groups together very different clinical problems that may well have different etiologies.) To avoid this problem, assume that Smith, Brown, and Jones are all depressed. Still, our evidence may indicate that the cause of Smith's depression may be biological; Brown's depression, a traumatic event; and Jones's depression, low self-esteem. If that is what our evidence were to show, then it would be reasonable and hardly intellectually dishonest to prefer the three separate explanations to the more unified account. Furthermore, if an analyst had data concerning the three patients, but the non-Freudian "three-separate-causes" hypothesis explained the data just as well *and* was just as plausible given our total evidence, then, as argued earlier, the analyst's hypothesis would not be confirmed.

Finally, let us change the example in one respect. Suppose that the non-Freudian and Freudian hypotheses are equally plausible except possibly for one thing: the latter is more parsimonious in that it cites a single cause for all three depressions. Would that tip the balance in favor of the Freudian explanation? I take up this issue in the next section, but whatever the correct answer, it has no bearing on the issue of differentialness. If parsimony, simplicity, and the like have separate epistemic value, then they can break a tie between rival theories that fit the observational evidence equally well. If and when that happens, there may be confirmation, but that would be no violation of differentialness. If a Freudian hypothesis is rendered more plausible than its rival because it is more parsimonious or systematic, then its rival is discounted by that fact. The rival would not be of equal or greater plausibility, so its existence would be no barrier to confirming the Freudian hypothesis even on a differential standard.

I conclude, then, that Wilkes is mistaken in implying that it would be intellectually dishonest in countering a Freudian etiologic hypothesis with one that cites three separate causes for three neuroses. Whether it is reasonable to prefer the more complex explanation depends on our total evidence, including the relative parsimony of each theory *if* such a feature is evidentially relevant. Wilkes also has failed to give any good reason to believe that a hypothesis can win evidential support even when its rival is just as plausible (or even more plausible). If she were to mean only that a *less* plausible rival is no impediment to confirmation, that would be a wholly trivial point, one not requiring any argument and one consistent with every claim made in Erwin (1988a).

I conclude, further, that one reasonable standard for evaluating evidence is a differential one. Evidence E confirms a hypothesis H *only if* it does so "differentially." E confirms H *differentially* exactly if E provides at least some reason for believing that H is true and does not provide equal (or better) reason for believing some rival hypothesis that is at least as plausible.

A differential standard by itself does not commit one to a demand for experimental evidence. However, it might do so when combined with certain empirical propositions about the plausibility of non-Freudian rivals. For example, Grünbaum (1984) argues that when data are collected in a psychoanalytic clinical setting, a suggestibility hypothesis often serves as a credible rival to certain Freudian hypotheses. Fine and Forbes (1986) argue against this position, but they also argue that even if it is correct, confirmation of Freudian theory may still occur. In arguing for a differential standard, I have disputed only the latter point. (The credibility of a suggestibility hypothesis is taken up in chapter 3, pp. 95–106). If it proves credible (more precisely, of equal or greater plausibility than its Freudian rivals), then this demonstration when combined with a differential standard will strengthen the case for insisting on experimental (or epidemiological) evidence. A differential standard, then, is by itself neutral between those who rest the case for Freudian theory partly or largely on clinical evidence and those who, like Grünbaum, argue for experimental requirements, but when combined with certain empirical evidence, it may favor the second position.

Simplicity

A second issue about evidential standards concerns the role of the so-called pragmatic virtues, especially simplicity, in tilting the balance in favor of Freudian explanations. Some writers distinguish between simplicity, parsimony, and comprehensiveness; others do not. For the purposes of this discussion, I use the term "simplicity" interchangeably with the other two.

In responding to my analysis of the Freudian experimental data (Erwin 1988a), Paul Kline writes:

> I now want to consider the claim explicit in part of Erwin's analysis and implicit in the rest—namely that many of the experimental findings cited in support of Freudian theory can be explained by other superior hypotheses. Where there are competing explanations the simplest is to be preferred: Occam's razor or the law of parsimony. (Kline 1988, 226; see also Erwin 1986a, and Kline's reply, 1986, 230–232).

Kline is suggesting here a general standard for theory selection: where there are competing explanations, the simplest is to be preferred. He also points out (1988, 226), that in judging the relative simplicity of a psychoanalytic explanation and a competitor, one may have to look not only at one experiment but at a number of them (a point on which I concur).

Other supporters of Freudian theory have proposed a standard similar to Kline's. For example, an APA subcommittee supporting the use of psychoanalysis in the study of history (American Psychiatric Association 1976, 19) proposes that one criterion for judging a psychohistorical assumption not susceptible to direct proof is this: that the assumption not be inherently unlikely and that it make comprehensible a series of events otherwise requiring a number of separate assumptions for their explanation.

If Kline and the APA committee on psychohistory are right, at least two important things follow. First, it makes it harder to demonstrate in certain cases, such as psychohistorical contexts, that we need experimental evidence. For in such contexts, the only plausible rivals may be discounted by an appeal to simplicity; experiments may not be needed. Second, as Kline suggests, the issue also bears on the interpretation of the Freudian experimental evidence. Where the experimental evidence is neutral between a Freudian and a non-Freudian rival, an appeal to simplicity may favor the Freudian explanation

One could reply to Kline and the APA committee as Hans Eysenck does (1986, 381): Freudian theory is not a single, unified theory; it is a collection of minitheories. This is an important point, one that to some degree *favors* the Freudian enterprise. Given the lack of unity, a disproof of certain parts of Freudian theory does not condemn the entire theory. The reverse point, however, is that one cannot argue that a Freudian explanation is simpler because it is part of a one large, unified theory. It is not. Nevertheless, Eysenck's point does not dispose of the entire issue. In certain cases, a Freudian can still argue that one of Freud's minitheories, say his theory of dreams or slips, provides a unified, comprehensive account of a wide range of phenomena. In such a case, it might be simpler to accept the minitheory than a number of separate hypotheses from commonsense psychology.

Another reply to Kline is that non-Freudian commonsense psychological explanations may themselves be systematic. Some philosophers argue that such explanations are part of a single theory, so-called folk psychology. That this "theory" is systematic and unified in the way that certain Freudian minitheories are may well be challenged, but folk theory is not the only alternative. In certain areas, Freudian theory must compete with rival, non-Freudian psychoanalytic accounts, as well as with cognitivist, conditioning, or biological hypotheses that are part of larger theories. This point, however, does not challenge the correctness of Kline's standard; rather, it questions its scope. Obviously, if the rival hypothesis is, all things considered, just as simple as the Freudian hypothesis, then we cannot use simplicity as a reason for preferring the latter. This platitude does not challenge Kline's contention that simpler theories are to be preferred.

Another, and more damaging, reply to Kline was suggested in the last section. As I noted in my reply to Wilkes, even if it is simpler to postulate one Freudian cause to explain three neuroses, nevertheless the empirical evidence may make it more likely that there are three different causes. Simplicity, quite clearly, is not the only epistemic value.

Most philosophers of science would not dispute what I have said so far about simplicity. I now want to raise a more controversial issue: Does simplicity have any epistemic value at all, as opposed to merely aesthetic or pragmatic value? More precisely, does the fact that one theory is simpler (more parsimonious, more systematic) than its rival count *in and of itself* as rational grounds for believing the theory to be true (or approximately true), even if those grounds can be overridden by observational evidence? As will be argued shortly, this issue is separate from the question, Does simplicity ever count as grounds for belief? Suppose that we have evidence that psychoses are primarily caused by biological factors. Given such evidence, the fact that a theory postulates a biological cause of a certain psychosis may count in its favor relative to a conditioning hypothesis. That does not mean, however, that we are entitled to infer a general epistemic principle (call it "Darwin's razor"): biological explanations are to be preferred. The issue about simplicity is the same as that raised earlier about thematic affinity: Does simplicity (or thematic affinity) *itself* have evidential value?

I will not review here all of the arguments used to prove that simplicity has epistemic value, but it seems to me, and to at least some other philosophers, that they have all failed. Consider a few examples.

One might argue that scientific realism presupposes that simplicity and the other pragmatic virtues have epistemic value. I doubt that one can show this, but if it were shown, another premise would still be needed: that scientific realism is true. That premise might become very implausible once it were shown that scientific realism is not true if simplicity, parsimony, etc. have no epistemic value on their own.

A second option is to try to find some a priori proof that simplicity has epistemic value. I do not think that this can be ruled out, but so far no such argument has been found that works. One could also argue on empirical grounds that most relatively simple theories are true. However, given the tremendous number of theories that the human race has formulated, who has such evidence either way? Even if one had such evidence, that would still fail to show that simplicity counts in and of itself as rational grounds for belief.

Another option is to claim that the world itself is simple, or that nature prefers simplicity. It is unclear what these claims amount to, but in any event those who make them fail to provide supporting evidence or explain how their truth would show that simplicity has epistemic value.

Perhaps the most preferred line of argument is to appeal to scientific practice. If this means an appeal to what scientists actually do, it has two problems. First, scientists disagree as to whether simplicity has more than aesthetic or pragmatic value. Second, even if they agreed, this might be because they accepted a false, or at least unwarranted, philosophical theory. Sometimes, and more plausibly, the appeal to scientific practice involves an appeal to scientific cases, such as the Copernican example. The problem here is that one must show not merely that the theory was accepted by scientists at a certain time but that there was warrant for doing so *and* that simplicity constituted part of that warrant. That is not easy to do.

Elliot Sober (1990) provides some nice case histories from biology that illustrate the difficulty. One concerns the controversy over units of selection. Some biologists have argued that group selection hypotheses are less parsimonious than hypotheses claiming that the unit of selection is the individual or the gene. If they were right to infer that the former hypotheses have a lower initial probability than rival hypotheses, this might appear to be an instance where parsimony makes an epistemic difference. However, as Sober demonstrates, it is not simplicity, but empirical details about natural selection that justify the initial assignment of a lower probability for group selection hypotheses. The general difficulty is this: In cases where simpler hypotheses should be preferred, how do we show that it is simplicity, and not empirical details, that supplies the justification? Perhaps the early Copernicans were justified in preferring the Copernican hypothesis, but perhaps that is because their background evidence made it implausible to believe that all those epicycles postulated by Ptolemy were real.

We have, then, two rival epistemic theories about cases where simpler theories are justifiably preferred. One says that simplicity itself constitutes part of the warrant; the other says that background theories and evidence alone provide the warrant. If we cannot point to something that favors the first explanation, there is at least one good reason for not according simplicity separate epistemic value. If we do not, then we do not have to answer the difficult question: Why would simplicity in and of itself provide a reason for believing that a theory is true?

It should also be noted that simplicity can count against a hypothesis. What I mean is not that it sometimes has independent negative value, but that given our overall evidence the simpler of two hypotheses is less likely to be true. Consider Ullmann and Krasner's (1969) case for explaining the etiology of all of the psychoses and neuroses in terms of a single cause: operant conditioning. They appeal to the parsimonious nature of their explanation, but in fact that feature counts against their theory. Given the evidence available to them in 1969, and the evidence has strengthened considerably in the last two decades, it was and is unlikely that all cases of depression, anxiety and phobias have the same type of cause as autism, schizophrenia, and what used to be called "manic-depressive disorder." The evidence is compelling, and was so even in 1969, that the causes of some or all of the psychoses are primarily genetic and biochemical, while at least some of the so-called neuroses are not. A theory that provided a unified account of the phenomena was less likely, not more likely, to be true, other things being equal, than a theory postulating separate types of causation. By itself, this does not tell against the view that simplicity in and of itself makes it more reasonable to believe a theory than its less simple competitors. A defender of that view can reply that in the Ullmann and Krasner case simplicity was overridden by empirical considerations. Still, there are problems. Suppose that we were to subtract bits of evidence supporting the multiple causation theory of neuroses and psychoses. If simplicity has separate epistemic weight, will we not reach a point where the theory has just a little bit of evidence but not enough to outweigh the simplicity of the Ullmann and Krasner theory? So even if the latter theory had no observational support, there would be no reason to prefer the multiple causation account despite its empirical backing.

Reflect on one more implication of the simplicity-has-separate-weight view. Suppose that, at a certain time, the operant conditioning theory of autistic behavior had exactly the same amount of empirical support as some biological account. On the theory that simplicity provides separate epistemic support, why could Ullmann and Krasner have not given the edge to their theory of autism by simply tacking on additional operant conditioning hypotheses about other clinical phenomena, provided that there was no counterevidence? They could then claim that their combined theory provided a more unified account than the biological view and, hence, was more likely to be true. I think that such implications are implausible, and they are avoided by the position that denies simplicity any separate epistemic weight. However, I cannot demonstrate the implausibility of either implication, so the simplicity supporter can reject the charge of implausibility, or perhaps explain why the view does not really have the consequences that I attributed to it. In the end the issue may turn solely on the first problem: is there any good reason to believe that simplicity in and of itself carries epistemic weight? If there is not, then we should not give it such weight, given that we have a plausible rival explanation of cases where we justifiably prefer the simpler of two rival hypotheses. The justification lies solely in our background theories and observational evidence.

The upshot of the above considerations is that Kline's standard should be rejected and the following standard should replace it: In order to confirm some hypothesis H, it may be necessary to rule out some rival, H_1, even if H is simpler. (Simpler theories are not always to be preferred.) There are three separate arguments for this standard.

First, even if simplicity does have independent epistemic value, a Freudian hypothesis may be less preferable because a rival is more plausible on empirical grounds. Second, again assuming a separate epistemic role for simplicity, the simplicity of a Freudian hypothesis may have to be balanced against other "pragmatic" features of rival theories (one kind of simplicity against another kind). For example, it may be simpler to accept a Freudian hypothesis that postulates a single cause compared to one that postulates three, but it may be more parsimonious to accept the latter. That may happen, for example, if the Freudian hypothesis commits us to new entities or processes, such as the id or Freudian repression, for which we have no independent evidence and the rival hypothesis does not do anything similar. Third, even if a Freudian hypothesis and a rival are evidentially tied except for the former being simpler, it is difficult to show that this fact *by itself* is a good reason for thinking that the Freudian hypothesis is more likely to be true. In fact, I do not think it can be shown at all. What one might do is something quite different. One might argue successfully, in a particular context, that our background evidence shows that the simpler of two competing hypotheses is more likely to be true. For example, suppose that we have grounds for thinking that various phobias form a natural kind and our evidence indicates that phobias *A, B,* and *C* are all caused by repressed infantile wishes. If experimental evidence is neutral between a Freudian and commonsense etiology for a fourth phobia, say agoraphobia, then our background evidence may support the Freudian hypothesis. However, in such a case, it is the background evidence and not simplicity that tips the balance. Furthermore, as the operant conditioning case discussed earlier suggests, the verdict can go in the other direction. If our empirical evidence suggests diverse causes for different types of phobias, then the fact that Freudian theory provides a single explanation counts not for it but against it (although, again, it is the evidence, not simplicity itself, that makes the epistemic difference).

Conclusion

For someone who disagrees with one or more of the previous arguments, some narrowing of our differences may be possible. Concerning simplicity, someone might say: Even if there is no independent argument to prove this, intuition supports the idea that simplicity and the other pragmatic virtues have separate epistemic value. However, they provide reasons to prefer one theory to another only if other things are equal. If the observational evidence favors the less simple of two hypotheses, then other things are not equal. We may have more reason in such a case to believe the less simple hypothesis.

To this sort of theorist, I reply that our differences about actual cases in the Freudian literature may be minimal. In cases where the Freudian hypothesis is preferable to a less simple rival, even though the experimental evidence favors neither, the only thing we may disagree about is the epistemic basis for the preference. The simplicity theorist says that simplicity itself is making the difference, whereas, I say it is our background theories and evidence. The only cases where we might disagree in our evaluations is where our background evidence does *not* make it more likely that the simpler of two hypotheses in a given area is more likely to be true, other things being equal. The simplicity theorist may still claim support for the simpler of two hypotheses even where they are tied on the basis of the observational evidence. In such a case, I would disagree and hold that neither hypothesis is supported. However, cases of this sort in the Freudian literature may be relatively few in number.

On the issue of differentialness, we need to distinguish between claims of strong and weak support when the differential condition is violated. Suppose that someone says that the evidential support for H can be so strong that we can be warranted in believing it despite the fact that we know that our evidence equally well supports an incompatible rival, G. I reject this position not only for the reason given in the first section but for the additional reason given in Erwin and Siegel (1989). On such a view, we can be warranted in believing a contradiction. In the case just mentioned, if we knew that G entailed not-H, then we could reasonably infer both H and not H on this "strong" nondifferential view.

A more plausible nondifferential view says merely that H and G can receive weak support even when the overall evidence favors neither. Someone who holds this position can make a mental adjustment when reading my assessment of certain Freudian evidence. If the differential condition is violated in a particular case, I will conclude that the evidence in that case is nonconfirmatory; my opponent will say that the evidence is weak but not necessarily nonexistent. I will still press the following questions: Of what value is evidential support for *P* that is so weak that it provides just as much reason to believe that *P* is false? and, What is the difference that matters between saying that *P* has no empirical support and saying that its support is so weak that it provides just as much reason to believe the negation of *P*? Still, if someone says that there is a difference that matters, then he or she can make the proper adjustment where necessary.

Inference to the Best Explanation

In Erwin (1986a), I criticize a study by Friedman (1952) on the grounds that a crucial premise in his argument is unsupported. The premise is that a subject's mention of a loss of tails in referring to a story about a broken toy elephant is a sign of unconscious castration anxiety. Paul Kline replies (1986, 230) that this is not a good criticism. Even if the validity of Friedman's castration fables has not been established, he argues, I fail to provide an alternative non-Freudian explanation of Friedman's findings. Kline concludes: "In this case, a sensible or even plausible one is extremely hard. It is up to the opposition to provide it" (230).

The issue raised by Kline's reply concerns an inference to the best explanation. Friedman uses Freudian theory to predict certain responses for his experimental subjects. His predictions are confirmed and, let us assume, there is no known plausible explanation of his findings other than the Freudian one. Does this give us at least some rational grounds for believing the Freudian account?

Kline raises the same issue in discussing Scodel's (1957) results. Scodel predicted, on the basis of Freud's orality hypothesis, that his oral-dependent subjects would prefer large breasts. They did not, so he inferred that the orality hypothesis had been disconfirmed. But he did not try to explain his findings. Kline argues (1981, 123) that the only plausible explanation is that the orality hypothesis is true, and the subjects were experiencing reaction formation. He concludes that the data confirmed, rather than disconfirmed, Freud's hypothesis.

One thing different about the Scodel experiment is that Kline brought in reaction formation after the fact, so to speak. Scodel himself did not predict that reaction formation would occur. However, I would agree with Kline that it does not matter that his interpretation was offered only after Scodel had published his findings. If his argument is cogent, why does it matter that it is *post hoc?* From a logical point of view, it does not matter.

Another issue raised by the Friedman and Scodel experiments concerns the status of auxiliary assumptions. Even if we grant that inference to the best explanation (hereinafter, IBE) is a legitimate form of inference, should we require that auxiliary assumptions invoked in an interpretation of an experimental test be warranted *before* IBE becomes applicable? Before arguing that the orality hypothesis plus the assumption about reaction formation best explains Scodel's results, do we first have to provide independent evidence that reaction formation truly did occur? Kline assumes that we do not.

Philosophers have debated a number of issues about IBE that need not concern us here. For example, is it the most fundamental form of non-demonstrative inference and is what is explained always, or just sometimes, the data that support the hypothesis being inferred? What *is* relevant here is the role IBE plays, and ought to play, in the inductive practices of psychoanalysts.

One such issue concerns the meaning of "best" explanation. Do we mean the best available (i.e., the best explanation that anyone knows of) or the best of all possible explanations? A second issue concerns the criteria for identifying the best explanation. Is the best the most plausible (i.e., the most likely) or is it something else? As to the second issue, Peter Lipton (1991) chooses the second option on the grounds that choosing the first (the plausibility option) would reduce IBE to triviality. Gil Harman, one of the first philosophers to explore IBE, notes (1992) that Lipton's is the right choice if IBE is to be an independent form of inference.

Lipton's idea is that we identify the best explanation by picking out the "loveliest." The loveliest excels in the pragmatic virtues: simplicity, precision, theoretical elegance, unification, etc. He claims, moreover, that the loveliest explanations are the likeliest to be true (Lipton 1991, 63). (If he were to deny this, he would have difficulty in explaining why the loveliness of an explanation is relevant to our being justified in inferring it to be true.) However, he does nothing to demonstrate the connection between loveliness and likeliness (see Achinstein 1992, 354–355), and, for reasons given in the previous section, I have doubts that this connection can be shown to exist. This is not necessarily a problem for Lipton, who is interested primarily in describing rather than justifying our inductive practices, but I am concerned here with their correctness. Because I see no way to establish the connection between loveliness and likelihood, I will not assume the former as a criterion of the best explanation. If using plausibility as a criterion were to totally trivialize IBE, then so be it: the only defensible version of IBE may be trivial. Someone who wants to render it nontrivial by appealing to the pragmatic virtues has the burden of showing that they are indicators of truth. For reasons given earlier, I doubt that this can be shown.

Leaving out the pragmatic virtues, however, does not completely trivialize IBE. It is not trivial to assert that the best available explanation (i.e. the most plausible one that we have come up with) is always likely to be true. Indeed, this assertion may well be false, as I shall soon argue.

I turn now to the first issue. Is the "best explanation" to be understood as the best available or the best possible? A number of philosophers appear committed to the former. For example, William Lycan (1988) states the rule of IBE as follows:

$F_1, \ldots, F_n$ are facts. Hypothesis H explains $F_1, \ldots, F_n$ ("explains" here is to be read in its nonsuccess sense, as "would explain if true"). No available competing hypothesis explains the F_1 as well as H does.
$\therefore$ (probably) H is true. (129)

The rule stated by Lycan appears to be relied upon very commonly in the psychoanalytic literature. An analyst quite often will tell a psychoanalytic story that makes sense of what the patient has said and done in the course of the analysis, and then offer as supporting grounds the fact that no other such explanatory story is available. For example, consider the case of the man who would not give his name. The analyst (Strean 1984) discusses a patient who refused for a year and a half to reveal his identity on the grounds that the government checks up on people. The analyst argues that the man did not know his real motive, which was his strong unconscious wish to be raped. When he was able to face up to this wish, he revealed his name. Or consider why a certain restaurant does not permit tipping. Bloom (1962) noticed two signs in a restaurant he visited in New York. One said "Hands never touch the food you eat at Chock Full O'Nuts." The second said: "Tipping is not permitted." Bloom points out that the word "tipping" in one sense means "to touch lightly." In premature ejaculation, however, the slightest touch can bring on an orgasm. So, Bloom reasons, the person responsible for the restaurant's policies had an unconscious fear of premature ejaculation; because he feared touching and unconsciously associated it with tipping, he decided to prohibit tipping. In cases such as these, the analyst typically does not provide independent empirical evidence for the interpretation, but infers it on the grounds that it offers the most plausible explanation of the facts of the case that one can think of. Freud appears to use the same sort of argument in his published case histories, such as the Dora and Wolf man cases.

I do not want to place too much stress here on what analysts appear to be doing. In some cases, analysts may, contrary to appearances, be offering a different sort of argument, or presenting an interpretation as a sheer conjecture and not arguing for it at all. Still, I believe that a review of the psychoanalytic journals would show that analysts quite often make use of an *IBE* that has the form laid out by Lycan. As noted earlier, Kline relies on this rule in his interpretation of certain psychoanalytic experiments, and I believe that Fisher and Greenberg (1977) in their review of the Freudian experimental literature do the same. Philosophers who support Freudian theory also frequently rely on some version of IBE that is close to Lycan's account. For example, Sebastian Gardner (1993) writes: "I will argue that psychoanalytic theory provides the most penetrating and satisfying explanation of irrationality. Given that irrationality is real, and requires explanation, this amounts to an argument for the truth of psychoanalytic theory" (1). Assuming that Gardner is referring to the most penetrating and satisfying explanation currently available, he seems to be presupposing Lycan's rule. Where he and Lycan might disagree is in the determination of the *best* available explanation. Lycan appeals to pragmatic criteria such as "simplicity," but he might consider "satisfyingness" too subjective to count as a justificatory reason.

Is an *IBE* legitimate, or as some would say "valid," that is, does it necessarily give at least some rational grounds for belief? Not if it takes the form stated by Lycan which I will designate as IBE_1. There are several problems.

One might be called "the problem of auxiliary assumptions." An experimenter who uses Freudian theory to predict certain observations must make additional assumptions to derive the prediction. Sometimes these auxiliary assumptions are credible and sometimes not. In Scodel's experiment, he assumed that the Thematic Apperception Test (*TAT*) measures oral dependency, something for which there is no credible evidence. Recognizing this lack of evidence, Kline (1981) is careful to say that if we set aside doubts about the TAT, *then* the Freudian explanation invoking reaction formation best explains Scodel's results. However, on IBE_1 (i.e., on the version I am considering), there is no need for such caution. A Freudian can combine the theoretical hypothesis with the auxiliary assumptions and argue that this new theory, the combination, best explains the finding and, consequently, is confirmed to some degree.

I am not suggesting that in every case auxiliary assumptions need independent support. In some cases, we might have empirical evidence that if some theory T and some auxiliary assumptions A can explain some evidence E, then it is likely that T and A are true. So, even if the assumptions that constitute A initially lack credibility, they may pick up support when E is discovered. For example, suppose that A_1 is the assumption that a patient was given zidovudine (AZT) for a period of 12 months. Owing to an administrative mix-up, there is some doubt, however, as to whether the patient was actually given AZT; he may have mistakenly been given a placebo. Suppose that we try to explain his remission in symptoms by postulating the ingestion of AZT as the cause. Depending on the severity of the symptoms, that hypothesis might have to compete with alternatives: the effect was due to a placebo treatment or temporary spontaneous remission. However, suppose we then obtain new data that rule out these alternatives. First, serum levels of viral p24 antigen have been reduced in the patient, suggesting a significant antiviral effect. Second, a variant of the human immunodeficiency virus (*HIV*) is obtained from the patient and is found to be significantly resistant to AZT. Finally, we have evidence that the baseline for such resistance is uniformly and significantly lower in patients who have not received AZT (Larder, Darby, and Richman 1989). Given this information, we can now argue as follows: The assumptions (A_1) that the patient did receive AZT during the 12-month experimental period and (*H*) that the drug produced the effects described above provide the only plausible explanation of the data. That fact plus background information about acquired immune deficiency syndrome (AIDS) in general and in particular about variants resistant to the *HIV* in patients not receiving AZT provide warrant for both A_1 and *H*. No independent support for A_1 is now needed.

My complaint about IBE_1, then, is that it does not distinguish cases such as the above from those where independent support for the auxiliary assumptions is needed. It permits the proponent of a theory in *any case* to form a new theory by combining it with auxiliary assumptions and then claim evidential support if the combined theory provides the best available explanation of the data. It is implausible, however, to think that this procedure will always guarantee confirmation where the conditions of IBE_1 are met, as can be seen from the following example.

Suppose that someone does a controlled study of the effects of Laetrile on cancer patients. The study is reasonably well designed except for one glaring defect: decrease in blood pressure is used as the criterion of improvement. If the mean decrease in blood pressure is significantly greater in the treated patients than in the controls, the experimenter may theorize that Laetrile cures cancer. If critics point out the obvious flaw in his reasoning, it would be no defense to say: "Well, now I have a new theory: that Laetrile cures cancer *and* a decrease in blood pressure correlates with cancer remission. My theory is the best available explanation of my results, so it is confirmed."

A second problem might be called "the problem of uncharted regions." In some areas of psychology, no one has tried to explain a certain behavior, perhaps because it is new or because no one has noticed that it forms a certain pattern, or for some other reason. At various junctures in the history of psychology, published reports began to appear for the first time offering explanations of perceptual defense, bystanders' failure to aid in cases of emergency, behavioral symptoms of so-called male menopause, sudden recall of infantile sexual molestation, etc. If IBE were acceptable, it would be comparatively easy to confirm new theories in these uncharted areas especially where there is a complex pattern of behavior to explain. Because the subject has not yet been studied in depth, the first theorist creative enough to develop a systematic theory may win by default. His or her explanation will be the best available because there has not yet been sufficient time for competing theories to develop. Yet in many such cases there is no evidence that the newly minted theory is true.

The two sorts of cases just discussed, those involving unwarranted auxiliary assumptions and those involving uncharted areas, are part of a more general phenomenon—a proposed explanation can achieve "the best" status simply because we can think of no other or because its known competitors are even less credible—yet the explanation may still lack credibility. Consider the scientific investigation of the shroud of Turin and the hypothesis that it was not a forgery (leaving entirely open whether it was or was not the shroud of Jesus). There were a wide variety of experimental findings that were potentially explainable by this hypothesis (see, e.g., the table in Heller 1983, 215–216). We now have new data that discredit the nonforgery hypothesis, but even before those data were obtained, the hypothesis was not confirmed even if it provided the best available explanation of the existing data. So, too, there are many cases where the best available explanations of the results of parapsychological experiments, of weeping statues, of reported visions of the Virgin Mary, and so forth., are simply not good enough: they are the best anyone has thought of, but they have no supporting evidence. Of course, the proponents of such explanations can challenge this verdict. In fact, anyone who wishes to stick to IBE can accuse me of begging the question in claiming that there are any cases where an explanation meets its conditions and yet has no warrant whatsoever. The burden of proof, however, lies with the defender of IBE$_1$. What reason is there to believe that merely because a causal explanation would explain certain, data if true, and is the best that anyone has thought of, this guarantees that there is some likelihood that it is true? It is no answer to say, Because if we did not argue in this way, we would be forced to accept a total skepticism. Perhaps some IBEs must be acceptable if skepticism is to be defeated, but that does not show that this particular form of it is acceptable. It is also not enough to appeal to the definition of "rational" or to evolutionary considerations about how IBE would have to work if we were to survive—unless it can be shown that this particular rule is supported by these considerations.

Because it does seem obvious that in some cases we may have no good reason to accept the best available explanation, perhaps I have been attacking a straw man. At least some of those who appear to rely on IBE₁ may be tacitly presupposing another condition: that the proposed explanation be not too implausible or, more strongly, that it have some initial plausibility. The addition of either condition would exclude some egregious cases of unwarranted explanations, but neither condition is strong enough. Peter Achinstein (1991) cites the case of Clerk Maxwell, who in 1860 published a paper providing the first unified treatment of the so-called transport phenomena of heat conduction, viscosity, and diffusion. Despite the fact that only his hypothesis, among those that were known to physicists, could explain all of the relevant gaseous phenomena, Maxwell did not believe that it was likely to be true. What he did believe, instead, was that some mechanical hypothesis or other was probably true yet his own hypothesis had some initial plausibility. It might be replied that the fact that the hypothesis had some plausibility and no competitors did constitute *some* evidential support for it, even if not enough to warrant Maxwell's believing it. Consider, however, some additional cases. A plausible explanation of why I cannot find my wallet, and perhaps the only one I can think of, is that my secretary stole it. He had the proper motive and once confessed to stealing something as a teenager. Yet I may have no evidence at all that he took the wallet. A plausible explanation of why the Dow Jones average dropped 10 points today is that the drop was triggered by the government's announcement of its cancellation of a defense contract. Even if that is the only explanation we can think of, the negation of that hypothesis may be just as plausible.

We might try strengthening our extra condition further. Lipton (1991) adds the requirement that the best explanation available must be good enough to make any inference at all. As Achinstein (1992, 355–356) argues, however, this veers between triviality and unclarity. It is trivial if we say that the best available explanation can be inferred provided that it is good enough to infer, and it is too unclear if we fail to explain what is meant by "good enough."

However we explain our extra condition, the basic problem is this. Our conditions are likely to be too weak unless they guarantee, for a causal hypothesis, that there is at least some good reason to believe that the set of proposed explanations contains the correct explanation. So long as it is just as plausible to believe that the correct explanation of the phenomena is one not yet formulated, there will be no good reason to believe the best of the available explanations. Why not, then, attack the problem directly and formulate the rule for IBE as follows? Call this IBE$_2$:

IBE$_2$: If our background evidence and theories make it somewhat likely that the correct explanation of data D is contained in a certain set, H_1 or H_2 or H_3, then we have some reason to believe H_1 if it provides the best (i.e., the most plausible) explanation among these competing hypotheses.

Critics of IBE are likely to respond that the above rule is trivial. Van Fraassen (1989, 49), for example, despite his criticism of IBE, accepts a similar rule, although he formulates it in terms of what one believes to be the likely alternatives, as opposed to what *are* the likely alternatives. He objects, however, that this commonsensible version of IBE cannot be "the cornerstone of epistemology": "This rule cannot supply the initial context of belief or opinion within which alone it can become applicable. Therefore it cannot be what 'grounds' rational opinion" (149).

I agree with van Fraassen's remarks about the cornerstone of epistemology and about the inability of IBE by itself to ground rational opinion. Nevertheless, I think the rule stated above is of some use. Consider Robert Gallo's (1987) reasoning concerning the cause of AIDS. In the early 1980s, there was a range of plausible hypotheses known to researchers. One was that the disease had no specific etiologic agent: the patient's immune system had simply broken down under chronic overexposure to foreign proteins carried by people's white blood cells or other infectious agents. Other hypotheses were that the Epstein-Barr virus or cytomegalovirus, members of the herpesvirus family, caused the disease. Additional hypotheses focused on various retroviruses: the agent was human T-cell lymphotropic virus type I (HTLV-I) or HTLV-II-or HTLV-III (*HIV*-1). There were, of course, many other hypotheses that were not taken seriously: perhaps the sheer quantity of sexual contacts caused AIDS; perhaps the communists were responsible. Such hypotheses were not taken seriously because they were just not credible given our existing evidence. As new evidence was discovered, only the retrovirus hypotheses remained plausible. Finally, the HTVL-III hypothesis emerged as the one that provided the best explanation of the data: hence, its confirmation. As van Fraassen says, IBE did not provide the initial context of belief; our background evidence played the primary role in doing that, that is, it made it somewhat likely that the cause of AIDS would be found among the specific factors that were taken seriously. In general, as long as our background evidence and theories can narrow the range of plausible hypotheses, both for theoretical and nontheoretical ones, to the point where there are good grounds to believe that a certain small set contains the correct causal explanation of certain phenomena, we can apply IBE in confirming or disconfirming the truth of hypotheses.

Van Fraassen also objects (149) that in some cases we may not wish to apply the rule even when it is applicable. Suppose it is likely that one of the first six horses in a certain race will win. If I have good reason to believe that the No. 1 horse is the best of these, then the best explanation of the crowd cheering at the end of the race will be that the No. 1 horse has indeed won, but if I have not seen the race I still may not be ready to say that this horse has won. In this case, however, it is assumed that the evidence favoring the No. 1 horse is not strong enough to warrant belief that it will win. Because of such cases, IBE should be formulated so that it does not guarantee that the best explanation is inferable, but more weakly, that we have *some* rational grounds to believe that it is true. Finally, van Fraassen makes the point (150) that where the likelihood of truth is not the sole basis for the choice of a theory, then the choice to accept must not be equated with the choice to believe. Again, I agree. For example, if our cognitive aim is to find the most useful theory or one that is merely empirically adequate, then choosing a theory and believing it are not the same. However, this point is consistent with the claim that IBE is of some use in deciding which theory to believe.

Can it not still be complained that when we use IBE to support an inference, it is really the empirical details, and not IBE, that does the epistemic work? In the case of reasoning about HIV, it was our background evidence and theories (but still theories warranted by evidence) that allowed researchers to narrow the set of plausible alternatives, and it was additional evidence that selected the best of the set. I think this is true—the empirical details are crucial—but there is still an epistemic role for explanatory considerations. One thing that made it likely that one of the initially, seriously proposed hypotheses was true is that each of these had the potential to explain the data. If it had been discovered that one of them would not explain the phenomena even if it were true, then it would have been reasonably rejected.

Whether or not the rule I stated is of any use, is there no more interesting and yet defensible version of IBE to be found? That depends on what we are looking for. In certain areas, we might have evidence for a certain assumption that makes it likely that the best available explanation for a phenomenon is true under condition C. For example, we might have evidence that if the experts in a certain domain have tried to find a reasonable competitor to the only known explanation but have failed, then the best available is probably true. We could then adopt the following rule:

IBE_3: In domain D, if the experts have repeatedly tried to develop a plausible competitor to T but failed, and T is plausible and explains the relevant data (if it is true), then infer T.

I assume, however, that philosophers looking to IBE as a substitute for the straight rule of induction would not be satisfied by such a rule. They were looking for a very general correct rule of inference, one not specific to any particular domain, and, perhaps, one knowable a priori. I am not arguing that there cannot be such a rule, but I see no reason to think that one can be formulated. The way in which a small set of competing theories is selected out by the evidence from the infinite set of possible theories may differ significantly from science to science, or even from case to case. Talk of IBE may remain a slogan that comes to little more than this (although this may be important): explanatory considerations play a prominent role in many justified inductive inferences.

How, then, does my position differ from that of those skeptical about IBEs (van Fraassen 1980; Achinstein, 1992, 259–278)? Not by very much. As already indicated, I agree that, so far, there is no account available that would justify making IBE the cornerstone of epistemology. Furthermore, if IBE_2 is the best we can do, then we cannot do very much; the rule is rather trivial. I am not convinced that it is totally trivial, however. As shown by the retrovirus case, what the rule tells us is to use explanatory power as a criterion for narrowing down the list of possible explanations. Include only those that if true would explain the data.

Explanation and Causation

The number of standards potentially applicable to Freudian claims is very large. Why discuss the particular ones assessed in this chapter and chapter 1? My answer is, in part, this: Because disagreement about them has played and continues to play an important causal role in controversies about the interpretation of the Freudian evidence. People familiar with the same evidence often disagree about Freudian theory or therapy partly because they disagree about one or more of these standards. However, if the capacity to generate disagreement were the sole criterion for deciding what to discuss, then it might be reasonable to be silent about the two standards to be discussed next; neither has figured prominently in the Freudian debates. Nevertheless, issues have been raised recently about each (Nussbaum 1991; Hopkins 1992; Grünbaum 1993). Moreover, the second standard, whether or not it is controversial, is also of potential significance in justifying a demand for experimental evidence (the subject of chapter 3). For these reasons, I will comment briefly on some questions that have been raised about each standard. The first standard I have in mind concerns explanation. It requires that for a hypothesis to be explanatory, it must meet the conditions of the deductive nomological (D-N) model of explanation as spelled out by Hempel and Oppenheim (1948). This standard is allegedly relied upon by Grünbaum in his (1984) critique of the Freudian clinical evidence. For example, Nussbaum (1991, 210) claims that for Grünbaum (1984) "there is nothing in Freudian explanations not captured by the D-N model." Nussbaum argues, however, that this standard is wrong. Psychoanalysis "resists placement" (202) under the D-N model for at least two reasons: (1) psychoanalytic hypotheses lack the predictive power of genuine D-N explanations, and (2) there is a difficulty in verifying that the postulated cause of a psychoneurosis is a particular repressed wish. Nevertheless, Nussbaum contends (193), something like the D-N model cannot be entirely dispensed with in Freudian explanations.

If we use the D-N model as a standard, then the problem for Freud's repression theory runs even deeper than a lack of confirmation and predictive power. Suppose that the theory were entirely true, that it had suitable predictive power and were empirically confirmed. It would still not meet the conditions of the D-N model. As Grünbaum notes (1984, 109–110), Freud's repression theory does not postulate a sufficient condition for the occurrence of a psychoneurosis. Freud did hold that repression of infantile wishes is an important causal factor, indeed a necessary condition, but he also allowed that unspecified biological factors also help determine whether or not a psychoneurosis develops. Given that the theory does not even purport to state sufficient conditions, the conjunction of it plus a statement of relevant initial conditions does not entail the conclusion that a psychoneurosis has occurred. Without such an entailment, a repression "explanation" of psychoneurosis is disqualified from being a D-N explanation.

We have, then, at least two choices: adopt a D-N standard and reject repression "explanations" as nonexplanatory (or, at least, as not providing *scientific* explanations) *or* refuse to employ the D-N standard. Malcolm Macmillan makes the first choice. In his evaluation of Freud's personality theory, he requires that for explanations to be adequate they be deductive in form (Macmillan, 1991, 508–509).

I choose the second option, mainly because I am persuaded by standard counterexamples to the D-N model interpreted either as stating necessary or sufficient conditions for an explanation (for a good history of the debates about the D-N model, see Salmon 1989). Grünbaum (1984) makes the same choice. Contrary to what Nussbaum asserts, he does *not* hold that there is nothing in Freudian explanations not captured by the D-N model, nor does he anywhere criticize Freudian theory on the grounds that it fails to measure up to D-N standards.

Readers familiar with the philosophical debates about explanation may notice that I have ignored a third choice. We could hold that Freudian explanations meet the standards of *either* the D-N model *or* Hempel's (1966) statistical model of explanation. However, because I think there are also problems with the statistical model (see Salmon 1989), I find this disjunctive standard unacceptable as well. There is no need, however, to examine here the putative counterexamples or possible replies. Philosophers who believe that either the D-N or the statistical model of explanation is defensible will probably insist on more rigorous standards than I intend to use. They are likely to object that even if Freudian theory meets all appropriate standards for confirmation, it (or part of it) still has a serious defect: it provides at best only an "explanation sketch," not a genuine scientific explanation. They might be right, but their position is not one that I intend to rely on. In what follows I do not presuppose any particular standard for a theory to be explanatory.

The next issue concerns causation. As already noted, Freud theorized that repression was a necessary but not a sufficient condition for the development of a psychoneurosis. (As Grünbaum points out [1993, 23; 1984, 110], repression is said also to be a "specific cause" of psychoneuroses, that is, it is claimed to be never, or hardly ever, a causal factor in the etiology of any other nosologically distinct syndrome. However, I will ignore this additional claim on Freud's part concerning "specific" causation.) Where a Freudian hypothesis postulates a necessary condition for the occurrence of some event or the development of some condition, we have at least one clear standard for judging the falsity of the hypothesis. If repressed homosexuality is said to be a necessary condition for developing paranoia, this implies that all those lacking repressed homosexuality (say overtly homosexual persons) will be nonparanoid. The claim would be refuted, consequently, if we were to find an overt (nonrepressed) homosexual who is also paranoid. Some Freudian causal claims, however, assert neither a necessary nor sufficient condition; they assert rather that a certain factor is *causally relevant,* either positively or negatively. For example, a Freudian may claim that the therapy contributes to the elimination of phobias, while conceding that other therapies are also effective in treating these disorders (so it is not necessary) and that psychoanalysis *by itself* will not provide a cure (so it is not sufficient). By what standard, then, do we judge these weaker claims of causal relevance?

Wesley Salmon suggests (1984, 185) the following answer. When we want to test for the presence of a cause-effect relationship, we need to seek evidence in the form of a statistically relevant relationship. To use one of his examples (186), suppose that I hypothesize that taking birth control pills contributes to the development of thrombosis. First, I develop an appropriate reference class, in this case, the class of women of child-bearing age. Second, I develop an appropriate attribute class, in this case, the class of women who suffer thrombosis. I then divide the original class of women of child-bearing age into two: the class of those who took birth control pills and the class of those who did not. Salmon's claim, as I understand it, is that to obtain evidence of causal relevance in this case, we would need to determine whether the frequency of thrombosis is greater in the first class (the pill taking group) compared to the second. To put Salmon's requirement in more general terms, suppose for some reference class C (say the class of patients suitable for analysis), X (e.g., psychoanalysis) is said to be causally relevant to the production of Y (say the elimination of agoraphobia). To test the hypothesis, we need to divide c into two sets, those receiving X and those not receiving it, and see if the frequency of y's (agoraphobia cures) is greater in the x class than in the non-x class. (Philosophers who accept a propensity rather than a frequency interpretation of probability might want to talk about an increase in probability rather than an increase in frequency of occurrence.) Grünbaum states essentially the same principle (1993, 163).

As Salmon notes (1984, 185) the above principle is neutral between different accounts of the nature of causation. One could accept it if one holds the traditional position that a cause is a sufficient condition (or a necessary condition, or both) for the occurrence of an effect or if one holds the newer view that causation is irreducibly statistical (Suppes 1970; Salmon 1984). On either view, however, there are some questions that need to be answered about Salmon's principle. For example, should it be interpreted as an evidential principle or as a "constitutive" principle, that is, one about truth conditions for causal judgments? There is a problem if we read it in the second way. There are possible cases in which x is positively relevant to y in some reference class c, but the frequency of y is greater in the non-x class than in the x-class. How can that be? Consider again the case of birth control pills and thrombosis. As Hesslow (1976) points out, it is plausible to believe that pregnancy is an even more potent causal factor for thrombosis than is the ingestion of birth control pills. In that case, let c equal the class of women of childbearing age and then divide it into two classes: women who use birth control pills and those who do not. We may find a greater frequency of thrombosis in the latter class even if birth control pills are also a contributing factor to thrombosis. The reason is this: Of the women not taking birth control pills, more are likely to become pregnant, and the pregnancy (being a more potent factor) may increase the frequency of thrombosis compared with those who took the pill and did not become pregnant. Salmon's reply to this example is that we need to change our initial reference class. Once we find that pregnancy itself is a causal factor, we should specify the reference class for the pill hypothesis as the class of women who do not become pregnant. For this class, we can then compare the incidence of thrombosis for women who take the pill with that for women who do not. The incidence should be higher in the former group if taking the pill makes a difference to the occurrence of thrombosis.

Salmon's reply was directed at Hesslow's counterexample to Suppes's probabilistic theory of causation. It may serve this purpose, but it does not, as far as I can see, save what I have termed "Salmon's principle" from failure *if* interpreted as a constitutive principle about causation. Before we obtain evidence about the causal role of pregnancy in producing thrombosis, the principle permits the selection of the class of women of childbearing age as the proper reference class. Yet, for the reasons given above, it is not necessary that the women in this class who take the pill will have a greater frequency of thrombosis compared with those who do not, even if taking the pill makes a difference. There are, moreover, other types of cases in which the principle fails if taken as stating a necessary condition for causal relevance. There is evidence that some psychological therapies actually make the client worse (Mays and Franks 1985). Suppose that, unknown to anyone, psychoanalysis has such a negative effect on victims of agoraphobia. Now consider the hypothesis that placebo factors present in the psychoanalytic setting contribute to the improvement of analysands who are agoraphobic. That hypothesis might be true, but the gain from the placebo factors might be offset by the workings of the therapy. Consequently, if we were to compare agoraphobic patients treated by psychoanalysis with those not treated by any therapy (and thus not subject to the placebo factors), the incidence of improvement might be exactly the same despite the positive relevance of the placebo factors. The latter make a difference, but that difference does not show up in our statistics because of the negative effects of the therapy.

Salmon's principle, then, might seem to be better interpreted, as both he and Grünbaum seem to intend (Salmon 1984, 185; Grünbaum 1993, 163), as an *evidential* principle. But, then, other questions arise. Does the principle state a sufficient condition—not for x being causally relevant to Y, but for obtaining evidence that the relationship holds? The answer is no, as both Salmon and Grünbaum would agree. We might, for example, find a higher incidence of y's in the class of those experiencing some factors x compared with those not experiencing x and yet be in no position to judge whether x made a difference to the occurrence of y or whether some third factor accounted for the correlation between x's and y's. For example, let our reference class be persons with agoraphobia who are suitable for analysis. If we divide this class into two, those who have completed analysis and those who have not, we might find that there is a greater incidence of elimination of agoraphobia in the treated class. Yet, it might be just as plausible to conclude that the so-called cures were due entirely to spontaneous remission and that the treatment made no difference.

Even taken as a necessary condition (which I believe is the very most that Salmon or Grünbaum would claim), some caveats are needed. Suppose that I claim that taking a new drug is causally relevant to the cure of some bacterial condition B, and I find that 80% of my patients with the B condition are cured within 2 weeks if they ingest the drug, but the cure rate is the same for those that are not given it. If that is all I know about the drug's effects, then I have no reason to think it effective in treating the B disorder. Suppose, however, that I know that streptomycin is effective in 8 out of 10 cases in curing the B problem in the same time period *and* that all of my patients not receiving the new drug had received this other drug. I might then have evidence that the new drug did indeed make a difference in curing the B problem. Analogously, I might obtain evidence that psychoanalysis generally helps in the elimination of phobias if it performs exactly the same as another treatment independently shown to be effective for the same problems. In these cases, we obtain evidence that x makes a difference to the occurrence of y despite the fact that a statistical comparison of the classes of x's and non-x's shows no increase in the probability of y for the former class. We can handle such cases by again specifying the reference class differently. If we have evidence that treatment T is effective in treating phobias, then our reference class for the psychoanalytic case should be the class of phobic patients suitable for analysis *who have not undergone T*. Still, the sorts of cases just discussed show that to get evidence that x is causally relevant to y it is not always necessary to do a comparison of x-cases and non-x-cases. Showing that a therapy equals or exceeds the performance of a therapy known to be effective is sufficient to confirm the hypothesis that the first therapy makes a difference.

There is also a problem about singular causation. There is an extraordinary case I discuss later (see chapter 6, p. 389) in which placebo factors apparently eliminated cancerous tumors in a dying man. The evidence of causation in this case was not obtained by doing a statistical analysis of cancer cases in which the placebo factors were present compared with cancer cases in which they were not. Indeed, were such a study undertaken, it is quite likely that no evidence of the causal relation in question would have been discovered. In other cases, such as those mentioned in the beginning of chapter 3, p. 136 (e.g., the use of shock in treating the self-injurious behavior of autistic children), evidence of causal relevance would likely show up if we were to do a statistical comparison, but our background evidence and well-confirmed theories make such a comparison unnecessary. We have evidence that x made a difference to the occurrence of y in *this* case whether or not we can reliably predict that it will do so in future cases.

James Hopkins (1992) also raises doubts about Salmon's principle, using an example discussed in chapter 1: Grünbaum's case of a woman who visits Frank Lloyd Wright's house Falling Water and then dreams of a house having the same details as Wright's house. Hopkins doubts that in order to have evidence of causal relevance here, we need to establish that certain correlations hold, such as "Whenever a woman dreams of an x, this indicates an increased probability that she saw an x the day before the dream."

I agree with Hopkins on this point, but I disagree with his alternative suggestion: that similarity in content between perception of the house and the dream provides evidence of causation. I argued against this view in chapter 1. My countersuggestion, as before, is that our background evidence and well confirmed theories provide the justification. To take a case discussed earlier, when Robert Gallo (1987) theorized that a retrovirus was an important contributing factor to the development of AIDS, he had some grounds for his view even before the relevant experiments were carried out. The grounds were provided by the prior evidence about the effects of retroviruses and the analogy between such effects and the symptoms of AIDS. To take a more familiar example, Salmon (1984) discusses our reasons for thinking that a baseball thrown with a certain velocity will shatter a pane of glass. Here, we can point to many cases where the shattering followed a ball hitting the window, but suppose I throw a watermelon through a window. For all I know, this may never have been done before. Still, I may know what broke the window without first inquiring as to whether throwing watermelons at a window tends to be followed by a shattering in greater frequencies than throwing nothing at similar windows. My warrant is provided by the analogy between the watermelon and baseballs (and other similar missiles) and the effects of hurling the latter at windows. When Ivan Lovaas and his colleagues (Lovaas and Simmons 1974) first used electric shock with autistic children, the experimental evidence on punishment and conditioning theory plus the base rates of injurious behavior for these children all combined to make it likely that the shock had made a difference. Similar background evidence of an analogous type can be pointed to in the cases of the placebo treatment of cancer and the woman who dreamt of a certain type of house.

Whether or not I am right about the role of background evidence, however, is not crucial to the present discussion. Here, I am arguing that cases of singular causation, as well as cases where a treatment's efficacy is established by comparison to a treatment of known effectiveness, create an apparent problem for Salmon's principle if interpreted as stating an evidentially necessary condition. However, the earlier cases, such as the birth control case, pose a problem for the principle if taken as a constitutive principle about truth conditions. So where do these considerations leave Salmon's principle? My suggestion is that we first modify it and then interpret it as an evidential principle. The modifications I have in mind, I suspect, would be acceptable to both Salmon and Grünbaum.

The first adjustment is that we state the principle so that it does not apply directly to cases of singular causation. Instead of talking about all causal hypotheses, we can restrict the principle to hypotheses that say of an event type x that it is *generally* causally relevant to the occurrence of an event type y. We thus avoid problems raised by cases (such as the placebo cancer case) where x makes a difference to the occurrence of y under a unique set of conditions that never again obtain. For some of these one-shot cases, we may have evidence of causal relevance despite our having no reason to believe that for a suitable reference class, the frequency of y-type events will be greater in the sub-class of x's than in sub-class of non-x's.

Salmon's principle can still be taken to be indirectly relevant to the confirmation of singular causal judgments in the following way. We might have grounds for concluding that x made a difference to y because of analogies to W's, whose effects, in turn, have been ascertained by comparing the class of W-type events with the class of non-W type events. However, I ignore this possibility in what follows.

The first modification to Salmon's principle has little effect on its usefulness if our sole goal is to assess Freudian theoretical and therapeutic claims. The reason is that such claims say what is *generally* causally relevant, not merely what happened on one or two occasions. A non-Freudian could easily agree that if Freudian repression ever occurs, it may have occasionally made a difference to the development of a neurosis or the content of a dream. Freudian theory goes far beyond such modest claims, however, and holds that such and such event is *generally* causally relevant to certain effects, or, in some cases, states that it is always relevant. Analogously, many generally ineffective psychological treatments might in a few cases contribute to a certain beneficial outcome, but if we are to recommend a particular treatment to future clients, we need to confirm that it *generally* (even if not invariably) makes a positive difference under certain specifiable conditions to at least one type of beneficial outcome.

The next modification is needed because of cases where an x-type event makes a difference that does not show up in the statistics because of countervailing factors, as in the pregnancy case and the case of the effects of placebo factors being offset by the harmful effects of a therapy. Actual cases of this sort are exceptional, but the number of possible different types of cases of this sort may be too large to permit inclusion in a manageable exception clause. So, instead of saying, "Except where there is a B case, or C case, etc.," we can simply refer to *countervailing factors*. By "countervailing factors," I mean factors that prevent the effects of x showing up in a statistical comparison even though x is generally relevant to the production of y. In other words, if we divide up the suitable reference class, the incidence of y's in the subclass of x's is not greater than in the non-x class *because* other causal factors are offsetting the effects of x.

We can now make the second modification in Salmon's principle and say: "Except where there is reason to believe that there are countervailing factors, to establish that x is generally causally relevant to the occurrence of y, we need to establish for some reference class c that the frequency of y's is greater in the sub-set of c's in which x occurs than in the subset where x does not occur."

Why accept the above principle? The argument for it is quite simple. If we claim that x is generally relevant to the occurrence of y, and not merely that it was relevant in one or two cases, then we imply that x generally makes a difference to the occurrence of y, at least for a suitable reference class. But to show that it generally makes a difference, we need to show that for that reference class (say the class of patients suitable for analysis), the class of x's contains more y's than the class of non-x's—unless we have reason to believe that this is one of the exceptional cases where there are countervailing causal factors.

Suppose that there are countervailing factors, but we have no reason to think that this is so. In that case, if our evidence indicated that there were at least as many y's in the non-x class as in the x class, then we might be in no position to infer that x was generally making a difference to the occurrence of y. It is not enough that there be countervailing factors: we must have grounds for thinking that they exist.

My modified version of Salmon's principle is an evidential principle in that it states what has to be done, in the nonexceptional cases, to get evidence that a claim of general causal relevance is true (it states a necessary but not a sufficient condition). However, the principle does not specify what type of evidence is needed to show that the frequency of y's for a reference class c is greater in the x class than in the non-x class; it does not specifically require that we do a statistical comparison of the class of x's and the class of non-x's. In some cases our background evidence and well-confirmed theory make such a statistical comparison unnecessary. Where such background evidence does not suffice, however, a statistical comparison of some kind will be required.

Finally, why not revamp Salmon's principle further and interpret it as stating a truth condition, although only a necessary one? Why not say "Except where there are countervailing factors, x is generally causally relevant to the occurrence of y only if for some reference class c, the frequency of y's is greater in the subset of c's in which x's occur than in the subset where x does not occur?" The problem with this formulation is that it relativizes causal relevance to a reference class, but the causal relation does not appear to be relative in this way. If I say that x is generally causally relevant to y, I imply that x generally makes a difference to y *period*—not relative to some reference class. The appeal to a reference class comes in only at a later stage, when I try to test the hypothesis.

Conclusion

It may be useful to identify those standards that I argued for and those I argued against:

1. First, I argued that for evidence to confirm a hypothesis, it must do so "differentially." This requirement was explained as follows: For any body of evidence E and hypothesis H, E confirms H differentially exactly if E provides at least some reason for believing H to be true and does not provide equal (or better) reason for believing some incompatible rival hypothesis that is at least as plausible.

2. Next, I argued against Kline's (1988, 226) contention, that where there are competing explanations the simplest is to be preferred. Most philosophers of science—and perhaps Kline himself, on reflection—would have trouble with that thesis. After all, even if simplicity counts for something, it has to be weighed against other epistemic considerations, such as initial plausibility as determined by relevant observations. However, I also argued that simplicity counts for nothing, that is, in and of itself. Of course, if we have empirical evidence for a certain domain that the simplest of known competing hypothesis is likely to be true, than in that case simplicity counts—but only in virtue of the prior empirical evidence.

Although I argued that simplicity in and of itself has no evidential value, I did not discuss other pragmatic virtues such as: elegance, precision, generality, and degree of unification. However, I believe that the arguments directed against appeals to simplicity as a separate epistemic factor would also tell against placing evidential weight on any of these other factors, except as dictated by independent empirical evidence.

3. Later, I argued against a rule of inference that Freudians (e.g., Kline 1986, 230; Bloom 1962; Strean 1984) often appear to rely on. This rule is captured by Lycan's (1988, 129) formulation of what philosophers call "inference to the best explanation." On this standard (referred to as IBE$_1$), it is sufficient for evidential support that a hypothesis explain certain facts better than any *available* competing hypothesis. I argued that this is not enough.

I also stated and accepted a weaker version of inference to the best explanation, referred to as IBE$_2$. On this version, certain data provide evidential support for *H* if it provides a better explanation of the data than any competing available hypothesis, but only if our prior evidence makes it somewhat probable that our list of available explanations contains the correct explanation. If, as I intend, observational evidence and logical consistency alone make an explanation "the best," then IBE$_2$ is uncontroversial and somewhat trivial (although I believe it to be of some use). Whether it is possible to formulate a more interesting but correct version of IBE, I leave open.

4. The next standard I considered is that a theory meet the deductive-nomological (D-N) requirements for a scientific explanation. It concerns not truth but a theory's capacity to explain. I argued neither for nor against this standard, but because it is controversial, I intend *not* to rely on it.

5. Finally, I argued for a variant of a principle for confirming judgments of causal relevance (Salmon 1984, 185; Grünbaum 1993, 163). However, I argued for certain changes in the more standard formulation in order to avoid some apparent counterexamples.

Chapter 3
Experimental versus Nonexperimental Evidence

I turn now to a set of issues concerning experimentation and Freudian psychology. Can Freudian theory be confirmed by uncontrolled clinical case studies? Or do we generally need evidence from well designed experimental studies (or perhaps epidemiological studies)? I focus initially on these two options, but others are discussed later. As a third option one might appeal to single subject experiments in a clinical setting; another possibility is to look to nonclinical, nonexperimental data, especially concerning the "psychopathology of everyday life."

Approaches to Clinical Confirmation

The Millian Approach

One way to approach the issue of clinical confirmation is to insist at the outset that in all cases of confirmation of causal hypotheses, an experimental standard must be met. This is the approach of John Stuart Mill and his followers.

In his *System of Logic* ([1843] 1973), Mill describes what he takes to be the most favorable case for establishing a causal hypothesis without experimentation. It is a case in which instances are sufficiently varied in their circumstances, and we are able to discover, either among the proximate antecedents or among some other order of antecedents, something that is always found when the effect is found, however various the circumstances, and never found when it is not. Yet, even in what is "certainly the most favorable case," Mill notes, we may discover through observation only a "uniformity in nature" (386), but cannot establish causation. For, suppose that by a comparison of cases of the alleged effect, we have found an antecedent which appears to be, and perhaps is, invariably connected with it. Until we have reversed the process, and produced the effect by means of that antecedent, we have proved only invariable antecedents within the limits of experience, but not causation. If, however, we do reverse the process and produce the effect, then we have performed an experiment. We are not relying simply on observation. Mill concludes

Until it had been shown by the actual production of the antecedent under known circumstances, and the occurrence thereupon of the consequent, that the antecedent was really the condition on which it depended; the uniformity of succession which was proved to exist between them might, for aught we know, be (like the succession of day and night) not a case of causation at all; both antecedent and consequent might be successive stages of the effect of an ulterior cause. Observation, in short, without experiment (supposing no aid from deduction) can ascertain sequences and coexistences, but cannot prove causation. (386)

Many experimental psychologists and some philosophers have accepted Mill's principle; some have used it to discredit the psychoanalytic clinical evidence. For example, in his classic paper on psychoanalysis, Ernest Nagel sets out what he describes as a *minimum* requirement for the reliable interpretation and use of empirical data: "In short, data must be analyzed so as to make possible comparisons on the basis of some *control* group, if they are to constitute cogent evidence for a causal inference" (Nagel 1958, 53).

If the Millian approach is correct, there can be an immediate and enormous simplification of the issues. All nonexperimental Freudian data, including those from clinical case studies, anthropology, and everyday life, can be disqualified: no experiment, no confirmation of causal hypotheses. There are, however, at least two problems with the Millian tradition, at least as carried out by Nagel. Psychologists in the operant conditioning paradigm have shown how causal hypotheses can be confirmed using various single subject (Barlow and Hersen 1984) experimental designs. No control group is needed, as the subject's own behavior in certain phases serves as an adequate basis for comparison. Because single subject experiments are still experiments, they provide no counterexamples to Mill's original dictum. Moreover, if they had been brought to Nagel's attention, he might well have dropped his demand for a control group. His main point, it appears, is to insist on Mills's original requirement: that we do experiments of some kind or other. Still, the issue of using single subject designs has become important given Marshall Edelson's (1984, 1988) arguments that they can be adapted for use in confirming Freudian hypotheses. If Edelson is right, then the Freudian tradition of relying on clinical case studies can be reasonably continued and yet Mill's experimental standard can be met.

Even though Mill can accept single-subject experiments, a more serious problem remains. How do we justify his basic principle, that confirmation of causal hypotheses always requires experimental evidence? He may appear to have an argument when he says "Until we have reversed the process and produced the effect by means of that antecedent, we have proved only invariable antecedents within the limits of experience, but not causation" (386). However, this is merely a restatement of his view that confirmation of causation requires experimentation. He does say later (386) that until we produce the antecedent and then the consequent, the uniformity "might, for aught we know, be (like the succession of day and night) not a case of causation at all," but this does not help. If the point is merely that we might be wrong if we have not performed an experiment, it is irrelevant to the issue of clinical confirmation. Even after we have confirmed a hypothesis, whether experimentally or nonexperimentally, it is still possible to be mistaken. We cannot achieve certainty, but is nonexperimental confirmation possible? If Mill's point, however, is that we can never know that a causal hypothesis is true until we have done an experiment, then he is, once again, merely restating his principle, although in a weaker form (weaker because the new version would rule out knowledge of causal connections without experimentation but would not necessarily rule out some weak form of confirmation).

So how does Mill know that his principle is true? It is unlikely that he or anyone else can know it *a priori:* It is surely not an obvious necessary truth that if *P* expresses a causal claim, it can be justified only by experimental evidence. Nor does it have empirical support; in fact the evidence shows that many causal claims can be confirmed without doing a controlled experiment. In Erwin (1978, 11–112, I discuss some clinical outcome hypotheses confirmed without experimentation. Grünbaum (1984, 259) gives additional examples from physics where, as he puts it, our background evidence serves as the probative equivalent of a control group, thus rendering experiments unnecessary. Many other examples can be found in evolutionary biology, geology, and astronomy. One might try to handle such counterinstances to Mill's principle by building into it a complicated exception clause, but, without rendering it trivial, that is no easy thing to do: the exceptions are quite numerous and diverse.

I will assume, then, that Freud was right in objecting to the idea that experimentation is *always* required to confirm causal hypotheses. It might still turn out that he was wrong about the prospects for clinical confirmation of his own theory, but to show that, something else besides an appeal to Mill's principle is necessary.

Shaping up Case Studies

A second way of approaching the issue of clinical experimental confirmation is to ask: What makes case studies (unless otherwise indicated, I mean uncontrolled clinical case studies) evidentially weak and what can be done to diminish their weaknesses?

Alan Kazdin (1981) makes a useful contribution concerning this topic. He proposes that five characteristics generally account for the evidential weaknesses of case studies. The first is the use of anecdotal reports, such as the client's or therapist's uncorroborated assertion that improvement has taken place. Kazdin regards this feature as being perhaps the most important obstacle to drawing causal inferences. We obviously cannot establish that *X* caused *Y* in a given case unless we establish that *Y* occurred. It might also be added that, given the tendency of some eclectic clinicians to mix ingredients from various therapies, firm evidence is also needed that a particular therapy, X, was used, if our hypothesis is about X. If we rely on only anecdotal evidence, we may not know if either the alleged cause or effect was present.

A second weakness of many case studies is the use of one-shot or two-shot assessments (e.g., post-treatment only or pre-treatment and post-treatment). With only one or two assessments, there is an increased difficulty in ruling out the possibility that change resulted from testing rather than treatment.

A third problematic feature of some case studies is that the problem being treated is either acute or episodic. Without experimental controls, it is more difficult in such cases to rule out the possibility that extraneous features caused an improvement. For example, if the subject is depressed during some months and not others, and improves after brief treatment, the change might well have occurred even if there had been no treatment. In contrast, it is more difficult to explain the elimination of a long-term, stable problem after brief treatment without appealing to the effects of the therapy

A fourth feature is the presence of gradual, weak effects. Such effects are easier to explain in terms of a spontaneous remission hypothesis, or some other rival hypothesis, compared to effects that are sudden and dramatic (so-called slam-bang effects).

The fifth weakness, which is present in every single-subject case study, is that it involves only one subject. This feature is often taken to be relevant primarily to external validity—How do we know that what worked with one subject will work with another?—but it is also relevant to internal validity. If the event Y follows the same putative cause, X, in a number of subsequent cases, and the cases are varied in relevant respects, we may have more right to be confident that, in the first case, X and Y were causally connected.

Kazdin points out that, to some extent, the epistemic weakness of case studies can be eliminated without transforming such studies into experiments. For example, a therapist can collect objective data in place of anecdotal information, assess performance on several occasions rather than one, and accumulate a number of cases that are treated and assessed in a similar fashion. Where these things are done, and a relatively stable problem is being treated and slam-bang effects are observed, it may be possible to support a causal inference. A group design using a control group would then be unnecessary.

In showing that clinical case studies can sometimes be fixed up, Kazdin strengthens the position of psychoanalysts who argue that clinical confirmation is feasible. However, some caution is needed. One could reasonably argue that in doing therapy, one needs to make decisions about the effectiveness of what is being done. Rather than merely guess, the therapist might follow some of Kazdin's suggestions and enhance the evidential value of the limited information available. Here, however, a lower standard is appropriate. In doing therapy, one does the best one can in figuring out the consequences of certain therapeutic strategies, but what is prudentially acceptable may not be acceptable from a scientific point of view. The best one can do in a therapeutic situation may not be good enough to meet minimal standards for confirmation of causal hypotheses.

Let us assume, however, that we are following Kazdin's advice not merely to enhance our therapy but to improve our chances of clinical confirmation. In that case, it should be noted that the advice is most straightforwardly applicable to the confirmation of certain behavior therapy outcome hypotheses. Even here, I have doubts that very much can be done to improve the evidential quality of case studies (see Erwin 1988a, 211–215). There is a further problem, moreover, if we try to apply Kazdin's suggestions to psychoanalytic outcome hypotheses given that the therapy typically last 3 years or more (see chapter 6, 237–238 for details). Finally, there is an even larger gap to close if we try to cross from the kind of clinical case study that Kazdin is discussing, one involving a relatively simple outcome hypothesis, to cases involving attempts at confirmation of Freudian theoretical hypotheses. One obvious difference is that the latter typically postulate unobservable causes; another is that they often talk about events that allegedly occurred in the distant past. A third difference is the serious epistemic problem of disentangling suggestibility factors from other causal factors in the psychoanalytic setting. This problem can also arise in assessing outcome hypotheses, but where it does, the prospect for shaping up case studies without transforming them into experiments is bleak. Moreover, the problem posed by suggestibility factors in confirming Freudian theoretical hypotheses in a clinical setting is even more insidious and more difficult to control than where we are concerned only with the cause of therapeutic outcomes.

Grünbaum's Analysis

A third approach to clinical confirmation forgoes any attempt to either state a Millian type of principle about causality *in general* or to fix up case studies, and tries instead to analyze the epistemic weaknesses of specifically psychoanalytic case studies. The philosopher Adolf Grünbaum takes this approach in a series of papers and two books (Grünbaum 1984, 1993). One of his major conclusions is that insofar as Freudian theory is based on uncontrolled clinical case studies, its evidential support is "remarkably weak" (1984, 278) and that to overcome this weakness, it is necessary to do well-designed experimental or epidemiological studies.

Grünbaum's arguments have attracted both a good deal of support and many criticisms. What follows is a discussion of the most important issues raised by the critics (for Grünbaum's responses, see his 1986 and 1993).

The Tally Argument

In his 1917 lectures, Freud raises an important issue about the possible role of suggestion in explaining his therapeutic results and his alleged psychological discoveries. He appears to answer this criticism by arguing that his therapy would not work unless his interpretations were true. Thus, he writes: "After all, [a patient's] conflicts will only be successfully solved and his resistances overcome if the anticipatory ideas he is given [by his analyst] tally with what is real in him" (1917, *S.E.*, 16:452).

Grünbaum (1984) paraphrases Freud's claim as implying the causal indispensability of veridical psychoanalytic insight into the etiology of a neurosis if it is to be permanently cured: no correct psychoanalytic insight, no cure. If we add the assumption that some of his patients have been cured—whether or not psychoanalysis produced the cure—we have an argument for the truth of at least some of Freud's interpretations. Grünbaum dubs this argument "the tally argument."

One question raised by some critics (Sachs 1989; Levy 1988) is whether Freud ever actually accepted the tally argument. On this question, I agree with Grünbaum. On balance, the evidence supports his interpretation (see Erwin 1993, 413–419), although I concede that the critics have made some useful points. A second question is this: If Freud did employ the argument, how important was it to his overall case for his theory? I am not sure how to answer this question, but I agree with the critics, as I think Grünbaum would, that it was hardly his only argument. Moreover, contemporary Freudians have offered additional arguments that are not dependent on any of Freud's arguments. So, disposing of the tally argument (as Grünbaum argues, 1984, 161–162, the first premise is false) is quite insufficient to rebut all claims of Freudian confirmation.

One final question is a hypothetical one: If Grünbaum were wrong, and Freud never employed the tally argument, how would this affect Grünbaum's arguments about the cogency of the Freudian clinical evidence? Some critics charge that it would do quite a lot of damage. For example, Paul Robinson (1993, 259) contends that Grünbaum's critique "hinges on" his construction and criticism of the tally argument, which, Robinson argues, was never accepted by Freud. This is Robinson's chief criticism of Grünbaum's arguments; in fact, except for citing one example taken from Freud and some criticisms of David Sachs (1989), it is virtually his only criticism. Other writers (Levy 1988; Richardson 1990) have made less sweeping criticisms, but have also implied that if Grünbaum is wrong in attributing the tally argument to Freud, this adversely affects his case against the Freudian clinical evidence. This is a mistake, as can be seen by looking at Grünbaum's argument.

In his 1984 book, part 1, Grünbaum argues that the clinical data that Freud and so many other analysts have relied on are unreliable because of the intermingling of suggestibility factors. Freud's solution to this difficulty was his appeal to the tally argument. That argument, however, is unsound as evidenced by spontaneous remission and the success of certain behavior therapies. In part 2, Grünbaum argues that other epistemic liabilities exist besides suggestibility *and* that even if the data were assumed to be epistemically uncontaminated, Freud's arguments for his interpretation of his clinical data would still not succeed (see Grünbaum 1984, 172). Suppose that Grünbaum were now to concede that Freud never endorsed the tally argument. Would that concession affect his criticism of the Freudian interpretation of the clinical data? It would not. Subtracting the tally argument from the Freudian corpus would do absolutely nothing to answer the criticism that the clinical data are contaminated or that Freud's arguments are flawed, even assuming no contamination; nor would keeping the argument in Freud's hands help his case, given that the argument is now known to be unsound. In short, Grünbaum's case against the alleged probative value of the Freudian clinical data does not rest, even in part, on his attributing the tally argument to Freud.

Suggestion and Placebos
As noted earlier, Freud was well aware of the possibility that his patient's responses were due in part to suggestion. But does Grünbaum make too much of this possibility? Fine and Forbes (1986) argue that he does: "What we find problematic is that this generic possibility, like Descartes' demon, relies on a general, always-available doubt, independent of any specific mode of instantiation or mechanism of operation. Used in this generic way, suggestibility, like its Cartesian counterpart, is just a place-holder for skeptical doubt, or fallibility" (238). Other philosophers have either seconded their criticism (Wollheim 1993) or made a similar complaint (Sachs 1989, 355). One response is to note that the criticisms of the Freudian clinical data in part 2 of Grünbaum's *Foundations* make no appeal to contamination by suggestibility. Thus, Grünbaum (1986), in reply to Fine and Forbes, writes, "If need be, I could and would rest my case on Part 2 alone" (277). This response is important, given the tendency of some critics to overlook its availability, but, of course, it does not render Fine and Forbes's criticism altogether irrelevant or unimportant. Grünbaum does make additional comments about their points (277; see also 275–276), but I believe there is more to say about what is really a large and complex issue.

To begin with, what is meant by "suggestion?" In a narrow sense, a therapist suggests an idea or course of action to a client by explicitly mentioning it in the course of the therapy. For example, an analyst may tell a client that her problem is due to penis envy. In hypnosis, the hypnotized patient may be instructed to stop smoking or to eat less. Freud, however, did not always use the term in this narrow sense; as Richardson notes (1990, 674), he seems to have meant a variety of things by "suggestion." Clinical psychologists and psychiatrists have followed Freud's practice of using "suggestion" in both a narrow and a wide sense. For example, Fisher and Greenberg (1977, 363), in speaking of suggestion, refer to such items as the reinforcement of certain types of patient communications, the presence of a prestigious practitioner, and the offering of an interpretation (whether or not it is correct). Grünbaum, too, uses "suggestion" sometimes to refer to the analyst's presentation of "anticipatory ideas," but also to conditioning factors. Finally, Fine and Forbes (1986, 238), although they mention no specific factors, note that "placebo effect" is sometimes used as an alternative to "suggestibility."

When "suggestion" is used in the wider sense, it means something like the presentation of a stimulus to produce an uncritical response, such as an action or the acquisition of a belief. So long as it is understood, however, that "suggestion" is not being used in what I called the "narrow" sense, it is not critical that we have an exact definition. If someone asks what we mean by speaking of suggestion in a clinical context, it is sufficient that we can specify the factors we are referring to; giving a general, precise definition is not necessary. Even if we can specify the factors, however, is the suggestibility hypothesis, like Descartes' postulation of an evil demon, that is, in Fine and Forbes's phrase, "just a place-holder for skeptical doubt, or fallibility?" In at least one very crucial respect, the two hypotheses are different. Descartes' hypothesis has at least a surface credibility no matter what the data are like. The theorist who appeals to suggestibility, in contrast, runs a real risk of invoking a hypothesis that is patently unwarranted, or worse. If I say that the elimination of the patient's brain tumor was possibly due to suggestion rather than his brain surgery, then what I say may be too incredible to take seriously.

Appeals to suggestion, then, are not seemingly plausible in some circumstances.

So far, I have not said anything incompatible with Fine and Forbes's comments. When they speak of the strategy evolved by "real science" (1986, 238), they seem to agree that the suggestibility hypothesis might have to be taken seriously in cases where it can be made specific, concrete, and testable. I have argued only that the hypothesis need not be irremediably vague and that unlike Descartes' demon hypothesis, it cannot *reasonably* be invoked come what may (of course, any hypothesis can be brought in if plausibility is of no concern).

Still remaining is the crucial question of whether the appeal to suggestibility in a psychoanalytic context is warranted. I will begin with Freud's therapy. The reason that suggestion needs to be taken seriously in evaluating Freudian therapy is that a solid body of evidence exists that placebo factors often do account for the elimination of a variety of (nonpsychotic) psychological problems. For example, it has been demonstrated that clients receiving a credible placebo, in some cases a sugar pill, will improve more than those in no-treatment or wait-list controls and as much as those receiving some standard treatment. In fact, some of the most effective treatments yet devised have sometimes performed no better than a placebo. For example, Beck's cognitive therapy for depression was studied in a series of well-designed experiments and initially produced better results than a placebo and, in some cases, a standard drug treatment. Advocates of the therapy thus anticipated favorable results in the recently completed National Institute of Mental Health study, probably the most sophisticated and most expensive experimental study of psychotherapy done to date.

The preliminary findings were announced at the 1990 meeting of the Association for the Advancement of Behavior Therapy and shocked some supporters of Beck's treatment. Clients receiving a sugar pill did approximately as well as those receiving the cognitive therapy. Furthermore, the sugar pill did almost as well as the remaining two treatments: a standard drug treatment and interpersonal therapy. There are also many studies in the behavior therapy literature in which a placebo treatment did as well as the therapy. There is also at least one such study involving psychoanalytically oriented psychotherapy (Brill et al. 1964). The placebo subjects received a sugar pill and brief interviews which were limited to 15 minutes so as to minimize any inadvertent psychotherapeutic effect. The placebo patients improved to approximately the same extent as those receiving the psychoanalytically oriented psychotherapy. Several other studies of insight therapies, reviewed by Prioleau, Murdock, and Brody (1983), have also shown a failure to outperform a placebo.

What accounts for the comparative effectiveness of placebos? Plausible candidates include the following: the client's expectation of being helped, the presentation of plausible sounding (even if false) interpretations, talking about one's problems to a credible therapist, the therapeutic relationship, and the therapist's demand for improvement. It is possible that some of these factors are generally more important than others and that different factors make a causal difference with certain clients and problems and not with others. Still, it would hardly be "real science" (Fine and Forbes's phrase) to bracket it off as a *mere* possibility that such factors make a clinical difference, given the repeated findings that sugar pills and various pseudotherapies can do as well with real patients as virtually any kind of psychotherapy studied to date (Prioleau et al. 1983), with the possible exception of behavior therapy and cognitive therapy. In the absence of a placebo control, the appeal to placebo factors as a rival explanation of psychotherapy outcomes can no more be dismissed as a Descartes demon-like hypothesis than can such an appeal be similarly rejected in the evaluation of drug treatments.

There are several questions about the role of placebos in outcome research. For example, does it even make sense to speak of a "placebo" when the term refers to a psychological treatment? (see Binns 1990, 534; and my reply, Erwin 1994). Even if it does, if we are interested in therapeutic efficacy rather than understanding why a therapy works, should we employ a placebo control group? These issues are taken up in chapter 6 (pp. 253–255).

I turn now to Freudian theory. What are the suggestibility factors that supposedly vitiate the probative value of Freud's clinical data for his theoretical claims? As with his therapy, there are more than one.

For example, investigators have found that individuals will enthusi-
astically accept bogus interpretations as accurate descriptions of
their personalities, especially if the interpreter is perceived as prestigious (see Grünbaum 1984, 240–241). Second, inaccurate interpretations have also been found to correlate with positive changes in
the patient's behavior (see Grünbaum 1980). Third, and very important, operant studies of verbal behavior show how the data of free
association are influenced by verbal cues, such as the therapist's
pausing, making certain reinforcing sounds (such as "uh-huh") and
giving evidence of paying or not paying attention. Judd Marmor
(1970) also reports that the theoretical allegiance of the therapist
influences the type of phenomenological data yielded in free association. Freudians elicit material about Oedipus complexes; Horney-
ites about idealized images; Alderians about feelings of inferiority,
and so on (for reviews, see Grünbaum 1984, and Fisher and Greenberg 1977). Before assessing the epistemic relevance of these factors,
I want to address an objection pressed by Sachs (1989, 353) and Levy
(1988, 198). Both point out that Freud tried to meet the charge of
suggestibility by relying on the coincidence of the free associations
of neurotic patients with the avowals of psychotic patients. Why do
such data provide "guarantees" (Sachs 1989, 534) that the free associations of neurotic patients are not due to suggestion? Freud's
answer is that the avowals of psychotics cannot be influenced by
suggestion, "Nor must we fail to point out that a large number of
the individual findings of analysis, which might otherwise be sus-
pected of being products of suggestion, are confirmed from another
and irreproachable source. Our guarantors in this case are the suf-
ferers from dementia praecox and paranoia, who are of course far
above any suspicion of being influenced by suggestion" (1917, *S.E.*,
16: 453).

At least two problems arise with Freud's "guarantee." First, we have
no independent evidence for Freud's claim that the associations of
his psychotic and his neurotic patients did coincide. Given the great
variety of ways in which the verbal responses of both groups could
have been both similar and different, how do we know that Freud
did not mistakenly emphasize the wrong similarities? The second
and more important problem concerns his claim that psychotic

patients cannot be influenced by suggestion. The only reason he gives for this claim is that psychotic patients are "of course far above any suspicion of being influenced by suggestion." Sachs and Levy give no reason at all. They apparently take the claim to be obviously true. The lack of empirical support for Freud's claim, however, is not the only problem. Solid evidence has been available for at least 25 years that the verbal behavior of psychotic patients, including schizophrenics, can be greatly influenced by suggestion. In fact, their verbal behavior has been shown to be influenced by the very same sorts of stimuli that affect neurotics, such as uttering "uh-huhs," moving about, and so on. In one early study, Krasner (1958) used a storytelling procedure to study the verbal responses of two men at a veteran's hospital who were diagnosed as having "schizophrenic reactions in remission" (364). In 25 sessions, each subject was asked to make up a story about at least four characters: a mother, a father, a child, and an animal. Krasner found that the experimenter could systematically increase the targeted verbal responses by nodding his head, smiling, and emitting an "hmm-hmm" sound. One interesting feature of the experiment, from a psychoanalytic point of view, was the targeted verbal responses: all references to the mother figure in the story.

Krasner's study may be of limited relevance to the present issue because his subjects were in remission and perhaps Freud's psychotic subjects were not. That problem does not arise, however, in certain other studies of psychotics. For example, Ayllon and Haughton (1964) studied three hospitalized female mental patients: two were chronic schizophrenics and one suffered from involuntary depression. None were in remission. In one case, a schizophrenic woman's delusional and neutral verbal responses either increased or decreased as a function of reinforcement or lack of reinforcement by the staff. The reinforcement consisted of listening to or taking interest in the patient's verbalizations, a point of obvious relevance to the practice of psychoanalysis. In a second experiment, the somatic verbal responses of two women (one a schizophrenic and the other a depressed patient) increased after reinforcement and were virtually eliminated when ignored. Salzinger and Pisoni (1961) were also able to condition affect responses in 10 female and 4 male hospitalized schizophrenic patients through the experimenters' use of such words as "hmm-hmm," "uh-huh," "I see," "yeah," and so on. In light of the results of these and other studies (e.g., Salzinger and Pisoni 1958), it can no longer be credibly maintained that psychotics cannot be influenced by suggestion.

I conclude that for both Freud's theory and therapy suggestibility factors are an important source of rival hypotheses. The hypotheses cannot be reasonably dismissed by saying that they are vague or that they are like Descartes' demon hypothesis. Questions remain, however, about the nature of the rival hypotheses and their epistemic role. For example, as to the hypothesis concerning Freudian theory and clinical data, what does it say? On Sachs's (1989, 357) interpretation, Grünbaum is saying that all of the Freudian clinical data may be due to suggestion. If that were being said, then the suggestibility hypothesis would be compatible with Freudian theory having strong clinical support. If true, the hypothesis would show only what is not at issue: that Freud's hypotheses lack certitude. If, however, "may," were replaced by "probably" in regard to all clinical hypotheses, then the hypothesis is implausible. It is unlikely that everything a patient says in analysis is due to suggestion. Something in between these extremes is needed. Perhaps the following will do (see Grünbaum 1984, 245, 246).

Because of the ubiquity in the clinical setting of those sorts of suggestibility factors found to influence clients' verbal behavior—the prestige of the analyst, the analyst's paying or not paying attention, or uttering reinforcing noises, or moving about, agreeing or disagreeing with the client's statement, and so on—there is no general, reliable way to tell which client responses are due to suggestion (in a broad sense) and which are not, unless experimental controls or some adequate substitute is introduced. Consider again a case discussed in chapter 1 (pp. 10–11). A schizophrenic woman drags a broom around a hospital ward all day and a psychiatrist gives a Freudian-like interpretation of her apparently ritualistic behavior. He says she drags the broom around because it is a phallic symbol. Suppose we know, however, that the behavior was conditioned deliberately by attendants who gave her cigarettes as a reward for dragging the broom. This, in fact, is what did happen (see Ayllon et al.

1965): The psychologists were trying to expose the baselessness of many psychiatric interpretations. If we know what caused the behavior, then we can know in advance that if the psychiatrist offers an argument for a rival hypothesis, the argument will lack cogency. Now suppose that many psychotic patients are dragging a broom around and we know that the psychologists had access to all of them. Even if it were unlikely that conditioning caused all of the responses, we could not appeal to observations of the broom-dragging to confirm nonconditioning hypotheses if we had no reliable way of telling which responses were conditioned and which were not. Analogously, in the absence of experimental controls, if the client improves in respect R, and placebo factors were present and were of the sort that often bring about that sort of change, then observation of the change is unlikely to confirm that the therapy caused the improvement.

In the case of Freudian theory, matters are more complex. Despite the ubiquity of conditioning factors, clinical data might disconfirm a Freudian hypothesis. To take a standard example, the observation of an overtly homosexual paranoid would disconfirm the proposition that all paranoia is due to repressed homosexuality. In addition, there might be some cases where a Freudian can argue cogently for some Freudian hypothesis or other by appealing to clinical data. Grünbaum, too, agrees that all the clinical data are not probatively irrelevant, but argues that they cannot bear the weight put on them by those who claim that such data typically can confirm or disconfirm Freudian hypotheses (1984, 245, 265).

It may be useful to summarize several points. First, a suggestibility hypothesis could be analogous to an evil demon hypothesis if it were invoked to show merely that a rival hypothesis lacked certitude. That may be the only comparison intended by Fine and Forbes (1986). There is, however, an important disanalogy, which is relevant to Grünbaum's argument. Insofar as the evil demon hypothesis has epistemic force beyond demonstrating a lack of certitude, it has this force no matter what our data are. That is not true of a suggestion hypothesis. As I noted in the case of brain surgery, an appeal to suggestion may lack all credibility given certain background evidence. Second, although unspecified talk of suggestion may be unclear, we can eliminate or at least diminish the unclarity by specifying which sorts of factors are being referred to. We can then address the empirical question of whether such factors are likely to be casually relevant in a specific context. Third, the suggestibility factors found to be casually relevant in the verbal conditioning studies—for example, taking interest in or ignoring a patient's verbalizations, moving about, saying "hmm-hmm," "yeah," and so on—are commonly found in the psychoanalytic setting. For that reason, they are an important source of epistemic contamination in the absence of experimental controls. Fourth, contrary to Freud, Sachs (1989), and Levy (1988), the verbal behavior of psychotics can be conditioned. The final point is the most difficult to state precisely. How much weight should we accord suggestion as an epistemic contaminant in a clinical setting? It is easier to give a precise answer if we are asking only about therapeutic outcomes. Although certain qualifications are needed, in particular relativization to a clinical problem, a rule can be stated. In the absence of a satisfactory placebo control, we are generally unwarranted in inferring that overcoming resistances, working through the transference, and other such ingredients of psychoanalysis produced the so-called cure.

It is much more difficult to state an analogous plausible general rule concerning Freud's theoretical hypotheses. One problem is that the presence of suggestibility factors may not prevent the confirmation of any and all claims that might be called a "Freudian hypothesis." For example, suppose we define "repression" by saying that: its essence lies simply in the function of rejecting and keeping something out of consciousness (see Kline [1971] 1981, 195). If that is all Freudian repression is , if there is no necessary link to the id or the ego, or even to a dynamic unconscious, then we may be able to confirm its mere existence on the basis of clinical data. In contrast, showing that repressed infantile wishes typically cause and maintain what Freud called "psychoneuroses" is obviously much more difficult. In trying to confirm the latter hypothesis in a clinical setting, the problem posed by suggestibility factors is much more formidable. It would be nice if we could sum up matters via a general rule, but I, at least, do not know how to do that. Even so, when evaluating alleged clinical confirmation of Freud's repression etiology (which is the subject of Grünbaum's *Foundations)*, the role of suggestibility factors needs to be taken seriously. The absence of an algorithm telling us how seriously to take it is insufficient reason for discounting it.

Besides lacking an algorithm, we also do not have a general, worked out theory of how such factors affect behavior. Does this disqualify a suggestibility hypothesis from being a credible rival to a Freudian explanation? Richard Wollheim apparently thinks so. Referring to Grünbaum, Wollheim writes (1993, 111): "He never proposes, nor feels the need for, any infilling when he invokes the possibility, indeed the likelihood, of suggestion as the real explanation of what the patient does. In the absence of such infilling, the situation is envisaged in the following way: (one) the analyst makes his wishes known; (two) the patient complies." If, in asking for "infilling," Wollheim is demanding a detailed theory of how suggestion works, he is setting too high a standard for taking a rival explanation seriously. On that standard, there would be no need to rule out the possibility of placebo factors in drug studies until we had a theoretical mechanism describing how such factors work. That is the wrong standard. If we have empirical evidence that certain suggestibility factors often cause such and such behavioral change, and that evidence makes a suggestibility explanation in a particular context just as plausible as some rival theory, no matter how detailed, then we need to discount the former if we are to confirm the latter. Fine and Forbes, whom Wollheim cites approvingly, deny this need (1986, 237–238). However, I have already criticized their view when discussing the differential nature of confirmation (see chapter 2, pp. 44–54).

Wollheim is right to demand that more be said than merely: the analyst makes his wishes known; the patient complies. However, we can do far better than this without having a full blown theory of how suggestion affects behavior. We can isolate particular suggestibility factors, introduce them under controlled conditions, and produce the sorts of behavior typically found in psychoanalytic clinical settings. That has already been done in the verbal conditioning studies referred to earlier. It should be stressed, moreover, that the concern is not merely that the patient complies with the analyst's wishes. The main problem concerns the analyst's influencing the patient's behavior unwittingly: by nodding, paying attention or not paying attention, making certain theoretical comments, etc. As Krasner's (1958) study demonstrates, an analyst can without realizing it cause a patient to continually make references to his mother by nodding his head, smiling, and emitting an "mmm-hmm" sound. I conclude that we cannot dismiss the need to rule out a suggestion hypothesis in interpreting clinical data merely because, as Wollheim puts it (1993, 111), we lack the "infilling." We may lack the infilling, but we do not lack the empirical evidence needed to make suggestibility and placebo explanations credible in psychoanalytic contexts.

Granted that the threat of contamination of clinical data by suggestion is very real, can anything be done about it? Perhaps, but if we are talking about the existing evidence, it is important to note that the measures taken so far are hardly sufficient. Tape recording analytic sessions, which is the main strategy that has been used, does not enable us to decide to what extent the client's responses were influenced by the analyst's noises, movements, pronouncements, questions, etc. Robert Wallenstein (1986) mentions some additional measures suggested by Clark Glymour (1974). The clinical evidence might have considerable force, Glymour contends, when, for example, the clinical proceedings show no sign of indoctrination, such as leading the patient and the like; when the results obtained fall into a regular and apparently lawlike pattern obtained independently by many clinicians; and when those results are contrary to the expectation and belief of the clinician.

These suggestions are useful beginnings, which is probably all that Glymour intends, but they are hardly enough. They barely touch the problem posed by the verbal conditioning studies: the analyst's influence can easily occur in a systematic way even in the absence of any attempts to indoctrinate the client. Still, I am not arguing that more cannot be done to weaken the credibility of suggestibility hypotheses. For those analysts who wish to continue psychoanalytic research in a clinical setting, this is a problem to be worked on. Success, moreover, may come in degrees. As Wallenstein (1986) notes, contamination of clinical data by suggestion is not an "all-or-none-affair." It is fair to say, however, that the problem has not yet been solved, and is a very serious one for analysts who wish to make their case largely by appealing to existing clinical data.

An Extension of Commonsense Psychology?

Some proponents of Freudian theory claim that it is an extension of common sense psychology. Given that commonsense psychological hypotheses can generally be confirmed without experimentation, the argument continues, the same can be done for Freudian hypotheses. Experimentation may supplement arguments appealing to clinical data or to data from everyday life but it is generally not required.

In some respect or other, Freudian theory *is* an extension of common sense psychology. For example, it is to some degree a conceptual extension insofar as it makes use of such concepts as "wish" and "desire." Yet that is no guarantee that its hypotheses can be confirmed nonexperimentally. If I say that autistic children who bang their heads against the wall generally do so because they find it rewarding to receive attention from their parents or hospital attendants, my hypothesis employs commonsense concepts, but that does not mean that I can confirm it without experimental evidence.

When Albert Bandura and his colleagues claim (Bandura, Adams, and Beyer 1977) that the enhancement of self-efficacy expectations makes an important difference to the effectiveness of certain therapies, he is tacitly using a concept of commonsense psychology; he is talking about a certain type of expectation. Yet he does not claim that he can warrant his hypothesis without doing experiments. It is difficult to see how he could do that.

Outside of clinical psychology, many commonsense theories have been formulated, for example, about the effects of corporal punishment on character, or the relationship between the death penalty and the homicide rate, that are extremely difficult to establish (if it is possible at all) without doing experiments.

Some writers suggest that instead of trying to confirm such general causal principles directly, we should focus on single cases. If we confirm a sufficient number of singular causal judgments, under varied conditions, we can then build up support for the general principles. We can try the same strategy in Freudian psychology. A problem arises, however, even for commonsense judgments, if we have no fund of evidence that a certain factor generally makes a certain sort of difference. It is one thing to be told that when a man put his sweater on, after the temperature dropped, he probably did it because he felt cold. Here, we can appeal to known facts about the general causal relevance of feeling cold under these conditions. It is quite different to be told that a paroled prisoner refrained from committing murder because he moved to a state that has the death penalty, or that another man has a sterling character because he was spanked (or not spanked) as a child. Without knowing how such factors as fear of the death penalty or corporal punishment generally affect people, it is usually difficult to establish the singular causal judgment.

It is not enough, then, for a theory to be an extension of common sense in some way or another (e.g., that it be a conceptual extension in the way just indicated). What needs to be shown is that Freudian theory is an extension of commonsense psychology in a respect that permits nonexperimental confirmation of its claims.

One way to argue this is to argue that commonsense hypotheses and Freudian hypotheses are alike in that both can be warranted by appeal to thematic affinities. Jim Hopkins (1988) gives this sort of argument. Another approach is to appeal, as Nagel does (1994b), to the principle that we can certify the cause of an action by figuring out what would justify it from the agent's point of view. I have criticized both the reliance on thematic affinities and Nagel's principle in chapter 1 (pp. 26–40 and pp. 13–19). I will assume, consequently, that using either strategy is of no help to Freud.

I turn now to other ways of arguing that Freudian theory is an extension of folk psychology in a way that matters epistemically.

Belief, Desire, and Action
Marcia Cavell (1993) replies to Grünbaum's (1984) contentions about the inadequacy of Freud's clinical evidence by claiming that the causal connection between repression and symptoms is fundamentally the same—though more complex and less obvious—as that between desire and action, action and belief. She continues: "If this

were so, then no inductive evidence of some special kind would be needed to establish a causal connection in any particular case" (80).

Grünbaum, she claims, tries to block this response by arguing (Grünbaum 1984, 79) that for repression and symptom-formation to be related as reasons to action, the cited reasons must be rational. This, in turn, implies, in the case of Freud's explanation of paranoia, that the paranoid unconsciously believes that his delusional conduct is a way of satisfying his homosexual longings. Surely, however, the paranoid does not believe this even unconsciously.

Although Cavell does not claim that repression can be understood as a straightforward instance of acting for reasons, she makes two replies. First, in discussing paranoia, Grünbaum speaks of an erotic wish, but on Freud's later instinctual model, the postulated wish is not itself erotic, but rather is a wish either to not acknowledge an erotic wish or to avoid something that makes one anxious. Cavell is partly right about Freud's later model, but she leaves out something important. In *Inhibitions, Symptoms and Anxiety* (1926, *S.E.*, 20:87–174) and, more clearly, in *New Introductory Lectures On Psycho-Analysis* (1933, *S.E.*, 22:5–182), Freud speaks of repression and the avoidance of anxiety, but he does not disavow his earlier claim that the etiology of psycho-neuroses involves erotic desires. Rather, he holds that there is an *initial* repression and repressions that occur later. The later repressions involve anxiety avoidance, but the initial repression is in response to libidinal demands (1933, *S.E.*, 22:94). When Grünbaum refers to the paranoid's erotic desires (1984, 79), he is talking about the desires that, according to Freud, are initially repressed, and that later lead through reaction formation and projection to paranoia.

Cavell's second, and substantive, point is this: if repression did display the full intentional structure, the repressed aims would be rational from the agent's point of view. If I thought (consciously or unconsciously) that I might be less anxious if I had a certain belief (say, a paranoid belief of some sort), I would have a good reason for acquiring it if I could. So, Grünbaum is wrong in saying that the agent's repressed aims would be irrational. This point is irrelevant to Grünbaum's criticism. His point (1984, 79) is not that the agent's symptom formation would be irrational but that there is no evidence that the agent has the belief that would relate the repressed wish to the symptom. Without such evidence, we lack grounds for assimilating the case to the practical syllogism. Thus, he writes, in reference to Freud's case of the man who forgot the Latin word *aliquis:* "This well-known case fails to conform to the practical syllogism. For there is not a shred of evidence that the male subject underwent his memory lapse in the unconscious belief—however foolish—of thereby realizing his desire (hope) that his paramour is *not* pregnant." (Grünbaum's emphasis, 1984, 77).

The same evidential problem arises in Cavell's example. We *might* be warranted in explaining the paranoid's acquisition of a belief in terms of a prior belief about the diminishment of anxiety, except for one problem: there is not a shred of evidence that paranoids typically have such a prior belief.

Cavell also tries to explain in terms of a belief-desire model (1993, 81) how lifting repressions removes symptoms. If one is doing x because one wants y, and then discovers that one had made a mistake, and wants z instead (or one does not want y on the whole), then one presumably will no longer do or want to do x. In the lifting of repressions, Cavell continues, one gains the insight that the desire for y is discordant with more highly valued desires, shifting the causal valences of belief and desire, altering behavior along the way. The same problem arises here as before. How does Cavell know, in the absence of any experimental evidence, that psychoneurotic symptoms are typically caused by repressed desires? How does she know that the two are even generally correlated, or that analysts often lift repressions, or that lifting repressions typically removes symptoms?

Apart from the two preceding examples, how does Cavell propose generally to warrant psychoanalytic causal hypotheses once they are expressed in belief-desire terminology? She could try Nagel's strategy, and argue that we identify causally relevant factors by figuring out which belief-desire set makes sense of the symptom or action from the agent's point of view, but as I argued in chapter 1 (13–19), that strategy is a failure. Cavell, however, does not rely on Nagel's tactic. Rather, she claims that psychoanalytic hypotheses have the same kind of predictive power as folk-psychological explanations, but she makes no attempt to show this. She fails to mention even one prediction that allegedly confirms a Freudian hypothesis. Instead, as Hopkins does, she appeals to thematic affinity (81). Because I have already objected to the reliance on thematic affinity in discussing Hopkins's views in chapter 1 (26–40), I will comment only on the two cases that Cavell mentions.

In the first, if I have evidence that you intentionally crossed the road, then I will assume that you wanted to cross the road, Cavell points out. I agree, but this does nothing to show that the warrant for my assumption is supplied by thematic affinity rather than background evidence about why people typically cross the road in such circumstances (for a fuller discussion of this point, see the discussion of thematic affinity in chapter 1, 26–40).

In the second case, if Cinderella daydreams of a handsome prince coming to rescue her, Cavell notes, we assume she wishes he might, and that the wish has caused the daydream. Again, there is no argument here that thematic affinity supports the causal inference. If I daydream about being president of the United States, figuring out, for example, how I might act if I were president, there is just as much affinity between my daydream and the wish to be president as is present in the Cinderella case. Yet, you would be mistaken in inferring that I wish to be president, and doubly mistaken if you concluded that this wish caused the daydream. Even if I were one of those people who secretly harbored such a wish, you would not have evidence for the causal inference if you were relying only on the affinity between the wish and the daydream.

In the Cinderella case, there is no need to fall back on thematic affinity: contextual clues in the story give us reason to think that she wants to be rescued by Prince Charming. Her subsequent behavior confirms the thought.

In brief, I deny Cavell's unargued claim (80) that if the relation between repression and symptoms were fundamentally the same as that between belief, desire and action, then no inductive evidence of a special kind would be needed to establish a causal connection in any particular case. Suppose that the relation were like this but it was unknown to us; indeed, suppose that we lacked evidence that repressed wishes were even generally correlated with neurotic symptoms. We might then be unable to warrant a Freudian explanation in a particular case unless we first obtained a special kind of inductive evidence, namely, experimental evidence, concerning the general causal relevance of repressions to symptom formation.

I am perhaps being unfair to Cavell. She may mean not that we would need no special kind of evidence if it were merely true, but rather if we were to have *evidence* that repression is related to symptoms as beliefs and desires are to actions. On that reading, however, she is clearly not answering Grünbaum's complaint. The complaint, as I pointed out earlier, is exactly that we do not have such evidence.

Edelson's Arguments

Marshall Edelson (1988, 329–330) also argues that Freudian theory represents an extension of commonsense psychology, but his analysis of how this bears on the justification of Freudian hypotheses is more complex than the accounts considered so far.

Edelson is concerned with the justification of clinical causal inferences apart from the issue of contamination by suggestion. That is, if we ignore the latter issue, can psychoanalytic inferences in a clinical setting be sometimes justified? Edelson's more modest goal is to show how *in the future* things can be done to warrant such inferences. Even someone skeptical of clinical confirmation can agree that this is a desirable goal, at least if psychoanalytic research should continue and if it is likely to be carried on, for the most part, in a clinical setting. Whether following Edelson's particular prescription will suffice to warrant psychoanalytic clinical inferences is another matter. I will argue that it does not suffice.

Edelson's more ambitious goal is to show that Freud has already succeeded in warranting some of his hypotheses. For example, he claims (328) that Freud justifies clinical causal inferences in the Rat Man and Wolf Man cases by giving not just some explanation but a *good* causal explanation. I assume that Edelson is not merely reporting what Freud claims, but rather is saying that Freud's inferences in these cases are, in fact, justified (see 327). If they are justified, then at least two things follow. First, some of Freud's hypotheses are already warranted, although it would be important to say exactly which these are. Second, clinical confirmation of Freudian causal claims without experiment, contrary to both Mill and Grünbaum, has been accomplished. In fact, if Freud's arguments in these cases are cogent, it is not necessary to appeal to commonsense modes of argumentation; it is enough to reconstruct Freud's arguments if the goal is merely to demonstrate the possibility of clinical confirmation. I deny, however, that the cogency of Freud's arguments in his case studies can be taken for granted given the serious criticism that scholars have made of them. See, for example, Grünbaum's devastating criticism of Freud's reasoning in the Wolf Man and Rat Man cases (Grünbaum 1993) and Esterson's (1993) incisive criticism of Freud's reasoning in his other published cases. Unless these criticisms are answered, one cannot take for granted that Freud's arguments in his published case studies are cogent.

We can, however, set aside the issue of what is demonstrated in Freud's case studies and still inquire about Edelson's arguments for justifying clinical inferences. If one or more of these arguments are successful, they may have been used by other analysts besides Freud, or they might be used in the future. There are three such major arguments, according to Edelson (327). One involves analogy, a second, a consilience of inductions, and a third, a concept of causal powers and an elucidation of causal mechanisms.

Analogy Edelson begins by citing a case in which a person says "This meeting is closed" instead of what he intended to say, namely, "This meeting is opened." Asked why he made the mistake, he is able to explain the slip. He remembers being reluctant to begin the meeting; he wished it were already ended. Edelson's strategy is to unearth the good reasons we would have for accepting the man's explanation and then to show that an analyst might have analogous reasons when the client is not aware of the cause of a slip. One question to ask, however, is whether the reasons cited in Edelson's made-up case really are good reasons. A second question is: In a typical psychoanalytic case, are there analogous reasons available?

Edelson's first reason for accepting the man's explanation is this: We have reason to believe that rational actions, such as closing a meeting, are generally caused by conjunctions of desire and belief. This is not a good reason (331). The most that we can infer from this assumption is that some belief-desire combination caused the slip; it would remain to be shown that the combination cited by the man was the real cause. However, even the more modest inference that the cause was a belief-desire combination is unwarranted. The man's action, as far as we know given Edelson's description, is *not* rational. He did not deliberately close the meeting; he made a slip of the tongue. Of course, given that this is a made-up case, we are free to stipulate that the slip was motivated, but we cannot infer that a slip was motivated in an actual case from the assumption that when people close a meeting, they generally do so because of a belief and desire. This case is different in that the action was unintentional. Unless we are taking for granted Freud's repression theory, we have no reason to believe that slips of the tongue are like rational actions in being *generally* caused by beliefs and desires.

Edelson's second reason is that there is a thematic affinity between the slip and the belief and desire. This sort of reason, according to Edelson, is quite important in justifying psychoanalytic clinical infer- ences. When the psychoanalyst adduces evidence for the existence and causal status of an oral, anal, or phallic wish or fantasy, his reasoning depends, in part, according to Edelson, on an appeal to thematic affinity. In fact, Edelson goes further: "Reasoning by appeal to thematic affinity is not only central in the explanatory strategies of psychoanalysis. It plays an important role in the definition of the domain of psychoanalysis" (332). Given what I argued in chapter 1 (pp. 26–40; see also Grünbaum 1993), I will simply comment that Edelson's second reason is also not a good one. If we had to rely on thematic affinity, then we would not be warranted in accepting the man's explanation of his slip.

Edelson's third reason is that, as a matter of common sense psychology, we believe, in some cases at least, that a person may have *direct access* to the causes of his actions. As an example, Edelson cites the case of someone who knows that he ran because he was in a state of terror. It could be argued that even in this case, the man does not know why he ran merely on the basis of introspection. He has direct access to the terror—he *feels* terrified—but he also has quite a lot of background information to support his inference. However, let us waive this objection and agree that commonsense beliefs about "direct accessing" of mentalistic causes are *sometimes* correct. Still, there is quite a lot of research in cognitive psychology demonstrating that when people introspect, they are often wrong about the cause of their behavior (Nisbett and Ross 1980). Worse still, if Freud's repression theory is true, there are many more cases when the cause that is seemingly "directly accessed" is not the cause; the cause is a repressed wish. So, in the case of the man who closed the meeting, how do we know, insofar as we rely on direct access, whether this is one of those cases in which introspection is reliable or one in which it is not?

Edelson's fourth and final reason (335) is that we assume that the person in such cases as the closing-the-meeting example can and will tell us directly, if nothing acts to prevent him, what conjunction of desires and belief, in conflict with other desires and belief, triumphed over these others to cause the mistake. This, too, is not a good reason. The most we have the right to assume here is that the person can and will tell us what he *thinks* to be the cause, if he has any belief about the matter. Unless we have evidence that the person making the slip is generally right in such cases, his opinion is not itself evidence that he is right. Moreover, in many cases, when people make slips they do not even have a view about what caused them. In such cases, Freud assumes, according to Edelson (336), that there must be some other causal process operating to prevent the person from being aware of the cause of his parapraxis, dream, or symptom. That is quite a large and unobvious assumption. Unless a Freudian can cite supporting evidence, appealing to it is not going to help warrant his or her clinical inferences.

There is no point in pursuing the analogies between the four reasons cited by Edelson in his model case, that of the man who inadvertently closed the meeting, and reasons typically available to the analyst. These reasons, either singly or in combination, fail to warrant the explanation given in Edelson's example. There is no reason to believe that they would be of greater use if available to the analyst. Perhaps the best of Edelson's reasons is the appeal to direct access. However, even if that could be defended, it is not relevant to the attempt to warrant psychoanalytic explanations of slips. In such cases, as Edelson is, of course, aware, there is a crucial disanalogy: the client has no direct access to the cause of his or her slip.

Edelson also appeals to analogical arguments to show that free association can reliably unearth causes of parapraxes, dreams, and slips.

First, Freud argues by analogy to the effects of interventions we carry out in practical actions to reduce the reluctance of those who wish to communicate their secrets to us. Edelson does not tell us what sort of interventions he has in mind in the non-Freudian cases. Sometimes we cajole people; other times we threaten or bribe them; still other times, we simply ask them to tell us their secrets. Without some specification of the method we talking about, it is impossible to know its degree of similarity to free association. Moreover, in assuming that in the psychoanalytic cases there is a secret to communicate, Freud and Edelson are taking for granted Freud's theory of slips; they are assuming that the cause of the slip lies in the person's unconscious. Without that assumption, there is no warrant for assuming that the client is keeping secret the cause of his or her slip If the cause is neurological or environmental, he or she may just be ignorant of the cause.

Second, Edelson draws an analogy with the effects of hypnosis, where a behavior is caused by an idea implanted in the subject's mind by the hypnotist. The subject has access to the phenomenology of mental states under hypnosis, but not later. Two questions should be asked about the analogy. First, are the phenomena in the Freudian case, unexplained slips, neurotic symptoms, and dreams, analogous in a causally relevant way? In one respect, they are: just as in the case of hypnosis, the subject is not aware of the cause of the phenomenon. However, that is also true in many other cases where there is no warrant for invoking a Freudian explanation, as where a subject feels a sudden pain, or hears voices when no one else is present, or suddenly acts out of character. If one is to invoke the rule, as Edelson does (336), "similar effects, similar causes," one has to have reason to believe that the effects truly are similar in a causally relevant way. The subject of hypnosis, say, raises his hand and later does not understand why he did this. Is this analogous to either my having a dream or forgetting a word in such a way that we have grounds for postulating the same cause? If the answer is yes, then why not say the same when I have an unexplained headache, a sudden moodiness, etc.? What is the difference? Suppose, however, that we were to have grounds for inferring similar causes (apparently not precisely similar: there is no repressed wish that causes the behavior of the hypnotized patient). We would still be without grounds for believing that the use of free association (or, for that matter, the analysis of dreams or transference, or the use of projective tests, etc.) is a reliable instrument for revealing the unconscious causes.

Third, Edelson draws (338) an analogy with the effects of "chimney sweeping" or "the talking cure" as reported in the "Preliminary Communication" (1893, *S.E.*, 2). A train of thought leads to the recovery of a traumatic memory, which is related by thematic affinity to a symptom. Several problems arise here. First, quite often in the case of slips and dreams, no traumatic memory is recalled. How does the analogy help in these cases? Second, when a traumatic event is seemingly recalled, it may well have not occurred—as in the Wolf Man's alleged punishment for masturbation or, more recently, in many cases of misremembered sexual abuse. Third, even where there is good evidence that the traumatic event did occur, thematic affinity is not good grounds for inferring that the event caused the neurotic symptom. In fact, in the one case that Edelson mentions, that of Anna O remembering the nausea brought on by seeing a dog drinking out of a glass, we now have reason to believe that her symptoms were not caused by that event but, rather, were physiological (Ellenberger 1970).

Freud's fourth justification for believing that free association works is based on an analogy with word-association experiments, which Freud believed provided reliable evidence for the existence, at least, of unconscious "complexes" (or conflicts or fantasies). However, the existence of unconscious conflicts is not at issue. The issue Edelson is discussing is: Does the use of free association provide reliable evidence that repressed wishes generally cause slips, dreams, and neurotic symptoms? Drawing an analogy between free association and word-association experiments does not answer this question.

Fifth, and finally, studies of art, literature, autobiography (the Schreber case), and jokes provide independent evidence, according to Edelson (339), for the kinds of mental operations postulated in

Freud's clinical causal inferences. Again, two questions. First, although psychoanalysts often invoke Freudian theory to explain works of art, jokes, etc., do they have warrant for doing so? Do we really have firm evidence in such cases that repressed wishes typically (or at least often) play a causal role? Second, even if we do, the issue is not, as it is in the case of word association experiments, merely the existence of causally efficacious unconscious mental events. What needs to be demonstrated is that free association is a reliable method for showing that such events occur *and* that they typically cause slips, dreams, and neurotic symptoms.

Edelson agrees (339) that none of the five justifications he cites is unassailable by itself, but contends that together they provide strong warrant for the credibility of clinical causal inferences in psychoanalysis. I disagree with the latter contention. For reasons I have given, the five "justifications" (or analogies) taken together provide no warrant at all for the sort of clinical inference that Edelson was trying to justify: one that infers the cause of slips, dreams, or neurotic symptoms based on the data of free association.

Consilience Edelson argues that if a number of risky inferences converge on the same conclusion, we may feel a great degree of confidence in the conclusion, and regard the evidence taken as a whole to be quite strong, especially where the inferences are based on very different *kinds* of information (340–341). As he points out, inferences by an analyst in an analytic situation may be based on such varied items as descriptions of early life experiences; reports by others about such experiences, patterns in the analysand's associations; descriptions of the analysand's current mental states, etc. Furthermore, the convergence of inferences concerning such very different things as parapraxes, dreams and symptoms, Edelson claims, justifiably increases our confidence in the inferred conclusion (341).

There is something right in what Edelson is arguing, but also something wrong, or at least controversial. What is right is the common idea that the warrant for a causal hypothesis may increase if we can point to different *kinds* of supporting evidence. Suppose I claim that the cause of a certain type of psychotic symptom is the ingestion of amphetamines in a certain dosage. To argue the case, I do a controlled experiment in which the symptoms are induced in subjects by giving them amphetamines (see Snyder 1975), whereas placebo subjects are shown to be symptom free. I can increase the probability of my hypothesis by replicating the experiment several times, but I can find additional support if I vary the experiment and obtain new kinds of data. For example, I might vary the experimental settings and the types of subjects. It would be even more impressive, if, for example, I could, by giving amphetamines, cause changes in brain chemistry that have been independently shown to correlate with the psychotic symptoms. So citing different *types* of evidence may provide greater warrant for a hypothesis than if the data are all of the same sort. This part of Edelson's argument is uncontroversial. Suppose, however, that I not do any of the above experiments; instead, I simply argue that my hypothesis would, if true, explain various types of data. It would explain why people with characteristics *A* and *B* display the symptoms in question, and why people with characteristics *C* and *D* do the same, and why certain brain changes accompany the symptoms. Now, my argument is considerably weaker. I may be able to say no more than my hypothesis, *H* (if true), provides the best available explanation of various types of data, D_1, D_2, and D_3; so, *H* is probably true. This sort of inference was shown in chapter 2 (pp. 62–73) to be fallacious.

   In his reply to Edelson, Grünbaum (1993, 159) gives a nice example of this type of fallacious argument. Suppose that everyone is a coffee drinker and there is a class of ailments that, unknown to me, remit spontaneously within 1 month of onset. I now hypothesize that drinking coffee for 1 month explains the remission of such symptoms. Suppose, further, that the ailments in the specified class are of very diverse kinds. I can now point to the great explanatory power of my hypothesis and its capacity to simplify (one postulated cause rather than many); yet, for all that, I still have no evidential support for my hypothesis.

   It might seem that I am begging the question in assuming in the above two cases that experimentation would be necessary to show, respectively, that the ingestion of amphetamines or coffee drinking was a cause. However, I am not assuming that; I have already conceded in discussing Mill's views, that background evidence can some-times obviate the need for a controlled study. What I am relying on is the thesis argued in the previous chapter: "*H* provides the best available explanation of data *D;* so we have some rational grounds for believing that *H* is true" is a fallacious inference. If it were a reliable mode of inference, this would be a boon not to psychoana-lysts alone. Behaviorists could argue that a conditioning hypothesis also has strong support: it explains not only the origin of phobias, anxiety states, and depression but also the etiology of autism, schizo-phrenia, and bipolar disorders (Ullmann and Krasner 1969). An analyst might be able to show that the Freudian account is superior, but that does not dispose of the epistemological point. Even if the conditioning hypothesis were the best available explanation, it would still not gain support merely from its potential to explain diverse kinds of data.

It may be that Edelson is not adopting the standard I am attribut-ing to him. In speaking of a number of "risky" psychoanalytic infer-ences that converge on the same conclusion, he may be assuming that, though risky, these inferences are warranted to some degree. In that case, however, he is assuming what he is trying to establish: that psychoanalytic clinical inferences are sometimes warranted.

I should add one additional point. Even if a group of inferences have some independent support, whether their convergence on a single conclusion increases that support is, as argued in chapter 2 (pp. 54–60), a contingent, empirical matter. As I noted there, the simplifying characteristic of Ullmann and Krasner's (1969) condi-tioning hypothesis counted *against* it rather than for it, if we had evidence that the psychoses had different types of causes from (what were then called) the "neuroses." Parapraxes, dreams and neurotic symptoms are, as Edelson notes (342), also unlike one another in various ways. Granted that there are some examples of motivated parapraxes and of wishes influencing dreams, still, does our overall evidence make it somewhat likely that all (or most) dreams, parapraxes, and psychoneuroses have a single type of cause or mul-tiple types of causes? That it is the latter is controversial, but *if* that is what the evidence indicates, then the simplifying power of the repression theory is not a virtue. It counts against the theory.

Successionist and Generative Conceptions of Causality Edelson's final argument utilizes a distinction between two conceptions of causality. In a successionist conception, a cause comes regularly before an event or state. If we know that the cause is about to occur, we can reliably predict its effect. Such a conception is especially useful, according to Edelson (345), in generalizing about the ways in which one moving body, hitting another, may be expected to change its motions. On this conception, explanation involves subsumption under a general law (346).

In the generative conception, in contrast, the cause is external; there is a "real" connection connecting cause and effect (347). Things have causal powers that can be evoked in suitable circumstances, but are not manifested under all circumstances. The generative conception is especially useful (345) in formulating theories that will explain illnesses in terms of viruses. Psychoanalysis, according to Edelson, utilizes a generative conception of causality. Freud, furthermore, does not use the covering law model of explanation (346).

Edelson's distinction closely resembles a distinction between two different philosophical theories of causation: what are sometimes called a "Humean view" (or a "regularity view") and a non-Humean view. The successionist view, at least, appears to be a variant of a Humean view. In the philosophical literature on explanation, such a view often, but not always, goes together with a covering law model of explanation. Grünbaum may or may not endorse such views, but contrary to Edelson's impression (347), whether he does or not, they play no role in his critique of the Freudian clinical evidence. In his 1984 book, Grünbaum points out that on Freudian theory, a repressed wish does not provide a sufficient causal condition for the development of a neurosis. That alone would disqualify the theory from providing an explanation that meets the conditions of a covering law model; the explanation cannot be deduced from the explanans if the explanans does not state a sufficient condition. Yet, as I pointed out in chapter 2, p. 75, Grünbaum nowhere criticizes Freudian theory on this account. He also does not commit himself to a successionist view of causation, one that denies "real" causal connections. In short, Edelson's distinction appears to be irrelevant to Grünbaum's critique. Even if it were shown that Grünbaum held a successionist view, it would need to be shown that holding the view affects one or more of his arguments. Edelson does make one attempt to do this, although he is somewhat (and rightfully) hesitant.

Philosophers such as Grünbaum and Glymour, Edelson notes, perhaps because they are working with a successionist view of causation, attack Freud's argument for the investigative powers of free association as a "causal inversion fallacy" (348). One commits this fallacy when, for example, one infers that a memory developed in free association *after* a dream was the cause of that dream (more precisely, not the memory but the event that is remembered is inferred to be the cause). Why call this a "causal inversion fallacy?" (Glymour, 1983) Glymour's point is this. There may not be any evidence of a causal connection, but if there is reason to infer a connection, one should infer that the dream, which came first, caused the memory, not that the remembered event caused the dream.

Edelson contends that the charge that Freud committed a causal inversion fallacy is based on three misunderstandings, two of which arise from a sucessionist account of causality. First, Grünbaum and Glymour ignore the fact that free associations are expressions of an enduring causal propensity of an entity having the power to generate certain manifestations; second, free associations are the products of a method that is intended to mitigate this causal process. Edelson, however, provides no reason to believe that either Grünbaum's or Glymour's argument presupposes a successionist view of causation, and the contention is implausible. Suppose that they were to adopt a generative conception of causality. That would not affect the reason that they charge Freud with fallacious reasoning. The reason, at least for Glymour's charge, is simply that Freud offers no cogent argument for his inference; he appears to infer from the fact that the memory came after the dream, that the event remembered instigated the dream. Grünbaum's argument is more complex, but it nowhere presupposes any particular view of causation.

Edelson can still reply that Freud is not really guilty of the causal inversion fallacy. Rather, Freud justifies his belief that free association is reliable by appealing to the five analogies discussed earlier (Edelson 1988, 337–339). Edelson may be right in thus absolving

Freud of any simple fallacy, but there are still two problems. First, as argued earlier, the five analogies taken together fail to provide any rational grounds for thinking that free association works. Second, Edelson fails to show that the charge of a causal inversion fallacy, mistaken or not, is based on a sucessionist account of causality. More generally, he fails to show that adopting a generative conception would have any effect on either Grünbaum's or Glymour's arguments.

Conclusion

Edelson has provided the most detailed attempt so far to show how psychoanalytic clinical inferences can be warranted nonexperimentally by treating psychoanalytic theory as an extension of common sense. That attempt, if I am right, fails completely. Could someone else do better? That remains to be demonstrated, but besides the failures of others (such as Nagel, Hopkins, and Cavell), there are two additional reasons to be skeptical about such attempts. First, as I pointed out earlier, we need to ask, In what sense is Freudian theory an extension of commonsense psychology? I have already conceded that it involves, to some degree, a *conceptual* extension insofar as it utilizes common-sense concepts, such as *wish* and *desire*. Even the idea of the unconscious is not that far removed from the commonsense idea that we sometimes engage in self-deception or, for other reasons, are unaware of our real motives. So a large part of Freudian theory is a conceptual extension of commonsense psychology, although not all of it is: postulating an id and superego involves the introduction of new concepts. Still, being an extension of common sense in this conceptual sense is no guarantee of initial plausibility, nor does it provide reason to believe that Freudian causal claims can be typically vindicated without experimentation. As I noted before, there are many hypotheses that utilize only commonsense concepts, but they are nonetheless speculative and are likely to remain so if proper experiments cannot be done or are not done. People have argued for centuries about the typical long range effects of spanking children, and yet even today the issues remain largely unresolved. Or consider various theories about the increase in the crime rate.

Many use only commonsense concepts—it is mainly due to poverty, or poor upbringing, or a lack of religious training, or watching violence on television, etc.—and yet they are all very difficult to confirm without experimentation. In short, being a conceptual extension of commonsense psychology is no guarantee of an "epistemic extension," of deriving some plausibility from background evidence gleaned from commonsense psychology. It is not surprising to be told, nor is it distinctly Freudian to say, that *occasionally* our parapraxes are motivated, or that sometimes our desires influence some of the details of our dreams. It is surprising, however, to be told that all (or most) of our slips, dreams, and psychoneurotic symptoms are caused by repressed wishes. That theory is not backed by evidence from commonsense psychology, and neither are Freudian claims about the oedipal phase, castration complex, penis envy, etc. On the contrary, such Freudian claims purport to provide explanations that rival commonsense explanations.

Those who talk about an extension of common sense often have in mind a methodological rather than either a conceptual or empirical extension. We typically use some procedure to warrant hypotheses in commonsense psychology. Using the same procedure in Freudian psychology, the problem then becomes: How do we specify the procedure and then show how it can be validly extended to Freudian psychology? As I argued in chapter 1 (pp. 13–19 and 26–40), the only two proposals in the literature, the appeal to either Nagel's principle or to thematic affinity, fail to work.

A second problem to consider, if we wish to treat Freudian theory as an extension of commonsense psychology but confirm it in a clinical setting, as Edelson proposes, is one discussed earlier: the difficult problem of disentangling suggestibility factors from other causal factors. Edelson temporarily sets that problem aside and tries to prove only the hypothetical: *if* that problem can be resolved, Freudian clinical inferences can be warranted in a clinical setting. At some point, however, one has to demonstrate the antecedent: that the suggestibility problem can be resolved (without experimentation). Drawing analogies between Freudian theory and commonsense psychology does not in any obvious way show how to resolve the problem. Nor does drawing an analogy between Freudian theory and Darwin's theory, as some writers do, including Edelson (1988, 339–340) and Robinson (1993), provide any obvious help with the suggestibility problem. What the latter analogy mainly does is to show how causal hypotheses can sometimes be confirmed without experimentation, but this is not an issue here. Earlier, I argued against Mill that such nonexperimental confirmation is sometimes possible. Indeed, there are sciences, such as geology and astronomy, where nonexperimental confirmation is quite common. If Darwin is to come to Freud's aid, something more than this needs to be shown. It needs to be shown specifically how Darwinian type arguments can be utilized in a psychoanalytic clinical setting to warrant hypotheses that are specifically Freudian. Given the arguments that I have made so far and those developed by Grünbaum (1984, 1993), the prospects for doing this are not bright.

Extraclinical Evidence

Grünbaum (1986) defines "clinical data" as data obtained from the psychoanalytic setting, including the analyst's observations of what the patient says and does. Richard Wollheim (1993, 103) replies that on this definition, the distinction between clinical and nonclinical testing is "ultimately untenable," as well as insensitive to Freud's overall project. To establish his contention, Wollheim cites an imaginary case. Suppose that the mother of the Rat Man had written down her observation that her son had not been punished for masturbation and her son read the comment to Freud during a clinical session. Freud's observation of this would count as "clinical data" on Grünbaum's definition but it would not count if, as actually happened, the mother did not write down her observation but reported it to Freud outside of a clinical setting. The difference would be inconsequential, Wollheim points out (108). Indeed, it would be, at least epistemically. However, the fact that the clinical-nonclinical distinction makes no epistemic difference in this one imaginary case hardly shows that the distinction is ultimately untenable. To say that the experimental-nonexperimental distinction is tenable, to cite a different example, does not entail that there is *no* case in which the distinction is irrelevant. One reason why the clinical-nonclinical distinction is of epistemological importance, of course, is that discussed earlier: there is a general problem about suggestibility in a clinical setting, but not, or least not the same, in a nonclinical setting.

Wollheim also makes the very different claim (107) that to define "clinical data" in the way Grünbaum does "certainly trivializes the issue." At first blush, it is not clear what the complaint is. In offering a stipulative definition of "clinical data," Grünbaum is not making a trivial claim; he is not making any claim at all. What issue, then, is trivialized by giving this definition? What Wollheim presumably means is that, on Grünbaum's definition, it is trivial to conclude that the clinical data are largely nonconfirmatory. If that is what he is claiming, that surely requires some sort of argument. Many analysts, indeed probably most, have claimed that the main evidential support for Freudian theory comes from clinical data, that is, data obtained in a psychoanalytic clinical setting.

There is no reason, however, to look only to clinical data, even if one believes that these are the main data. One can appeal to experimental data or to extraclinical nonexperimental data, especially data concerning the psychopathology of everyday life. Grünbaum does not maintain in any of his writings that either option cannot be exercised. One needs to ask, however, how good this extraclinical evidence is. I briefly comment on the nonexperimental data here; issues about the experimental data are discussed in part II.

There is one advantage in looking to nonclinical data to support Freudian theory: the suggestibility problem is diminished and perhaps in some cases is avoided altogether. There is, however, an epistemic tradeoff. Analysts have long relied on clinical data for at least two reasons: (1) it is alleged to come in a richer form than that found outside of a clinical setting, and (2) even if the analyst is not performing an experiment there is at least an opportunity for careful and systematic observation and recording of what the patient does. By switching to nonclinical data, we may lose these two advantages. Nevertheless, let us try the switch.

In an important paper, David Sachs (1989) argues that Grünbaum ignores a great deal of extraclinical (nonexperimental) evidence. He points out (in section 4 of his paper) that Freud tried to support his doctrines by appeal to diverse phenomena such as psychotic manifestations, the vagaries of sexual orientation, jokes, taboos, myths, and so on. Some of these sources of support, he claims, are impressive and some negligible. At this point, he does not identify the "impressive" sources, or give any argument that they exist. However, in subsequent sections he does give illustrations of the type he has in mind.

Sachs's first example concerns what he terms "accumulated parapraxes" (365). A woman acquaintance of his was anxious about an impending appointment with a gynecologist; the appointment concerned a question, Sachs says, that was "charged with anxiety." To some degree, the anxiety was not consciously experienced. While the person anticipated the appointment with a barely felt anxiety, she, untypically, forgot first her purse and later her car keys. She then made an engagement that conflicted with her doctor's appointment. When she remembered the latter, she tried to postpone it, or she recalled it when the time for keeping it had passed. This is only one case, but, Sachs suggests, our acquaintances may well tell us of similar ones.

The case discussed, and others like it, provide no support for Freudian theory. Given the description of the case, there is no reason to believe that a repressed motive was present. Even if there were, evidence would still be needed that the repressed motive caused the forgetting. How is the forgetting to be explained if we do not postulate a repressed motive? One plausible answer is that the woman's anxiety interfered with the ability to concentrate, and the lack of concentration caused the forgetting. Some or most of her anxiety may have been below the threshold of consciousness, but that alone would not support any distinctively Freudian thesis. Freudian and non-Freudian alike can agree, for example, that a student's nervousness can affect test performance even if the student is not aware of being nervous, or that feelings of anxiety that exist in the so-called preconscious can affect mental functioning.

Sachs's next example, or rather class of examples, concerns the Freudian interpretation of symbols. As Freud notes (in a passage quoted by Sachs), his views on the interpretation of dream symbols was based not only on his studies of dreams but also on his purview

of fairy tales, myths, jokes, folklore, and poetic and colloquial linguistic usage. After Freud developed his views on symbolism, many
investigators tried to confirm them through experimental tests. The
results have been equivocal (see pp. 165–172), but what is at issue
here is not what these experiments show, but rather, apart from the
experimental studies, what grounds we have for thinking that
Freud's theory of symbols is correct. The only grounds offered by
Sachs is a statement by Freud that he partly italicizes, "If we go into
these sources in detail, we shall find so many parallels to dream-sym-
bolism *we cannot fail to be convinced of our interpretations*" (quoted in
Sachs 1989, 364). Non-Freudians have not generally been convinced
of Freud's interpretations, but even if they had, that would not have
provided firm support. Given that the Freudian theory of symbolism
is not self-evident, agreement about its correctness hardly suffices
without independent corroboration. Perhaps Sachs's use of italics
was not intended to signal an endorsement of Freud's reason for
accepting the Freudian view; however, he gives no other reason.

Sachs's next two examples involve what he calls "tendentious"
(367) forgetting. The first example is Freud's Signorelli case and the
second is his *aliquis* case. Both of these cases, Sachs contends, have
the same phenomenological features (except for the first, which is
absent in the *aliquis* case): (1) the context in which the name was
forgotten was directly preceded by talk of thought on another topic,
which the forgetter broke off or suppressed; (2) the substitute names
were displacements of the forgotten one; (3) besides those external
associations, an internal, disagreeable content associatively linked
the later topic, especially the bearer of the forgotten name and the
vivid detail, to the early, broken-off topic; and (4) the disagreeable
content motivated forgetting the name (365–366). Sachs contends
that Grünbaum fails to notice this distinctive ensemble of phenomenological features and, consequently, fails to see that it may require explanation as a whole.

I have several questions about Sachs's contention. First, if the goal
is merely to explain the forgetting of the name Signorelli and the
Latin word *aliquis,* why insist that the above ensemble of features be
explained as a whole? As Sachs notes, Freud claims that this ensemble appears with uncommon frequency in cases where a name is

forgotten and the other names come to mind. However, as Sachs concedes, Freud offers no evidence for this claim (although Sachs suggests a way of obtaining such evidence). In the absence of such evidence, I ask once more: Why insist that this particular ensemble of features be explained *as a whole?* Why believe that what caused the forgetting is also causally relevant to the other features that Sachs isolates? Second, and of more importance, are all four of the features that Sachs mentions present in the Signorelli case? We can take Freud's word concerning the first feature in the Signorelli case, the breaking off of discussion of a previous topic, but what about the second feature? How does Freud know that the substitute names that came to mind were *displacements* of the original name in Freud's *technical* sense of being a defense product? He says the following about this displacement: "The process that should lead to the repro-duction of the missing name has been so to speak *displaced* and has therefore led to an incorrect substitute" (Freud's emphasis; *S.E.,* 6:2). Freud is making a causal claim here. How does introspection suffice for him to know that it is true? Contrary to what Sachs says, features (*3*) and (*4*) also fail to qualify as "phenomenological" fea-tures if this means that their presence can be confirmed by intro-spection or casual observation. In fact, to assume that the last feature was present, that the disagreeable content motivated the forgetting of the name, is to assume question-beggingly without argument that part of Freud's *explanation* of the forgetting is correct. In short, even if we concede feature (*1*), neither Freud nor Sachs establishes the presence of *any* of the remaining three features alleged to be present in the Signorelli case. The same comment applies to the *aliquis* case, except here matters are even worse. As Sachs notes, the first feature was absent; so, as far as we know, *none* of the four features cited by Sachs were present. In short, his whole argument for Freud's expla-nation in either case collapses. Finally, even if Freud or Sachs knew that the forgetting in the Signorelli and a*liquis* cases was motivated, how does either know that repression was involved? Sachs does not claim to know; he interprets Freud as talking about material that was suppressed rather than repressed. Sachs may be right; as he notes, Freud sometimes uses the term "suppression" in the *Psychopathology* *of Everyday Life* (1901, *S.E.*, 6: 1–279). However, when Freud tries to state his view with care, he uses the term "repression": "We shall, I think, have stated the facts of the case with sufficient caution if we affirm: *By the side of simple cases where proper names are forgotten there is a type of forgetting which is motivated by repression*170 (Freud's emphasis; 1901, *S.E.*, 6:7). Suppose, however, that we go along with Sachs and interpret Freud as requiring only that the motive for forgetting be outside of consciousness, not that it be repressed into the unconscious. In that case, however, we would be left without a distinctively Freudian claim. Non-Freudians can agree that *sometimes*—how often or even when may be unknown—a motive we are unaware of may contribute to our forgetfulness. Let us take one of Sachs's examples: I may forget to return a borrowed object because I want to keep it, and yet I may be unaware of that desire (at least until someone brings it to my attention). To take another example from Charles Darwin (cited by Sachs 1989, 368): I may be more motivated to forget a fact that disagrees with my theory than one that supports it. Darwin apparently had this motive, but it was not repressed; on the contrary, he was sometimes aware of it. In sum, Sachs's examples of tendentious forgetting provide no support for any distinctively Freudian theoretical hypothesis unless evidence is provided that a repressed wish preceded *and* caused the forgetting.

Sachs's final two examples concern slips of the tongue discussed by Grünbaum (1984). In the first case, a man is giving a lecture on human sexuality and instead of saying "organism" says "orgasm." As Grünbaum points out, this is not an instance, as far as we know, of a genuine Freudian slip. The mistake can be plausibly explained in terms of what the lecturer is conceptually preoccupied with combined with an appeal to phonetic similarity. There is no reason to think that the slip was motivated, let alone motivated by a repressed wish. The second example involves a man who sees a woman's exposed bosom and says "Excuse me, I have to get a *breast* of *flesh* air." I have already discussed this example in chapter 1 and shown that it does not require a Freudian explanation. Sachs's point in discussing these two slips was not to provide evidence for Freud's theory of slips, but to show how thematic affinity plays a crucial role in validating Freudian hypotheses. As I argued in chapter 1, he fail to show this; furthermore, thematic affinity *should* play no such role: it does not provide good evidence of causal connections.

Much of Sachs's paper is concerned with subtracting from the Freudian corpus arguments that he believes are mistakenly attributed to Freud and adding others that Grünbaum does not discuss. As I noted in connection with the tally argument, however, subtracting bad arguments does nothing by itself to improve Freud's case, although in some instances it might enhance his reputation. As to the undiscussed arguments, I do not question the reasonableness of Sachs's bringing them to our attention. However, given the vast amount of arguments that Freud employed in his long career, the additional clinical arguments used by his many followers, and the hundreds of Freudian experiments, it is always possible to confront a critic of Freudianism with arguments that he or she has not discussed. What needs to be ascertained is this: Are the newly cited arguments cogent? Those that Sachs appeals to are not. Either singly or in combination, they do virtually nothing to strengthen Freud's case.

Freudian Infrastructure

Some writers approach psychoanalysis by concentrating on what are called its "empirical components": they try to test propositions implied by Freudian theory (plus certain additional assumptions). For example, instead of trying to confirm directly Freud's view of the successive stages leading to paranoia, they try to confirm the implied correlation between paranoia and latent homosexuality. The reason for focusing on the latter is that it is "closer to the observations" and, hence, easier to confirm or disconfirm than is the existence of the underlying theoretical structure, or so it is argued.

Richard Wollheim, in his reply to Grünbaum (Wollheim 1993), argues that it is a mistake to concentrate on the so-called empirical propositions and ignore their theoretical underpinnings. For if we confirm only the empirical correlations, but not (what Wollheim calls) the Freudian "infrastructure," we confirm nothing of specifically psychoanalytic concern (105). If such correlations hold, this would confirm psychoanalytical theory, Wollheim notes (105), to no higher degree than some theory that behaviorism might have inspired, whereas, if they fail to hold, this may be explicable in terms of, say, some defense mechanism.

I agree with Wollheim's observations, provided that a few caveats are added. The finding that certain implied correlations do not hold might have a *plausible* psychoanalytic explanation (which would "cancel" the disconfirmation) but then again it might not. In the latter case, the correlation's failure to hold would have negative epistemological significance. For example, refuting the claim of an exceptionless correlation between paranoia and latent homosexuality would disprove Freud's theory of the etiology of paranoia if it entails the correlation. Second, given the differential standard argued for in chapter 3, if a behaviorist inspired theory's explanation of a certain correlation were at least as plausible as the Freudian, then the correlation would provide no evidence at all for either theory. Third, even if finding a correlation between, say, paranoia and latent homosexuality did not confirm Freud's etiological theory, the finding might still provide a useful first step in some further argument for the theory. So I think it is a bit too strong to say that in establishing the correlation, we would "have nothing of specifically psychoanalytic concern" (105). I am not sure that Wollheim would disagree with any of these three points, but even if we disagree and I am right, none of them affects his main argument. What he mainly tries to show is that bringing in Freudian infrastructure is of help in attempts at both clinical and nonclinical (nonexperimental) confirmation.

Wollheim's first example of Grünbaum's allegedly ignoring Freudian infrastructure concerns free association. Under the guise of making a methodological point about free association, Grünbaum (1984) is denying, according to Wollheim (104), one of Freud's substantive beliefs about the mind. Freud believed that free association provides valuable evidence for the causes of symptoms and dreams, according to Wollheim, because of what he also believed about how symptoms and beliefs are formed *and* the residue that this leaves in the mind. More precisely, Freud believed that it is intrinsic to the symptom and the dream that they are invariably formed, formed by the patient, along an associative pathway, which, setting off from a desire that the patient is no longer able to act upon in any straightforward fashion, terminates upon the symptom or belief. In stating Freud's belief, Wollheim is paraphrasing part of the repression theory. It is not clear at all that Grünbaum denies Freud's belief; rather, he asks for evidence that it is true. One way allegedly to get evidence is by using the method of free association. If the empirical underpinning of that method is challenged, it clearly is of no help to then turn to the repression theory to underwrite it *unless* we already have evidence for that theory.

Even if Wollheim intends some distinction between the repression theory and the belief he attributes to Freud about how dreams and symptoms are invariably formed, it does not affect my point. Appealing to Freud's belief does not help to certify the free association method unless we have some evidence that the belief is true. Furthermore, confirming this one belief would not be enough. As Wollheim notes (104), Freud has a second assumption; it, too, is crucial to his argument. He assumes that in free-associating, the patient will retread, if not the original associative path, then one sufficiently related to it, although in the opposite direction. It was Freud's "expectation," says Wollheim (104), that this would happen. Without some supporting evidence for thinking that his expectation would be fulfilled, however, appealing to it would not strengthen Freud's argument.

Concerning Freud's second assumption, Wollheim might be presupposing evidence gleaned from outside Freudian psychology concerning word associations. However, he mentions no such evidence, and I know of none that would support specifically the idea that in free-associating, the patient moves backward along the original associative path (or one close to it) that began with a repressed desire and ultimately led to a symptom or dream.

Wollheim's second example of a neglect of infra-structure concerns the explanation of the Rat Man's neurosis in terms of punishment by his father for a sexual offense, say masturbation. As Wollheim is aware, there is reason to doubt that such a punishment ever occurred, but let us ignore this point. Wollheim calls the explanation of the Rat Man's neurosis a "contextualized" explanation and claims that it is licensed by Freud's developmental theory (105). It is not clear that this part of Freudian theory would by itself license the explanation. although it might provide some indirect support. However, the real problem is that appeal to the developmental theory is not of any use unless there is evidence for it. Here and elsewhere, Wollheim appears to take for granted that one Freudian proposition can be confirmed by certain data if we assume other Freudian propositions even if they, in turn, lack empirical support. He may not be assuming this, but when he brings in propositions about Freudian infrastructure, he nowhere cites any evidence in support of the relevant theoretical propositions. Without support, we are simply adding a premise to an overall argument that then becomes at least as weak as the reason for believing the premise about the infrastructure.

Wollheim's third example was alluded to earlier. In discussing the correlation between paranoia and latent homosexuality, Wollheim says (106) that Grünbaum ignores, or at least does not grasp, the methodological import of the Freudian infrastructure that mediates the correlation. Wollheim is referring here to Freud's theory of how paranoia develops in certain stages, starting from unconscious acceptance of the proposition "I love him," which is transformed into "I hate him," which later becomes "He hates me." Again, however, the same problem arises as before. Appealing to the theory of stages is of no help in warranting the confirmation unless there is reason to accept the theory. Here, I may misunderstand Wollheim's point, which may be merely that the concern should be to confirm Freud's theory of how paranoia develops and not merely the correlation between latent homosexuality and paranoia. If that is his only point in discussing this example, then I agree with him, but then the example is not even intended to show how bringing in the Freudian infrastructure would aid attempts at clinical confirmation.

Another example concerns the use of Freudian categories in describing what the analyst observes. To confirm Freudian theory on the basis of what the patient says or does, the clinical material must be subsumed, Wollheim claims, under Freudian categories (108). The patient has to be identified as, say, presenting *anal material* on a massive scale; resorting to *phantasies of omnipotence; fragmenting, assaulting* or *idealizing,* etc. I agree that if such categorizations were warranted, this might help, but this is just another case of establishing Freudian theoretical propositions. If all the analyst observes is the patient saying or doing something, how does he or she know that the patient is presenting genuine anal material or phantasies of omnipotence as opposed to what Freudian theory, mistakenly or not, *calls* "anal material" or "phantasies of omnipotence?" Once more, appealing to other parts of Freudian theory is not going to strengthen the argument for the hypothesis being tested unless these parts in turn are empirically supported. Wollheim also adds that we should consider the material brought up in the transference or what motivated the production of that material. However, the same problem arises. If the analyst restricts himself to what he observes—the patient said such and such or did this or that—it has to be shown how this will help confirm Freudian theory. If, however, the analyst appeals to Freudian theory to infer what the transference material means or what its unconscious cause is, then support is needed for that section of Freudian theory.

Wollheim adds three additional points. First, to clinically confirm psychoanalytic propositions, we must assume other psychoanalytic propositions about, for example, symptom formation, the mechanisms of defense, the stages of libidinal organization, etc. However, Wollheim does not claim that we now have evidence for these other Freudian assumptions; rather, we have a hope that we someday will obtain such evidence. He writes: "In the first place, if psychoanalytic hypotheses are to be clinically tested, then we must assume, for the duration of the test, certain more general psychological principles for which *the hope must be that eventually tests will be devised,* presumably of an extra-clinical kind, that will establish them." (italics added, 109). If what Wollheim says here is accurate, then *presently* there are no cogent clinical arguments for Freudian theory; all such arguments must assume psychological principles that have not yet been tested.

This concession on Wollheim's part creates a puzzle. Let us assume that he is right: clinical confirmation of particular psychoanalytic hypotheses requires that we assume the truth of other parts of Freudian theory, but these in turn have *no empirical support* (indeed, there is only a hope that the means for testing them will eventually be devised). If Wollheim is right, we have an alternative argument for Grünbaum's (1984) conclusion that the support provided by the clinical evidence is, at best, remarkably weak.

Why would Wollheim provide such an argument and yet persist in his efforts to answer Grünbaum's criticisms of the Freudian clinical evidence? The answer may be that he is not trying to refute such criticisms. He may see no need to do so, perhaps because he believes that Grünbaum's (1984) book is only about the issue of testability. Thus, he claims (102) that Grünbaum concentrates entirely on the testability (i.e., the clinical testability) of Freudian theory. This is mistaken. Grünbaum's *Foundations* is partly about testability issues, but quite a large portion of it is about the weaknesses of the current clinical evidence.

Wollheim also suggests (103) that the tally argument is discussed in *Foundations* to rebut Karl Popper's charge that Freudian theory is untestable and that Freud himself was indifferent to this. This, too, is mistaken (although it should be noted that Wollheim is hesitant about his interpretation). The point of discussing the tally argument is not to answer Popper, but to deal with Freud's attempt to dispose of the suggestibility problem.

Wollheim's second point (109) is that confirmation of the correlations that assume the Freudian psychological principles (which are to be tested later extraclinically) will confirm the principles to some degree—though no more than any other set of credible principles. I have already commented on this claim: if the rival principles are at least as credible, there would *no* confirmation of the Freudian principles.

Wollheim's third point (109) is that something established in a clinical setting may later be relied on in an extraclinical study. I agree, but the point is trivial. To take Wollheim's example, if there is evidence that what the patient says about his life history actually happened, then we are free to appeal to this report in an experiment. (I am not complaining about Wollheim reminding us of this obvious point; rather, I am merely commenting that it does not, and probably was not intended to, show how appeal to Freudian infrastructure aids in clinical confirmation.)

Wollheim also raises the following question (111): If psychoanalytic theory is an extension of commonsense psychology, how is the latter tested? However, he does not try to answer the question. My answer is that the antecedent of Wollheim's question is false. As I argued in chapter 1 (pp. 13–19), in discussing Nagel's views, and earlier in this chapter (pp. 106–124), in any way that matters epistemologically, Freudian theory is *not* an extension of common sense.

Wollheim also raises two other major points: one concerns the distinction between clinical and extraclinical testing (107–108); the other is about suggestibility issues (110–111). I have answered both points above.

I close with two comments. First, Wollheim fails to show how paying attention to Freudian infrastructure will help at all in attempts at clinical confirmation. Second, all of his arguments taken singly or together fail to provide any cogent reason to doubt the soundness of Grünbaum's critique of the Freudian clinical evidence.

Single Subject Designs

So far, I have been discussing clinical evidence obtained from *nonexperimental* Freudian case studies. But why restrict the discussion in this way? Behavior therapists have developed, and used in a clinical setting, a variety of single subject experimental and quasi-experimental designs. Both types involve the manipulation of an independent variable, but in using a quasi-experimental design, the investigator is unable to control something needing control, such as the assignment of subjects. One of the simplest of the single-subject designs is the *ABAB* design, alternatively referred to as the *ABA* design, when the last phase is omitted (Barlow and Hersen 1984). In the initial *A* phase, there is an absence of treatment and a measurement of "baseline" behavior; in the *B* phase (or experimental) phase, treatment is administered; in the second *A* phase, treatment is withheld; and then given again in the next *B* phase. If the behavior reverts to or approaches baseline when the treatment is withheld, evidence is provided that what occurred in the treatment phase was responsible for the initial behavioral changes. As Kazdin (1980, 176) points out, the evidence can be very persuasive when the target behavior can, in effect, be turned on and off as a function of the intervention. There is a problem, however, if the investigator wants to demonstrate that a specific element in the treatment phase made the difference. That may not be possible where an *ABAB* design is used and a placebo hypothesis is plausible. If the placebo factors accompany the intervention, they may, for all we know, be responsible for turning the target behavior on and off. There are, however, many variants of the basic *ABAB* design and some can be used to rule out certain placebo explanations (see Barlow and Hersen 1984, 330).

Can variants of the *ABAB* design or other single-subject designs be used to test Freudian hypotheses in a clinical setting? Marshall Edelson (1984) argues that they can. Some of his points concern only what is logically possible or bear only on issues about falsification. I agree with these points, but they are not relevant to the present discussion. I also agree that *if* Freudian researchers continue to confine most of their research efforts to a clinical setting, they would do well to heed Edelson's advice and at least explore the possible use of single subject designs. In stimulating discussion of the possible application of single subject designs to Freudian clinical settings, Edelson has performed a valuable service. Having said this, I now want to express some significant reservations.

At the moment, I am discussing Freudian theory; outcome hypotheses are discussed in chapter 6. One question that should be asked now is this: How successful have behavior therapists been in using single subject designs to confirm *theoretical* hypotheses? I will not say that there have been no such successes, but almost all of the cases cited by Barlow and Hersen (1984) and Kazdin (1980) involve the testing of outcome hypotheses. Such cases almost always involve observable interventions, and observable and measurable behavioral changes. It is far from evident that single subject designs can also be used to confirm theoretical hypotheses that postulate unobservables, such as repressed wishes, or that talk about childhood events that cannot now be observed or manipulated. Talking in general terms, then, about the power of single subject designs to test causal hypotheses is not enough; they may be applicable to certain types of causal hypotheses but not to others. We would need to

discuss the details of their application to specific hypotheses. Grünbaum (1993) has done this to some extent, and his results cast
serious doubts about the feasibility of Edelson's proposals. However,
there are so many different types of Freudian theoretical hypotheses
and so many variants of single subject designs, that the subject warrants more discussion. It is possible that some such designs, perhaps
some not yet developed, will some day prove useful for confirming
some Freudian hypotheses. My point is that we should not infer that
this is likely from the fact that behavior therapists have been successful in using such designs for testing outcome hypotheses of a relatively narrow type.

A second question is more pertinent to the issue of interest here:
the state of existing evidence. How many applications have been
made so far of single-subject designs in Freudian settings? Edelson
cites only three, although, to be fair, his purpose is not to establish
Freudian tenets but to provide counterexamples to someone who
says that such applications are logically impossible. His first example,
Josef Breuer's treatment of Anna O, does not concern Freudian
theory. The second case, Freud's Rat Man case, involves a disconfirmation. As far as I can see, Edelson does not claim that the case
provides convincing evidence for any part of Freudian theory (see,
as well, the discussions by Glymour 1974, and Grünbaum 1984). The
third case is that of Miss X (Luborsky and Mintz, 1974). There are
problems with Edelson's derivation of a test hypothesis in this case
(Grünbaum 1988) and with his interpretation of the results (Erwin
1986b). In the end, however, Edelson (1984, 146–147) concedes that
no causal hypothesis was confirmed, and is content to say merely that
a Freudian hypothesis ran the risk of being falsified. That leaves
Edelson with *no* examples of actual confirmations of Freudian theory by use of single subject designs.

Since the publication of Edelson's book, there have been some
other attempts to apply single subject designs in Freudian clinical
settings, for example, Weiss, Sampson, and the Mount Zion Psychotherapy Research Group (1986). Some of this work is examined in
chapter 5, pp. 224–235. There is, however, very little to examine.
The vast majority of experimental studies are extraclinical studies.
Whether or not single subject designs will eventually prove fruitful

in confirming Freudian theoretical hypotheses in a clinical situation, that possibility has not yet been realized in any systematic way.

Conclusion

Grünbaum's (1984) powerful critique of the Freudian clinical evidence has received many challenges, but, if I have argued correctly (and see, as well, Grünbaum 1986, 1993; Erwin 1993), the challenges have been unsuccessful. The critique stands. Before saying what follows from this, I should say something about what does not follow. First, both Grünbaum and I have been talking primarily about clinical *validation*. Although there are also difficulties in attempting disconfirmation, they are not as great. Clearly, it is generally easier to disconfirm "All S is P" than to confirm it. (I assume, given the standards argued for in chapter 2, that finding one S that is a P, or even many such P's, is no guarantee of confirmation.) I, at least, do not deny that clinical disconfirmation of some of Freud's ideas is possible.

Second, there are many hypotheses that an analyst might consider in a clinical setting that are quite obviously nonpsychoanalytic (e.g., "The patient is jealous of his older brother's success") or resemble psychoanalytic views but are not distinctively psychoanalytic ("The patient is unaware of why he wants to succeed"). I have not argued that these non-Freudian hypotheses are unconfirmable in a clinical setting, and neither has Grünbaum.

Third, there may even be some distinctively Freudian hypotheses that are confirmable in a clinical setting. Grünbaum, Edelson, I, and others have been discussing primarily Freud's repression theory, basically the view that dreams, parapraxes and psychoneurotic symptoms are caused by repressed wishes. However, I should add that most of the epistemological problems discussed in this chapter also arise in trying to get evidence for the existence of the mental apparatus postulated by Freud, the existence of an oedipal phase, and many other Freudian views. If someone wants to argue that the epistemological problems are real enough, but that such and such a Freudian theoretical hypothesis is significantly different from the repression theory, the burden of proof lies on him or her to state the hypothesis and show how clinical evidence or some other type of nonexperimental evidence confirms it.

Fourth, as should have been clear from the context, I have been discussing what either has been done in the way of clinical confirmation or what is practically feasible. I have no doubt that a clever philosopher can describe a logically possible situation in which clinical confirmation occurs. Finally, as Grünbaum now agrees, despite all of the arguments, one cannot rule out altogether the possibility that some ingenious strategy will be developed some day to make clinical confirmation feasible. Freudian experimenters have been quite clever in developing experimental tests; perhaps those who advocate clinical testing may prevail in the end. But that remains only a possibility. What the arguments presented by Grünbaum, myself, and others show is that there is a *strong presumption* that Freud's repression theory is not confirmable without experimentation. The presumption is strong enough to infer, unless there is a countershowing, that the existing Freudian nonexperimental evidence is generally nonconfirmatory, at least for the repression theory and very likely for most other parts of Freud's overall theory (but I will note some possible exceptions in the chapter 7, pp. 283–285).

Although the following is not intended to sum up this entire chapter, it might be useful to say again what some of the general epistemological problems are if we do not have experimental evidence. First, if we are looking to confirmation "on the couch," there is the very serious problem of contamination by suggestibility factors. That problem may be chipped away at, but as of now it remains a large obstacle to clinical confirmation. Second, even apart from suggestibility factors, there remains the difficulty of ruling out plausible explanations posed by rival theories. Some of these theories are psychoanalytic but non-Freudian (although it should be stressed that analysts who look to one of these newer theories have to explain how *they* can be confirmed without experimentation; for some of the problems and the state of the evidence for these theories, see Eagle 1984; 1994). Edelson (1988) holds that only theories in rival psychoanalytic paradigms need to be ruled out, but the differential standard argued for in chapter 2 (pp. 44–54) implies the opposite. *Any* plausible alternative to a Freudian hypothesis needs to be disconfirmed even if it comes from cognitivist, behaviorist, or common sense psychology. Some behaviorist theories may immediately be ruled out if they bar all appeals to cognitive factors, even the subject's awareness, but some behaviorist-inspired conditioning theories do not do that. When all of these theories are allowed to compete, ruling out alternative plausible explanations is often not possible unless experiments are done.

Third, even in the absence of plausible rivals, the causal principle argued for in the previous chapter needs to be satisfied by Freudian hypotheses that make a general causal claim. Except where there is reason to believe that there are countervailing factors, to establish that X is generally causally relevant to the occurrence of Y, we need to establish for some reference class C that the frequency of Y's is greater in the sub-set of C's in which X occurs than in the subset where X does not occur. Thus, suppose that an analyst somehow establishes that his neurotic patients generally have one or more repressed wishes. He or she would still be in no position to infer a causal connection between repressed wishes and neurosis unless there were evidence that for the suitable reference class, say the class of all adults, the incidence of neurosis is greater for people with repressed wishes than for people without them.

Meeting the above standard, moreover, is necessary but not sufficient. Mill's problem remains. Suppose we find repeated instances of A being followed by B and non-A's being followed by non-B's. Unless we can manipulate A and thereby produce B—that is, do an experiment—it is often difficult to know whether the correlations held because A caused B in each instance or whether some third factor caused both A and B, which are not causally connected. Mill exaggerates the difficulty; sometimes our background theories and evidence make experimentation unnecessary. Nevertheless, there is a general epistemological problem here, and it is far greater when we are trying to confirm very general causal principles. No doubt, we can know without experimentation, for example, that Smith's feeling guilty about the way he treated his wife explains why he bought her flowers. It is quite a bit more difficult, if there is no random assignment to comparison groups and no manipulation of the putative cause, to get evidence that in all or most cases, when such and such behavior occurs, guilt is the cause. In trying to confirm Freudian theory, however, we are trying to warrant not merely hypotheses about singular causation but rather general, even if not exceptionless, causal principles. What often happens in practice is that supporters of the theory will say: Freudian theory provides the only available explanation of such and such data, so the theory has evidential support. As argued in chapter 2 (pp. 62–73), however, this type of argument is not good enough.

Part II

Chapter 4
The Pre-1980 Experimental Evidence

At this point, I am now presupposing the evidential standards argued for in chapter 2. Several other assumptions should be made explicit. The first two concern the demarcation of the subject matter.

First, I am interested primarily in Freud's theoretical and causal hypotheses. There are well known problems in drawing any general, philosophically interesting distinction between theoretical and observational hypotheses (Achinstein 1965; Maxwell 1962), but I am not presupposing that any ontological or epistemological significance attaches to the distinction or that it can be clearly drawn in all cases. In some cases, hypotheses will be hard to classify; it will be wise, then, to inquire about their empirical support and not be too strict about whether they fall within the guidelines of the discussion. A second point concerns *Freudian* theory. I will not be discussing what Crews (1986) calls a "watered-down" version of the theory, but instead will discuss only what Kline (1981) terms "distinctively Freudian" hypotheses. (Unless otherwise indicated, all references to Kline's look will be to the 1981 edition.) Consider, for example, common sense talk about defense mechanisms. It is obvious even to non-Freudians that people sometimes rationalize their behavior or blame others for faults that they themselves possess; so "rationalization" and "projection," in some sense, do occur, even if there are no unconscious conflicts and no Freudian psychic apparatus. To assert that such things occur, however, is not to endorse any hypothesis that is distinctively Freudian, or that is in any way controversial. I am primarily interested, then, in hypotheses that are peculiar to Freudian theory or to it and some neo-Freudian version of it.

Although some distinction of the sort mentioned is needed here, drawing a clear line between distinctively Freudian hypotheses and counterfeits will be problematic in certain cases. Again, wisdom dictates flexibility. We can ask about the evidence for the hypothesis and simply note that it is unclear whether or not it is "distinctively Freudian".

Finally, some simplifying assumptions need to be made because of the sheer number of experimental studies available for consideration. There are more than 1500 such studies, most of which were published before 1980. My strategy will be to focus on the best designed studies that appear to support some aspect of Freudian theory. Following Kline (1981, 44), I will consider only published studies. His grounds for omitting from discussion unpublished doctoral dissertations is that almost all of the worthwhile research that they report appears later in published papers. I will also not consider studies that have been rejected on sound methodological grounds by those sympathetic to Freudian theory, such as Kline (1981) and Fisher and Greenberg (1977, 1985). Because of the very valuable work of these reviewers, my task is made much easier. They have already weeded out many studies that are nonsupportive; there is no need to repeat their arguments here. Despite their criticisms of many studies, however, both Kline and Fisher and Greenberg argue that core parts of Freudian theory are supported by some of the experimental studies. Kline (1981, 447) concludes that although the theory should not be retained as a whole, much of it has been confirmed. Fisher and Greenberg argue for a similar conclusion. In this chapter, I will consider studies published prior to the appearance of the works by Kline (1981) and Fisher and Greenberg (1985). In most cases, these are pre-1980 studies; post-1980 research is discussed in chapter 5.

The Kline Reviews

As noted earlier, Paul Kline has reviewed most of the Freudian experimental studies published before 1980. He sums up his findings as follows: "The status of psychoanalytic theory must now be clear. It must be retained not as a whole but only after rigorous objective research has revealed what parts are correct or false or in need of modification. But, as has been shown in the book, much of it has been confirmed (Kline 1981, 441).

In his summary (432–433), Kline lists 16 "verified concepts," including "Oral character," "Repression and other defenses," and "Sexual symbolism outside dreams." Each of these 16 "concepts," or headings, picks out one or more Freudian hypotheses said to be confirmed by the experimental evidence. Some of Kline's interpretations of the evidence have been challenged (Eysenck and Wilson 1973; Eysenck 1985; Erwin 1980, 1986a) and Kline, in turn, has replied to these challenges (Kline 1978, 1981, 1986). Before turning to the relevant issues, it might be useful to locate areas of agreement.

Kline and I agree, in opposition to Popper, that most of the central parts of Freudian theory are testable in principle. Concerning testability, we disagree only about certain of Freud's metapsychological hypotheses. Kline holds that some are untestable, whereas I doubt that this has been demonstrated (Erwin 1988b). Kline and I agree, further, that it would be unreasonable to dismiss Freudian theory *a priori* on the grounds that it is pseudoscientific. (One might stipulate that a theory is "pseudo-scientific" if it is not supported by empirical evidence, but then the judgment that a theory is pseudoscientific ordinarily cannot be made *a priori*.) We also agree (Kline 1988, 255) about the weakness of the Freudian (nonexperimental) clinical evidence. Finally, I find little to disagree with concerning Kline's illuminating discussion of most of the hundreds of experimental studies that he reviews. Our disagreement concerns mainly the evidential value of a relatively small number of studies. I would concede, moreover, that in some cases the evidence is very difficult to interpret and reasonable people may well disagree about its scientific worth.

Part of the disagreement between Kline and me turns on issues about the plausibility of non-Freudian rival explanations, the validity of certain dependent measures, and the meaning of certain Freudian claims. In some cases, however, Kline and I may also disagree about the evidence because of certain philosophical differences. For example, although he is interested in the truth or falsity of Freud's theoretical claims, he may not accept the scientific realism that I argue for in Erwin, 1992 and am now presupposing. He writes: "In any case, modern philosophies of science regard scientific theories not as pertaining to some truth in the real world but simply as describing phenomena more or less elegantly and accurately. Thus, there is no difficulty in having more than one theory, although a unification is preferable on grounds of elegance" (Kline 1986, 224). In contrast, I interpret Freudian theory so that it *does* pertain to some truth in the real world and not simply as "describing phenomena." Although I am not certain of this, Kline's position sounds very much like the constructive empiricism of van Fraassen (1980), which I discussed in Erwin, 1992. On that view, it could be argued that it may be reasonable to accept two conflicting theories in the same domain if both are empirically adequate, that is, if what they say about *observable* things and events is true. A scientific realist, however, will typically not be content with this state of affairs, but rather will seek additional evidence to choose between the two theories. Kline and I may also disagree about certain epistemological issues, such as the role of simplicity in theory confirmation. As I proceed, I will mention such disagreements where they seem to affect our evaluation of the experimental evidence.

In the following discussion, I am guided by Kline's useful format. In his summary (1981, 432–433) of verified concepts, he lists for each one what he calls "exemplar investigations." These are generally what he takes to provide the strongest support for Freudian theory. I focus on these "better" studies, but I do not limit the analysis to them.

Oral Character

Under this heading, Kline (1981, 432) cites two studies: Goldman-Eisler (1950) and Kline and Storey (1977). The first study tested the Freudian view of the origin of the oral personality. The theory holds that oral character traits originate from repressed or deflected oral impulses that are dominant during the nursing period and that have undergone transformation into certain behavior patterns by the process of reaction formation, displacement, or sublimation (Goldman-Eisler 1948). In her 1951 paper, which also includes the results of her 1950 paper, Goldman-Eisler distinguishes between what she calls "factor I" and "factor II." The first refers to a cluster of traits assumed to correspond to the syndrome of oral pessimism and the second refers to oral optimism. The main positive finding was a correlation between Factor I (oral pessimism) and early breast-weaning. It should be noted that even if a causal connection were established between these two items, this would not necessarily support the Freudian explanation of the connection (in terms of repressed or deflected oral impulses that are transformed by reaction formation, displacement, or sublimation). However, the establishment of a causal connection between early weaning and oral pessimism would itself be of interest. Was it established? Three things had to be done: (1) the presence of the putative effect had to be demonstrated; (2) the presence of the putative cause had to be shown; and (3) a causal connection rather than a mere correlation between the two factors would then have to be demonstrated.

There are reasonable doubts that any one of these three things was done. Concerning the alleged effect, the only evidence for the validity of the rating scales used to measure both oral pessimism and oral optimism was face validity. As Kline notes (1981, 15), face validity is not considered to be satisfactory for personality tests. As to the alleged cause, how did Goldman-Eisler identify the subjects who were weaned early? She relied on reports of their mothers concerning events that had occurred at least 15 years earlier and were thus subject to distortions of memory. I think that Kline and I agree here. He refers (1981, 70) to the "dubious nature" of both the breast-feeding data and the validity of the scales. Finally, even if a correlation had been established, how does that prove a causal connection? Kline (1981, 70) comments that in studies where the data are not ideal, unless it can be shown that the measures are not only in error but are actually measuring some other factor, any correlation is support for the theory. This is very dubious. If the theory postulates a causal connection between *A* and *B*, finding a correlation between the two need not be evidence for the theory. Suppose that a correlation is found between drinking Coca-Cola and a decrease in mortality from heart attacks. We might have available a much more plausible explanation of the correlation than that which credits the Coca-Cola drinking for the fewer heart attacks. Even in the absence of such a theory, our background evidence might make the Coca-Cola theory too implausible to be acceptable without additional evidence. As argued in chapter 2 (pp. 44–54 and pp. 62–73), if a superior or equal rival is not eliminated, or the tested theory is too implausible even in the absence of known rivals, then confirmation is not forthcoming. Someone who accepts these general considerations concerning confirmation might still question their applicability to the Goldman-Eisler study. If a correlation had been established between early weaning and oral pessimism, would the differential condition have remained unmet? The answer is yes if, as Eysenck and Wilson argue (1973, 62–63), a genetic explanation is just as plausible as the Freudian explanation.

Because of the dubious nature of the breast feeding data *and* the validity of the scales, *and* a lack of any argument for a causal connection, the Goldman-Eisler study does not provide any firm evidence for any part of Freudian theory. If Kline and I disagree here, our disagreement is slight. He takes the study to provide some support for the Freudian position, but adds that it cannot be considered as proof or very strong evidence (1981, 71). The Goldman-Eisler study also had some negative findings, but I agree with Kline that these do not constitute disproof of the Freudian position.

In the Kline and Storey (1977) paper, the authors list four propositions about orality. The first asserts merely the existence of the syndrome (or that there are two syndromes, the oral pessimistic and optimistic personalities). The rest concern either etiology or the mouth as an erotogenic zone in early childhood. As the authors note (317), their investigation concerned only the first proposition. No evidence was provided concerning the meaning or etiology of the oral personality, but evidence was provided for the existence of the syndrome.

Besides the two exemplar discussions just mentioned, Kline discusses other studies that bear on either the existence or etiology of the oral syndrome. The interpretation of the evidence from these studies is discussed in the section on oral erotism (below).

Anal Character

Under this heading, Kline refers to two exemplar items, a paper and a book. Both were written by him (Kline, 1969, 1979). Because he claims to establish only the existence and not the etiology of the anal character, I also postpone discussion of the anal character until the conclusion of the next section.

Oral Erotism

No links between personality and child-training procedures
[note added by Kline 1981, 432].

Under this heading, Kline lists two exemplar studies. The first, done by Kline and Storey (1980), studied hypotheses derived from Freud's theory of the etiology of the anal character. One hypothesis, for example, asserted that dentists are more oral sadistic than medical controls; another that oral optimists like milky, warm foods, whereas oral pessimists like hard, crispy, bitter foods. Kline concludes (1981, 126) that the study fails to confirm the psychosexual etiology of oral traits, although the confirmation of three of the eight hypotheses does "perhaps confirm a limited aspect of the theory." I see no argument that the study specifically supports the existence of oral erotism, but Kline and Storey's main argument (109) for the phenomenon is based on other exemplar study (Levy 1928) in combination with another study carried out by Yarrow (1954).

Levy (1928) studied the etiology of thumb-sucking. He noted (109) that of 94 children who did not suck their thumbs, 99% had "satisfactory, spontaneous withdrawals" from their mothers' breasts. Only one did not. In contrast, 20 of 28 finger-suckers fell into an "unsatisfactory" feeding category. The category includes withdrawal from feeding done to excess or lack of milk, forced withdrawal from the breast due to time-regulated feeding, and feeding without sucking.

In evaluating the Levy study, it should be noted, first, that it was a retrospective rather than an experimental study. Levy had to rely on the recollections of parents about their infants' feeding experiences; as both Kline and he note, such data are not trustworthy. Furthermore (although this is not decisive), he did not claim to be testing any Freudian hypothesis. Levy noted (915) that there are various theories about the etiology of thumb-sucking, including Freud's, but he does not argue in favor of any one of them. Nor is it obvious that his findings, even if taken at face value, support Freud's claim of oral erotism. Suppose that we set aside concerns about the validity of the parents' recollections. What do Levy's data suggest? That feeding difficulties of various kinds during infancy can make a difference as to whether a child subsequently sucks his or her thumb? Of the 28 thumb-sucking cases, the breakdown was as follows. In eight cases, feeding difficulties did not contribute to the thumb-sucking for there were no such reported difficulties. In six cases, there was spontaneous withdrawal from the breast due to excessive flow of milk; in five cases, there was spontaneous withdrawal from the breast or bottle for various reasons; in seven cases, the child was pulled away from the breast or bottle at termination of an assigned period of time; and in two cases, during an early period, the children were fed with a dropper. In some of these 20 cases of "feeding difficulty," the child was apparently still hungry after the feeding was completed, but no data were provided as to how many experienced inadequate sucking. I see no ground, then, for the following claim by Kline (even assuming that the dubious nature of the data is ignored): "Nevertheless, the main conclusion still holds—finger- or dummy-sucking seems to be a compensation for insufficient sucking during infancy" (Kline 1981, 104). Finally, even if the conclusion were demonstrated, that would still not show oral erotism. To demonstrate the latter, it needs to be argued not merely that infants find sucking pleasurable but that the mouth is a source of *sexual* pleasure.

Apart from the points already made, it should not be overlooked that Levy studied a relatively small number of cases; it is important, therefore, to check the findings of subsequent researchers. As Kline points out, some of these studies are in agreement with Levy, but others are not (e.g., Sears and Wise 1950). At best, the overall evidence appears inconsistent. Kline takes a later study (Yarrow 1954) to offer a plausible explanation of these apparently contradictory findings, one that closely fits Freudian theory. However, Eysenck and Wilson (1973, 32–35) provide several alternative non-Freudian explanations of Yarrow's findings that are just as plausible as Yarrow's. First, the main positive finding—that thumb-sucking is related both to brief feeding and late weaning—can be explained in terms of the conditioning principle that intermittent reinforcement results in greater resistance to extinction. Second, all of Yarrow's data came from retrospective reports by the mothers of the children who were studied. Not only are there general grounds for not trusting such reports but there is a specific reason for being skeptical in this case. The mothers of those children who did not suck their thumbs were aware that their children did not have this problem. They were more likely, then, than the mothers of thumb-suckers to take credit for their children's lack of a problem by reporting that a great deal of time was spent patiently feeding the infant and that the infant was weaned early. One does not have to postulate conscious deceit here; it is enough that the desire to impress the doctor may well have influenced what they *seemed* to remember. As Eysenck and Wilson also point out, Yarrow was not able to manipulate the methods of child rearing of his subjects and was thus not able to rule out genetic explanations of his findings.

Levy (1934) also did an *experimental* study of sucking that appears to support the results of his earlier findings. However, his subjects were puppies; whether the experimental results are applicable to human infants is unclear.

In sum, I take the studies of oral erotism to be inconclusive. Some of the studies (both for and against) are retrospective rather than experimental; the results are mixed; and even the positive results of Levy (1928) bear on the etiology of thumb-sucking but not, at least not directly, on the existence of oral erotism.

Conclusion

I have not discussed all of the studies that Kline evaluates, but the inclusion of other studies would have no effect on the following points. First, for reasons mentioned earlier, the overall evidence does not lend strong support to Freud's postulation of oral erotism.

Second, Kline and I agree that the total evidence neither confirms nor disconfirms Freud's theory about the origin of either the anal or oral syndrome. Third, Kline concludes (1981, 128) that there is good evidence to support the existence of the anal syndrome, some evidence (but not as strong) in support of the existence of the oral syndrome, and no evidence in support of any other hypothesized psychosexual dimensions. Kline bases his conclusions about the existence of the oral and anal syndromes on a number of studies, including the well known Beloff (1957) paper and works by a colleague and himself (Kline and Storey 1977; Kline 1969, 1979). I do not discuss these studies because I agree with Kline's conclusion; where we may disagree concerns its implications for Freudian theory.

In "Character and Anal Erotism" (1908. *S.E.* 9:167–175), Freud notes that certain people are remarkable in having a regular combination of three peculiarities: they are exceptionally orderly, parsimonious, and obstinate. He also notes that the last two qualities hang together more closely than the third, but holds that in some way all three go together. He concludes with a theoretical explanation of the origin of the cluster: the permanent character traits are either unchanged perpetuation of the original impulses (connected with anal erotism), or are sublimations of them, or are reaction formations against them. If one suspends judgment about this explanation and affirms merely the existence of the cluster of traits, then one is not affirming any part of Freudian theory. In fact, the assertion that the cluster exists amounts to no more than the relatively trivial claim that some people are orderly, parsimonious, and obstinate. Why use the term "oral" at all to refer to this cluster of traits except for the fact that Freud used the term in this way? Freud did so, however, because he hypothesized a causal connection between the appearance of the cluster and anal erotism. Eliminate the connection and you eliminate the rationale for using Freud's terminology. If Kline and I disagree here it is because Kline (1981, 128) breaks Freudian psychosexual theory into three components, one of which is the assertion of the existence of certain constellations of personality traits, such as the anal and oral syndromes. If one accepts this breakdown, then one is forced to conclude that the confirmation of the existence of the syndrome is confirmation of part of Freudian theory. I do not, however, accept the breakdown.

Consider an analogy. Freud's theory of dreams implies the existence of dreams, but confirmation of that fact would not confirm part of his dream theory for two reasons. First, that dreams occur is not a theoretical hypothesis; and second, it is not distinctively Freudian. Similar remarks apply to the existence of the anal and oral syndromes. First, Freudian psychosexual theory is supposed to explain the etiology of the syndromes; to assert that some people have some of the character traits that make up the syndromes is not to assert any theoretical proposition. Second, even if one classified the proposition as "theoretical," it is not distinctively Freudian.

Some of the work that Kline cites does support something more interesting than the claim that at least one person is parsimonious, orderly, and obstinate; it also provides evidence that in certain normal and abnormal populations, the traits tend to cluster together. However, even this more interesting claim, as Eysenck and Wilson (1973, 96) point out, is not distinctively Freudian. I would also add that it is not theoretical. In sum, I agree with Kline about his first two categories (the anal and oral character) but not the third (oral erotism). I am also not persuaded that confirmation of the existence of the oral and anal character is sufficient to confirm any part of Freudian theory.

The Oedipus and Castration Complexes

Kline discusses the Oedipus complex and the castration complex together. I shall do the same. In support of the Oedipus and castration complexes, Kline lists one exemplar study for each complex (Friedman 1952 and Stephens 1961, respectively). He also argues that "good evidence" is provided for the Oedipus complex by Hall (1963) and for the castration complex by Friedman 1950; Schwartz 1956; Sarnoff and Corwin 1959; and Hall and Van De Castle 1963 (Kline 1981, 158)

Hall's (1963) paper purports to confirm the existence of the Oedipus complex by comparing male and female dreams of strangers. Five hypotheses were said to be derived from Freud's oedipal theory. Hall concludes (1963, 122) that four were confirmed. Examples are (1) that in all dreams there would be more males than female strangers; and (2) that there would be more male strangers in male than in female dreams. These and the remaining three hypotheses do not follow directly from Freud's oedipal theory, but they can, of course, be derived from it when conjoined with suitable auxiliary assumptions. The issue I want to raise is this: Is confirmation of these hypotheses sufficient to confirm the theory from which they were derived? Or is it also necessary to consider rival hypotheses? Hall (121) says that it is unnecessary to consider rivals provided that the theory maintains (a) its heuristic value, (b) its capacity of making sense of a wide variety of phenomena, and (c) its ability to generate correct predictions. I argued in chapter 2 (pp. 44–54), however, that plausible rival hypotheses must be discounted if confirmation is to occur. Because plausible rivals may be available even when Hall's three conditions are met, his conditions are not sufficient for confirmation. It might be said, in reply, that this general point about confirmation does not matter in this case because plausible rival explanations cannot be found. That, however, is not true. Eysenck and Wilson (1973, 123–124) have little trouble finding such explanations. For example, why should there be more male strangers in male dreams? An obvious reason is that at the time of Hall's study (1963), many more men than women worked and, consequently, men were much more likely to meet male strangers. Why should there be more aggressive encounters in dreams with male strangers? A likely answer is that male strangers tend to be more aggressive. Hall's failure to rule out such plausible rivals to his oedipal hypothesis means that his data fail to provide strong confirmation, if any confirmation at all (see Eysenck and Wilson 1973, 167).

Kline also cites Stephens' (1961) findings as evidence for the existence of a castration complex. Stephens used the anthropological data of Whiting and Child (1953) to determine the presence in 72 primitive societies of assumed antecedents of castration anxiety. The antecedents include such items as overall severity of sex training and severity of punishment for disobedience. No attempt was made, however, to establish empirically that such items really are antecedents of castration anxiety. Without such evidence, the results do not confirm the existence of a castration complex.

The remaining three studies (Friedman 1950; Sarnoff and Corwin 1959; Schwartz 1956) all rely on the validity of projective tests to support their conclusions. For example, Friedman used "castration fables" to measure castration anxiety. In these fables, a child finds his toy elephant broken, and the subject is asked to say what is wrong with it. If a subject mentions, say, the loss of a tail, then this is assumed to be a sign of high castration anxiety. No attempt is made, however, to establish this assumption; no evidence is offered that castration fables measure castration anxiety at all. Without such evidence, the results of the study cannot be interpreted as confirming the hypothesis being tested. A similar comment applies to Schwartz's (1956) use of Thematic Apperception Test (*TAT*)–like pictures to confirm hypotheses about castration anxiety (see Eysenck and Wilson, 1973, 136–139).

The remaining study, by Sarnoff and Corwin (1959), tested the hypothesis that persons who have a high degree of castration anxiety would show a greater increase in fear of death after the arousal of their sexual feelings than those who have a low degree of castration anxiety. To measure the latter variable, they used a cartoon from the Blacky Test. It shows two dogs; one is standing blindfolded, and a large knife appears about to fall on its outstretched tail. The second dog is an onlooker. The subjects were asked to rank three statements attributing varying degrees of anxiety to the onlooking dog. Most subjects (36) ranked highest the statements attributing the least anxiety. These subjects were categorized as having low castration anxiety; the remaining subjects (20) were placed in the high castration anxiety group. No evidence was provided that this classification was correct. The high anxiety subjects might been experiencing a greater degree of castration anxiety, but they could just as plausibly have been *consciously* reminded of the fragility of their genitals (a non-Freudian explanation); or they might have been conjecturing how other people, such as the drawer of the cartoon, might interpret the cartoon; or they might have been more concerned than the other subjects about the mistreatment of dogs. Many other conjectures are also plausible including that of Eysenck and Wilson (1973, 153), that the high anxiety subjects had a particular personality dimension, such as a general tendency to be anxious or emotional.

It might be replied that even in the absence of evidence for the validity of the Blacky Test, there remains the problem of explaining Sarnoff and Corwin's data. Since Freudian theory alone does that, there is confirmation of part of Freudian theory. One counter reply is that a non-Freudian view, one that points to a greater *conscious* concern about one's genitals among those who are more distressed about the thought of dying, can equally well account for the data (see Eysenck and Wilson 1973, 155, for details). Another counter reply, which I want to press, is that the failure to validate the Blacky Test may itself be a bar to confirmation even without anyone having a non-Freudian explanation of the overall data. This raises a general epistemological issue about the need to confirm auxiliary hypotheses, one that applies to a number of Freudian experimental studies. For that reason, I defer discussion until I consider Kline's (1986) response to some of my criticisms.

I conclude that the studies by Friedman (1950, 1952), Stephens (1961), Hall (1963), Schwartz (1956), Sarnoff and Corwin (1959), and Hall and Van de Castle (1963) all fail to provide any firm evidence for either the Oedipus or castration complexes. Kline does discuss other studies, but these, he claims, provide either no support or less support than the studies that I have discussed.

Id, Ego, and Superego

N.B. Validity of experimental personality variables uncertain

[note added by Kline 1981, 432]

This hypothesis is distinctively Freudian if it asserts the existence of what Freud meant by id, ego, and superego, and does not say merely that there are three major motivational factors in human behavior of some unspecified sort (a claim that Plato endorsed). Interpreted in a distinctively Freudian manner, the hypothesis is not confirmed by either of the two major studies cited by Kline (Cattell 1957; Cattell and Pawlik 1964) because there is no evidence that the three factors picked out in these studies are identical to the id, ego and superego. In fact, what corresponds to the id in Cattell's work is not unconscious; consequently, it is clearly different in a crucial respect from the id of Freudian theory. Kline and I, at most, disagree only marginally on this issue. He takes the Cattell studies to be "strikingly suggestive" but not to provide "definitive proof" (Kline 1981, 436).

Repression and Other Defenses

Kline concludes (436), first, that the experimental studies of Dixon (1958) and Blum (1955) are "laboratory demonstrations" of repression. Second, he argues that the other Freudian defenses have not been confirmed to the same degree, but that the percept-genetic studies of Kragh and Smith (1970) go a long way toward doing this (subject to a certain qualification about their measures of defense). Third, he makes a point about the relative importance of repression that is worth quoting: "Nevertheless repression is probably the most important of these defense mechanisms in Freudian theory since the whole dynamic view of mental life turns upon this concept. Thus the fact that it has been so powerfully supported means that one of the cornerstones of psychoanalytic theory as a whole still remains" (436).

I agree with Kline's comment about the importance of repression, but we should distinguish between the concept and the theory in which it is embedded. The theory of repression holds, among other things, that repression is causally implicated in an important way in the etiology and maintenance of neurosis, in originating slips of the tongue and other parapraxes, and in determining dream content. It is not surprising, then, that Freud described the theory as "the cornerstone" on which the whole structure of psychoanalysis rests (1914, *S.E.* 14:16). If the theory of repression is confirmed, then, even if the id, ego, and superego and the Oedipus complex are mere fictions, a very central part of Freudian theory has empirical support. Conversely, if, as Grünbaum (1984) argues, the theory is not well supported, then more than Freudian theory is affected. Any theory that presupposes the theory of repression, that is, virtually any psychoanalytic theory, has a serious epistemological difficulty to face. Next, consider the concept of repression (which is obviously central to Freud's theory of repression). If it applies to nothing, then the "cornerstone" of Freud's overall theory is not even approximately true. However, as Grünbaum points out, establishing merely that repression occurs is quite far from establishing the truth of the theory that attributes such causal importance to the phenomenon. In short, demonstrating that repression occurs is *necessary* for confirming Freud's "cornerstone" theory, the theory of repression; such a showing, however, is clearly not *sufficient* for confirming that theory.

Even if we focus on the more restricted claim about the mere existence of repression, there are problems despite the impressive array of evidence that Kline surveys. An important part of this evidence comes from studies of perceptual defense. Concerning one of these studies (Blum 1954), Kline concludes (223) that it seems to provide "incontrovertible evidence" for perceptual defense and hence the Freudian concept of repression. Kline also argues (221) that the work of Dixon provides "firm evidence" for repression, and (26) that the work of Blum and Dixon together is sufficient to show that this defense mechanism exists. In contrast, I have argued that the Dixon and Blum studies, and the perceptual defense literature in general, fail to establish the existence of Freudian repression (Erwin 1984a, 120–125). Part of my doubt concerns the concept of perceptual defense and part concerns Freud's concept of repression. The reasons for my skepticism are given in chapter 5.

Kline also appeals to the Levinger and Clark (1961) study of emotional factors in the forgetting of word associations. He takes their results to "show conclusively" (208) that forgetting word associations is related to the emotionality of the stimuli. Levinger and Clark, in contrast, are much more modest about what they found: "The results of this study merely demonstrate certain correlations between these variables. Yet, in the writers' opinion, they lend some support to the hypothesis that emotional factors can determine forgetting"(202). Even if the emotionality hypothesis were strongly supported, there is another link in Kline's argument that is questionable. From the assumption that there is a causal connection between forgetting associations and the emotionality of the stimuli, he concludes the following without the aid of any additional premise: "This, therefore, is a clear example of Freudian repression" (Kline 1981, 208). The logical gap between premise and conclusion can be bridged by assuming Kline's definition of "repression," but as I have argued elsewhere (Erwin 1986a), there is, according to Freudian theory, more to repression than merely a denial of entry into consciousness. At the very least, a dynamic unconscious must be causally linked to that denial. If that is right, then Kline's assumption about what is sufficient for repression is incorrect. What we are left with, then, is some evidence (strong evidence, if Kline is right) that the emotionality of verbal stimuli can affect the forgetting of associations, but no evidence from the Levinger and Clark (1961) study for Freudian repression. Other evidence in favor of the existence of repression is culled from the work of Lloyd Silverman and from studies of percept genetics. Because I discuss Silverman's research in chapter 5, I will not discuss his work here, but focus instead on research on percept genetics (Kragh and Smith 1970; Kragh 1955; Sharma 1977, and Westerlundh 1976).

In an early paper on percept genetics, Kragh (1960) points out that there are similarities but also important differences between his work and studies of perceptual defense. In a typical study he and his associates use a tachistoscope to present what are called "DMT" and "MCT" pictures to groups of subjects at increasingly greater exposure times. One picture shows a boy with a violin, the head and shoulders of a threatening and ugly man having been inserted to the right of the boy. A parallel picture shows a young man centrally placed and an old ugly man above him. The subjects are instructed to make a drawing of what they have seen without paying any attention to whether their impression is correct or not. If they feel unable to make any kind of drawing, they are allowed to make markings instead. Kragh (1960) uses the term "hero" to denote the person who is seen (drawn, marked) by a subject at the place of the main person in the picture. A "secondary" figure is the person seen at the place of the secondary person in the picture. Results are scored using Freudian defense categories. For example, a drawing is classified as "repression" if the hero or the secondary figure, or both, have the quality of stiffness, rigidity, lifelessness, or of being "disguised," or if one or both are seen as animals. What evidence does Kragh (1960) provide to show that repression is the cause of the subject's drawing the figures in this way? None at all. He simply stipulates that "repression" and other Freudian categories will be applied if certain kinds of drawings are made. Without such evidence, the studies of Kragh and his associates, whatever their value in distinguishing between psychiatric groups, provide no warrant for accepting the existence of any Freudian defense mechanism.

Kline (1981) makes the following comment about this lack of evidence: "Regrettably the only evidence for the validity of the DMT and MCT defense mechanism variables is effective face-validity. That is, if one examines what behavior is actually entailed in obtaining a score for a given mechanism, one makes a value judgment that the behavior resembles closely what Freud described as the appropriate mechanism"(234). One may make such a judgment (I am not sure why it should count as a value judgment), but without supporting evidence it would be unwarranted; it is not self-evident or obviously true that such drawings are caused by the operation of Freudian defense mechanisms.

In reply to the above criticism, Kline (1986) writes: "Now my case is this, not that the drawing is 'caused' by repression (strange word for a philosopher) but is an 'example' of repression, and similarly for the other defenses." Here is the problem I see with this reply. One might stipulatively define "repression" or, say, "reaction formation" so that the terms apply whenever subjects give a certain type of response regardless of what accounts for the response. This is apparently what Kragh and Smith do; at least, that is how Kline interprets their work. He notes (1986, 211) that in their view, when a subject says that the ugly threatening voice is angelic, such a response is *by definition* a reaction formation. However, as Kline himself stresses (1981, 198) the Freudian theory of defense mechanisms postulates that a response is due to or related to an unconscious attitude. Clearly, then, if one stipulates that a response is by definition a reaction formation *even if* it is not due to an unconscious attitude, then one is using "reaction formation" in a non-Freudian sense. The same comment applies to the term "repression" and to the terms for the other defenses. Verbal stipulation, then, does not settle the issue of whether the drawings of Kragh and Smith's subjects were due, at least in part, to the operation of some Freudian defense mechanism. Empirical evidence is needed to establish this. I infer, however, that Kline now agrees with these points. In a more recent paper on the DMT (Kline 1987, 55), he questions its validity, and points out that DMT responses do not constitute scientific evidence for defenses.

Apart from the work of Kragh and Silverman (and their respective associates), Kline regards most of the research he reviews on the defense mechanisms other than repression as being not well enough designed to permit either refutation or confirmation of Freudian theory (Kline 1981, 251). One exception is the work by Dollard and associates (1939) which, Kline claims (237), demonstrates "beyond all reasonable doubt" the occurrence of displacement. However, I regard this work, for reasons given elsewhere (Erwin 1984a, 122), as not supporting either displacement or any other Freudian defense mechanism. The key reason for being skeptical is the loose, non-Freudian usage by the authors of defense mechanism terms. "Displacement," for example is applied in any case where aggression directed at a given object is prevented and is then redirected toward another object (Dollard et al. 1939, 40) no matter why the redirection occurs. It does not even matter whether the subject is aware of his or her reason for redirecting the aggression, as is the case in one of the author's examples (106). To take another of the authors' examples, consider kicking a chair rather than one's enemy. The explanation of this behavior might be, as postulated by Freudian theory, that the ego is protecting itself from the instinctual demands of the id; but the behavior might also result from response generalization or from some conscious cognitive factor. To assume that the kicking of the chair is *automatically* a case of "displacement," no matter what its explanation, is to use the term in a sense that bears little resemblance to its Freudian counterpart.

This leads me to a general point about the Freudian defense mechanisms. I do not regard the experimental evidence that Kline relies on as providing firm evidence for the existence of any Freudian defense mechanism; these studies are even less satisfactory if interpreted, contrary in most cases to the intentions of the authors, as providing good evidence for the causal role of the defense mechanisms in the etiology of neuroses, slips, or dreams. Still, is it not obvious that people sometimes displace their aggression, repress their feelings or rationalize their actions? As Kline notes (1981, 238), is there not considerable anecdotal evidential support for, say, displacement? Can we reasonably deny, to use his example (238), that a clerk who is annoyed by his boss might be quick to kick his cat? I do not deny this; what I deny is that the kicking of the cat is necessarily due to Freudian displacement. The man in Kline's example may even be aware of why he is quick to strike his cat, which rules out Freudian displacement. More generally, I have no doubt that in some folk theory sense people "rationalize," "repress," "project," etc., but that is not evidence for the operation of *Freudian* defense mechanisms. Concerning these, Freud writes:

These observations provide good grounds for reintroducing the old concept of "defense," which has have the same purpose—namely, the protection of the ego against instinctual demands—and for subsuming repression under it as a special case. . . . It may well be that before its sharp cleavage into an ego and an id, and before the formation of a superego, the mental apparatus makes use of different methods of defense from those it employs after it has reached these stages of organization. (1926, *S.E.*, 20:164).

As the above quotation makes clear, Freud linked his concept of defense to the mental apparatus that he postulated. The concept applies to those processes having a particular purpose: the protection of the ego against the instinctual demands of the id. As Adolf Grünbaum has pointed out to me, one might disconnect Freud's concept of defense from that of the id, ego, and superego. Nevertheless, one must retain at least the link to a dynamic unconscious. As noted earlier, Kline appears to agree, given his remark that essentially all the defense mechanisms postulate a response due to or related to an unconscious attitude (Kline 1981, 198). If one deletes even the link to the unconscious, then what is left over and above the commonsense concepts of "displacement," "repression," etc.? As far as I can see, nothing, or at least nothing of theoretical importance. Some Freudians might reply that they intend nothing more. The existence of the defense mechanisms is one thing; the existence of the id and ego or the unconscious is a completely separate issue.

In that case, I have two further questions. First, why all of these sophisticated experiments with their multivariate statistical techniques, galvanic skin responses (*GSRs*), tachistoscope, and DMT cards if their only purpose is to demonstrate what anecdotal evidence has already amply confirmed? Second, given that it was known long before Freud was born that some people kicked their cat instead of their boss or blamed others for faults they themselves possessed, why call the confirmation of such things the confirmation of "distinctively Freudian" hypotheses?

The next four categories to be discussed contain hypotheses pertaining to Freud's theory of dreams. Kline notes (1981, 267) that this theory is fundamental to the Freudian corpus and that its falsification would cast considerable doubt on much of psychoanalytic theory. In fairness to Freud, it should also be noted that its confirmation would mean support for a central part of his overall theory.

Kline reviews a large number of studies bearing on Freudian dream theory. Some of the experiments are interesting and most of the results are congruent with the theory. Congruence, however, is not necessarily support. It takes considerable effort to figure out exactly which parts of Freud's dream theory are supported by which studies. I begin by examining studies concerning sexual symbolism outside of dreams.

Sexual Symbolism Outside of Dreams

The studies reviewed under this heading do not concern dreaming, but they are relevant nevertheless to one aspect of Freudian dream theory. The theory holds, in part, that certain objects that commonly appear in dreams, such as trees, poles, and other elongated items, represent sexual organs. If we assume that similar symbolic relationships exist in unconscious thought processes when a person is awake, then we can predict, for example, that drawings or pictures of poles and trees also symbolize sexual organs. By confirming this prediction, we can obtain indirect evidence for Freud's views about dream symbols.

The first supportive study reviewed by Kline was carried out by Hammer (1953), who used the HTP (House-Tree-Person) projective test to study genital symbolism. Subjects were asked to make a drawing of a house, a tree, and a person. On the assumption that a chimney, for example, symbolizes a penis, it was predicted that subjects suffering from castration anxiety would omit the chimney when drawing a house. They might also draw a tree, if it too represents a penis, as being cut down. In drawing a person, the castration anxiety subjects might, for example, omit the hair or draw the person as decapitated. Such features were in fact found in the drawings of the treatment group in statistically significantly greater numbers than in the control group. The latter group was composed of 20 men who had undergone operations other than sterilization. The treatment group consisted of 20 prisoners who were tested before and after undergoing sterilization. Given the correctness of the predictions about the castration anxiety subjects, Kline (1981, 268) takes the results to provide strong support for Freud's theory of sexual symbolism.

Why believe, it might be asked, that Hammer's treatment subjects were suffering from castration anxiety? Kline offers no direct evidence for this assumption, but appeals to the clinical finding that many patients tend to equate sterilization with castration. For example, in one sample, when asked to describe what they expected sterilization to be, many patients indicated that they expected to be castrated. If Hammer's treatment subjects were like these patients, however, then they were consciously afraid of castration. Given that they were not repressing their fear, therefore, they were *not* suffering from castration anxiety.

Still, even if the clients consciously believed that they were to be castrated, did not their fear affect the way they constructed their drawings? Indeed, it might have. Even if a tree does not in all contexts represent a penis, it would not be surprising if subjects who feared imminent castration, and who might well have equated castration with the loss of their penis, might draw a tree as if it were cut down or draw a person as if he or she had been decapitated. In short, for these subjects under these extreme conditions, trees and chimneys and so forth might have been associated with sexual organs, but this is no evidence that all people—or even these subjects in more benign contexts—have similar associations.

In addition to the Hammer study, Kline cites (285) 15 other studies with positive conclusions concerning symbolism. One of these (Moos and Mussen 1959) found no differences in sexual symbolism between psychotics, neurotics, and surgical controls, a finding that is not distinctively Freudian. Another study (Meissner 1958), which Kline rates only as "fair," found evidence of death symbolism in adults. The rest of the studies were about sexual symbolism in adults and children. There are patterns in the overall data, but also apparent inconsistencies. For example, as Kline notes, Levy (1954) found no evidence of sexual symbolism among the children he studied, although that might have been because of the method he used. Cameron (1967) found that adolescents preferred male sexual symbols, but his results were partly inconsistent with the findings of Forster and Ross (1976). Accord's (1962) results supported the hypothesis that sexual symbolism occurs in subjects aged 17 years or older, but not in subjects aged 14 years or younger. The findings concerning adults have been more consistent. Kline (283) even claims that there have been *no* findings contrary to the theory, but such results were found by Eysenck and Soueif (1972) who studied young adults with a mean age of 20 years (451 males, 445 females). The authors tried to replicate the work of Jahoda (1956) and McElroy (1954), who found that their male subjects preferred rounded shapes and that female subjects preferred rectilinear shapes. If we can reasonably assume that people generally tend to prefer shapes representative of the sexual organs of the opposite sex, then we can infer that the subjects' indicated preferences is evidence of sexual symbolism. Eysenck and Soueif, however, obtained negative results. This could be taken as evidence that for their subjects, the rounded and rectilinear shapes did *not* represent sexual organs. We might object to this interpretation if we give up the assumption that people generally tend to prefer shapes representative of the sexual organs of the opposite sex; however, that would undermine much of the positive evidence cited by Kline (including that of Jahoda 1956; McElroy 1954; and Cameron 1967).

The discrepancies in the data (e.g., the negative results of Levy 1954, and Eysenck and Soueif 1972) and the uncertainty about certain axillary assumptions (e.g., about preferences for shapes representing sexual organs of the opposite sex) would require discussion *if* the issue were the universality of "Freudian" sexual symbols. Even more important would be the small number of subjects and very narrow experimental contexts that have been surveyed. However, I do not think that Kline's conclusion is that for all people, no matter what the context, elongated or pointed shapes, for example, always represent the penis and rounded or curved shapes always represent the vagina. Any such extreme conclusion would at best be only weakly supported by the data. Kline's "basic conclusion," as he puts it, is much more modest: it is that Freudian sexual symbolism does occur among adults and probably occurs among children (285). My disagreement with this conclusion concerns only the use of the term "Freudian." It was known long before Freud wrote, as Eysenck (1985, 122–123) stresses, that sometimes sharp and pointed objects represent the male genitals and curved objects, the female genitals. That such symbolization does occur, either among adults or children of certain ages, is probably true, but this contention is not distinctively Freudian.

It should also be noted that the finding that sexual symbols sometimes occur outside of dreams is of limited relevance to Freudian dream theory. If it had been established that in all contexts, except for dreams, a pole, say, represents the penis, then this might provide grounds for thinking that a pole in a dream always has the same symbolic status. In dreams, too, it could be argued, it invariably represents a penis. However, the much weaker conclusion that sometimes a pole represents a sexual organ does not by itself support the inference about dreams.

Psychological Meaning of Dreams

Under this heading, Kline discusses Hall's (1966) book which interprets the results of a number of earlier studies done by him or a colleague. Of those that Kline reviews, he (Kline) regards (295) all but two as failing to provide any strong support for Freudian theory, although together they may, he suggests, furnish "slender" support. The two exceptions are papers by Hall (1963) and Hall and Van De Castle (1963). The first purports to confirm the existence of the Oedipus complex and the second the castration complex. The fact that the Oedipus complex can be observed in the content of dreams, Kline argues (295), indicates that there is psychological meaning in dreams and also supports Freud's view that the dream is the royal road to the unconscious. I argued earlier, however, that neither the Hall (1963) nor the Hall and Van De Castle (1963) study confirms the existence of either the Oedipus or castration complex. So, I will not discuss either study here.

Kline also claims (295) that the work of Lee (1958) provides powerful support for Freudian dream theory. The part of the theory that is relevant concerns dreams as wish fulfillments. As Grünbaum (1984) notes, the early Freud held that repressed infantile wishes are the causal instigators of all dreams. Such wishes are, of course, not conscious wishes. Later, in 1933, Freud acknowledged exceptions to his universal hypothesis. He thus modified it and held that, although the dream is an *attempt* at the fulfillment of a wish, the attempt sometimes fails. Even with this modification, however, Freud's hypothesis receives no support from the study by Lee (1958), who examined the dream reports of Zulu women. Some of the dreams manifested a desire to have a baby, a desire, Lee notes, that is quite strong among many Zulu women, but many of the dreams evidenced no instigating wish at all. This finding can be accommodated by saying that perhaps the attempt at wish fulfillment failed in the latter cases, but there is no support here for the ideas that *all* dreams are attempts at wish fulfillment. At best, the Freudian hypothesis is not disproved; it is clearly not supported. Even in the cases where the dream manifested a wish to have a baby, this wish was not, as far as is known, a *repressed* wish. In fact, some of the subjects who had such a dream expressed to the investigator their strong conscious desire to have a child.

Kline (296) takes the Lee study to provide "powerful evidence" that in a sample of Zulu women certain common dreams do reflect wishes, in accordance with psychoanalytic theory. Agreed. However, that finding is also in accord with non-psychoanalytic theory which holds that *sometimes* unfulfilled *conscious* wishes can affect one's dreams. As Grünbaum notes (1984, 219), the idea that *some* dreams are to be regarded as wish fulfillments was a commonplace idea in prepsychoanalytic psychology. This idea, then, did not originate with Freud.

Sexual Symbolism in Dreams

As far as I can ascertain, Kline relies on one study in this category, an ingenious study done by Berger (1963). Berger tried to determine whether verbal stimuli would be incorporated into dream events and whether such incorporation would be dependent upon the significance of the stimulus. The subjects were four male and four female normal volunteers. Galvanic skin responses were recorded while a list of words and names were read to them, including the names of current and past boyfriends and girlfriends. The two names selected as "emotional stimuli" were either the name of the current friend and previous friend which evoked a GSR of the greatest amplitude, or the names of two past friends also evoking GSRs of greatest amplitude. From a list of names not evoking any GSR, two neutral names were chosen. There were thus four stimulus names.

The subjects later fell asleep to the accompaniment of "white noise." Five to 10 minutes after the onset of rapid eye movement (REM) sleep, a stimulus name was played repeatedly on a tape recorder. The subjects were later awakened and questioned so as to elicit dream reports, which were recorded. The subjects were then allowed to fall asleep again until the next REM period, during which the procedure was repeated. This time the particular name presented was chosen randomly from the four stimulus names used for the particular subjects. A total of about 10 dream reports were elicited from each subject during the four to six nights of sleep. The four stimulus names were later played to each subject as he or she lay awake in the same room where the sleeping had occurred. The subjects then chose the one following playback of each of their dream reports, which they considered most appropriate to the dream. An independent rater, a colleague of the experimenter, was given the same task. Both the subjects and the independent judge were able to match correctly the names presented with the associated dreams more often than would be expected by guessing correctly.

Before relating the results to Freudian theory, one should ask to what extent the stimulus names really did appear in the subjects' dreams. For example, one subject correctly selected Rosemary as the stimulus name that preceded one of his dreams. His reason? People in the dream *arose* to go out. It could be argued that the name Rosemary thus appeared in the dream in a disguised form, but it could equally well be argued that the subject was merely speculating, on the basis of some free-associating, that the name Rosemary appeared in the dream. In another case, the subject chose the name Sheila because at the time of his recall of the dream he thought of one of the dream characters, an Indian, as a sheik. The subject's choice was correct, but did the name Sheila appear in the dream? If we say no in this and other cases, we are left with no explanation of how the subjects and judge were able to be right, not always but more often than would be expected by chance. If we say yes, however, that puzzle remains. For even if the names Sheila and Rosemary, to take the two cases just mentioned, did appear in the dreams, they were so well disguised that it is not clear how the subjects and judge were later able to recognize them.

Even if we agree that some of the stimulus names did appear in some of the dreams, how does this support Freudian theory? Berger (1963, 736) points out that his experiment was not designed to test any Freudian hypothesis, but claims that the results appear to support Freud's views concerning the function of dreaming. The fact that external stimuli were woven into the dream in some cases supports Freud's idea that the dreamer "seeks an interpretation of external stimuli" in order to "rob them of reality." The purpose of this is to avoid waking up. However, Berger also concedes (736) that an underlying unconscious wish of the dreamer could not be ascertained from the manifest content of the dream alone. Nor was any evidence presented that the stimulus names were in any way threatening or disturbing to the dreamer. We are left, then, with the finding that in some cases, names of present or former friends were presented to sleeping subjects and subsequently appeared in their dreams in a distorted fashion. There was no evidence that the dreamer deliberately created the distortion or was even motivated to do so in order to "rob them of reality." I see no argument, then, that the findings even taken at face value (i.e., if the skepticism expressed earlier is ignored) support Freudian theory about the function of dreaming, that is, that dreams are "the guardians of sleep."

Kline also takes the Berger study to support the view that Freudian sexual symbols occur in dreams. As evidence for this, he points out (311) that a few of the dreams where a stimulus symbol was incorporated contained Freudian sexual symbols. Earlier, I expressed some reservations about the claim that there was such incorporation; I now want to raise a different issue. How did Berger know that sexual symbolism occurred in any of his subjects' dreams? In one dream, said to be remarkable for its sexual symbolism, the dreamer and his girlfriend had to take a lamp back to town. They were standing near a fireplace and the girlfriend was holding the lamp. Either the lamp or the fireplace could have symbolized sexual organs, but then, again, they might not have. Berger offers no argument, either for this or any other dream, that sexual symbolism actually did appear. Kline, in discussing Berger's work (311), refers the reader to the studies listed on p. 285 of his book. However, as argued earlier, these studies support only the contention that certain items *sometimes* represent sexual organs, not that they invariably do so.

Even if Berger did not establish this, I assume that many non-Freudians, such as Eysenck (1986), would agree that sometimes items appear, both in and outside of dreams, that represent sexual organs. This claim is not made by Freud alone. Freud's distinctive contribution was to add that the symbolic relationship is invariable. A stick in a dream always represents a vagina, etc. Freud's contention, however, is not confirmed by the Berger study or any of the other studies that Kline discusses. Freud, of course, also offers a causal explanation of why certain symbols appear in dreams: they are the product of the work of the dream censor. Kline agrees (436) that this hypothesis has not been empirically confirmed.

Sexual Nature of Dreams

Kline relies here primarily on an experiment performed by Karacan et al. (1966). The investigators studied the effects of anxiety in dream content on erections during sleep. It was hypothesized that less anxious dreams would be reported when subjects are awakened from REM periods with full erection than from REM periods with an irregular or no erection. One problem faced by the investigators was to determine which dreams (and to what degree) had anxiety content. To address this problem, they used two measures of anxiety: the Gottschalk content analysis technique and the Nowlis adjective checklist. On the first measure, the main hypothesis was supported; on the second, it was not. Assuming equal credibility of each measure, the evidence, then, was inconsistent and did not unequivocally support the hypothesis. Kline, however, reaches a different conclusion. He says (307) that in view of the encountered problems in attempting to score dreams for anxiety, the fact that scores on one of the measures were related to the subjects' erection may be taken as evidence for the hypothesis. I see no reason to accept this point. If both measures are problematic, and I think they are, then even if the results on both agreed, it would be problematic to say that anxiety dreams had been correlated with lack of penile erection. The disagreement between the measures only adds to the uncertainty. In the absence of evidence of superior credibility for one of the tests, there is no warrant for taking the positive results at face value and ignoring the contrary results.

Even if the major hypothesis of Karacan et al. is supported, why infer support for Freudian theory? There is nothing distinctively Freudian about the idea that if a dreamer experiences anxiety while dreaming, this can inhibit erection. Kline (307), however, infers something further from the hypothesis of Karacan et al., namely, that instinctual impulses are expressed in dreaming, but he gives no grounds to support this additional inference. Later, in discussing the overall results of studies of dreams and erections, Kline reaches the following conclusion: "It is probably the case that erection *per se* does not imply the sexual etiology of dreaming. The fact that it can be affected by some dreams certainly imputes psychological significance to dream content and to this extent the phenomenon is in accord with psychoanalytic theory" (319). I agree with these comments, but would also add: it is not only Freudian theory that attributes psychological significance to dream content or allows, as is obvious, that *some* dreams have a sexual nature.

The remaining group of hypotheses concern the etiology of various sorts of psychological disorders. Kline (388, table 10.2) finds

strong support for the Freudian view of the origin of paranoid schizophrenia and appendicitis; *support* (but not quite as strong) concerning the etiology of depression and phobias; and only *slight support* or
no support concerning homosexuality, asthma, peptic ulcer and colitis, stuttering (except for the work of Silverman), anorexia nervosa,
and alcoholism. Kline's general position, with which I agree, is that
where the evidence is slight or nonexistent, that is because of a
failure to do adequate tests; a falsification of Freud's views cannot be
reasonably inferred from the lack of evidence. I will begin the discussion by examining studies of the origin of paranoia and paranoid
schizophrenia.

Paranoia and Homosexuality

As Kline notes, Freud held that the persecuting delusions of the
paranoid are due to repressed homosexuality and the operation of
the defense mechanisms of reaction formation and projection. In
the mind of the paranoid, "I love him" becomes "I hate him," as a
result of a reaction formation that serves as a defense against homosexuality; "I hate him" then becomes, by projection, "He hates me."
Because Freudian theory requires that the homosexuality of the
paranoid be repressed, a difficult epistemological dilemma arises. If
the paranoid overtly evidences his or her homosexuality, then it is
not repressed and thus Freudian theory is contradicted; if the paranoid, on the other hand, never displays any homosexual behavior,
then it is difficult to confirm the presence of homosexuality. Investigators have tried to circumvent this dilemma by obtaining *indirect*
evidence of latent homosexuality. One way of doing this is to use
projective tests, such as the Rorschach and TAT. The weakness of this
approach is that the tests themselves need to be validated. Thus, the
studies by Zeichner (1955) and Watson (1965), which Kline cites as
providing "some" support, are suspect because of their reliance on
unvalidated projective tests. It should also be mentioned that Watson
(1965) disconfirmed one of his three predictions. Kline (338) explains away this failure as possibly due to the invalidity of the
Masculinity-Femininity Scale. I agree, but doubts about the depend-

ent measures should also be extended to the TAT-like pictures and other scales that Watson relied on to obtain his positive results.

Two similar studies, Klaf and Davis (1960) and Moore and Selzer (1963), found correlations between homosexuality and paranoia. Kline does not place much weight on either study, although he does say that they offer some support or very limited support. The study by Klaf and Davis (1960) compared 150 male paranoid schizo-phrenic subjects and 150 nonparanoid non-psychotic subjects. One of the findings was that the paranoid group were seven times more frequently preoccupied with homosexuality than the control group. In Moore and Selzer's study the investigators substituted nonpara-noid schizophrenic subjects. Their findings were similar to those of Klaf and Davis. Both of these studies were retrospective rather than experimental. In addition, as far as is known, their subjects were not repressed homosexuals. Consequently, no support is provided for Freud's view of the origin of paranoia. In fact, Klaf and Davis found that their paranoid subjects had twice the incidence of *overt* homo-sexual experiences compared with the controls; furthermore, 30% of the paranoid schizophrenic subjects in the Moore and Selzer study (1963, 742) exhibited overt homosexuality. In the absence of some explanation, these findings appear to refute rather than sup-port Freud's view that *repressed* homosexuality plays a causal role in the etiology of all instances of paranoia.

Of the remaining studies that Kline discusses, two are said to provide *strong* support for Freudian theory. In the first, Daston (1956) studied recognition times for words judged to have homosex-ual, heterosexual, and nonsexual meaning. The words were pre-sented through the use of a tachistoscope. Daston assumed that faster recognition times for the homosexual words indicated homo-sexuality. However, as Fisher and Greenberg point out (1985, 265), one could just as reasonably assume that if the paranoids subjects were anxious about their homosexuality, they would have slower recognition times for homosexual words; on that assumption, Freu-dian theory is disconfirmed. However, in the absence of evidence either for or against Daston's crucial assumption, his findings are neither confirmatory nor disconfirmatory. Even if the foregoing objection were overlooked, Daston's findings would at best support the presence of repressed homosexuality in paranoids; as Kline notes (333), the experiment does not bear on the etiologic significance of repressed homosexuality.

The study on which Kline apparently places the most weight (as evidenced by its being listed as an "exemplar study," 433) was done by Zamansky (1958). This study has been singled out by several writers (Eysenck and Wilson 1973; Erwin 1986a; Grünbaum 1986) possibly because of Kline's suggestion (335) that some reactions to the study illustrate how far some non-Freudians will go to deny any aspect of the theory. Zamansky tested five hypotheses that he claimed to be reasonable if one accepts the Freudian thesis that paranoids are characterized by strong homosexual desires. The hypotheses were tested by presenting in a tachistoscope-like viewing apparatus pairs of pictures (e.g., of males and females, and of scenes with and without "homosexually threatening" items). Two of the five hypotheses were not supported, which could be taken as evidence against the initial Freudian assumption if Zamansky's other assumptions are all warranted; if the conjunction of his five hypotheses is reasonable given the initial assumption that paranoids are characterized by strong homosexual needs, then the falsification of even one conjunct would falsify the assumption. However, not all of Zamansky's other assumptions are warranted. One crucial assumption, for which he provides no evidence, is that if the subjects look longer at pictures of males than females when the subject's task is disguised (they were told to determine which picture in each pair was larger), that is because the subjects are repressed homosexuals. Another unwarranted assumption is that when the question of preference for male or female pictures is made explicit, and so more conscious, unconscious defensive forces are set into motion and this causes the preferences of the paranoid subjects to approximate those of nonparanoid persons. The failure to provide evidence for either assumption renders Zamansky's results neither confirmatory nor disconfirmatory for the hypothesis that all or most paranoids are repressed homosexuals.

Why did Zamansky's paranoid subjects look longer at the male photos? One cannot be sure. But one plausible explanation, suggested by Eysenck and Wilson (1973), is that being generally suspicious and finding males more of a possible threat, paranoid subjects are likely to pay more attention to pictures of males. Why, however, did the paranoid subjects state a greater preference for pictures of women than men? Eysenck and Wilson suggest that the subjects, after being shown pictures of homosexual encounters, were worried about being labeled homosexuals. Kline (335) is skeptical about both of these replies, especially the second. As to the first, he asks (231): Why the connection between suspicion and length of looking, between men and threat? In reply, I would say that if someone is generally suspicious, it is not implausible to think that this might make a difference as to how long he or she stares at a certain picture. Whether it did so in the Zamansky study is speculative, but is this speculation any less plausible than the speculation that people who gave no sign of being homosexual stared at the pictures of men longer because they were latent homosexuals? As to Eysenck and Wilson's second explanation (the "suspicion of the shrink" hypothesis), it is not needed. If one looks at Zamansky's table (1958, 306), one finds that the mean of the verbal choices of the paranoid subjects was almost identical to that of the control group. In other words, when asked which picture they preferred, both the paranoid and control subjects expressed roughly the same preferences; both groups tended to prefer the pictures of women. No special explanation is needed to explain why the paranoids expressed these preferences that is not also needed for the control group. The most likely explanation for both groups is that they really did prefer the pictures of women. Their staring longer at the pictures when presented tachistoscopically was simply not a good measure of the paranoid subjects' preferences.

Appendicitis and Birth Fantasy

The basic hypothesis considered in this section is that some event in real life gives rise to birth fantasies which initiate acute pain in the right iliac fossa leading to the diagnosis of acute appendicitis and appendectomy. This hypothesis is, at best, a peripheral part of Freudian theory. Freud did say concerning the Dora case: "Her supposed attack of appendicitis had thus enabled the patient . . . to realize a fantasy of childbirth" (quoted in Eylon, 1967, 268). However, it is unclear from this quotation whether Freud wished to claim that it is *generally* true that birth fantasies cause appendicitis. Even if he did, the hypothesis seems to implicate very little, if any, of the rest of Freudian theory.

Marginal or not, Kline argues that the hypothesis is supported by a study done by Eylon (1967). Even if that were true, the support is rather weak. His treatment group consisted of only 35 subjects. Surely, replication would be necessary if one wished to provide strong evidence that birth fantasies are *generally* implicated in the etiology of appendicitis. Even if we are content with a much weaker claim, that birth fantasies at least partly caused appendicitis in Eylon's 35 subjects, there are several reasons why the evidence is suspect.

It should be noted, first, that according to the typically used criteria (Campbell and Stanley 1966), the Eylon study is not an experimental study. There was no manipulation of an independent variable and no random assignment of subjects to an experimental and control groups. Merely pointing out that the study is not truly experimental does not in itself disqualify the evidence obtained, but the lack of random assignment does increase the chances that differences between the "experimental" and control subjects explain the differences in outcome, despite Eylon's attempt to match the two groups. Eysenck and Wilson (1973, 292) suggest that differences in the types of health conditions and operations between the two groups might explain the results. This may not be right (see Kline's reply, 1981, 364), but before accepting Eylon's interpretation of his results further examination of his two groups is warranted.

The first ground for suspicion is very general and fairly weak, but there are other more concrete reasons for doubt. For example, Eylon tested not one, but four hypotheses. Although they are logically independent, at least two of the remaining three bear on the plausibility of the etiologic hypothesis. *All* of these remaining three hypotheses were disconfirmed, thus reducing the likelihood of a causal connection between birth fantasies and appendicitis. Third, even Eylon's first hypothesis was disconfirmed. He then charged his definition of "birth event"; only after doing so, did he find a statistically significant correlation of the type he was looking for. Finally, we need to ask: What was the main finding? After charging his definition of "birth event," Eylon confirmed the following hypothesis: The proportion of appendectomies among surgery patients who have a birth event in their personal history (BE group) will be significantly higher than the proportion of appendectomies among surgery patients who do not have a birth event in their personal history (NBE group).

In the new definition, a "birth event" included a wedding at which the subject was present, or a birth or expected birth was present (provided that the birth occurred 6 months before or after the subject's operation and involved parents, spouse, siblings, children, aunts, uncles, or first cousins). No evidence was provided that the subjects who experienced such "birth events" typically fantasized about childbirth. Nor is the assumption particularly plausible. Is there any evidence that people who attend weddings or who learn that a cousin or aunt had a baby typically fantasize about childbirth? Even if we assume, without evidence, that such fantasies were present, we have at best an unexplained correlation between the presence of such fantasies and appendicitis. In the absence of some plausible mechanism to explain the connection, that is a very frail reason for inferring a causal connection. If we do not posit a causal connection, it might be replied, then we have no explanation of why the correlation was found. True, but even in the absence of other reasons for doubts, that is insufficient reason to infer a causal connection. This last reply of mine again raises a general issue that arises in other cases besides the Eylon study: If the tested hypothesis explains the experimental data and no *known* rival hypothesis does so, or, at least, not as well, is this sufficient for confirmation? For reasons given in chapter 2 (pp. 62–73), the answer is no. I return to this issue when I consider Kline's replies (1986) to my criticisms.

Phobias

Under this heading, Kline cites only one study, a psychometric study by Dixon, De Monchaux, and Sandler (1957) of 125 men and 125 women. Even if the study had no glaring methodological problems, replication would be needed before the evidence could be accepted as being firm. In addition, it would be necessary to consider rival theories about the origin of phobias (e.g., Eysenck 1983a) and data about behavior therapy successes with phobic patients which are difficult to explain if Freud's etiologic claims are correct. There are, in addition, several methodological problems with the study of Dixon et al. One of these is the lack of evidence for the validity of the dependent measure. Two other difficulties concerning factor analysis are pointed out by Kline (378). Because of these problems and doubts about the background evidence and the absence of replication, the authors' results provide, at best, very weak evidence for a Freudian view on the etiology of phobias. Kline agrees about the internal difficulties of the study, but concludes (379) that the results give "qualified support" to Freudian theory.

Depression

The single study cited under this heading is also a psychometric study carried out by Leckie and Withers (1967). Some of the problems that arise in interpreting their results are similar to those discussed above. First, replication is necessary before we can infer firm support for a Freudian view of the origin of depression. Second, it is necessary to consider rival theories, both biological and cognitivist (e.g., Beck 1976), and outcome data concerning the use of drugs, behavior therapy, and cognitive therapy in treating depression. Finally, even if the foregoing are ignored, there is a serious deficiency with the study. Evidence is needed to confirm the validity of the scales used by Leckie and Withers.

Libidinal Wishes and Psychopathology

The work cited under this heading has been performed by Silverman (1976) and his colleagues. This is in some ways the most interesting of the works reviewed by Kline. Silverman made a serious attempt to replicate his original findings, to rule out alternative hypotheses, and to answer those who disagree with him. Despite its virtues, however, there remain serious doubts about whether Silverman's experiments provide any firm support for Freudian theory. Because the studies in question span both the pre-1980 and post-1980 periods. I postpone giving my reasons for skepticism until chapter 5.

This completes my discussion of the Freudian hypotheses claimed by Kline to have experimental support. I turn next to the reviews by Fisher and Greenberg (1977, 1985). After completing this section, I present some general conclusions about the scientific value of the pre-1980 Freudian experimental evidence.

Because so many of the more important experimental studies reviewed by Fisher and Greenberg have already been discussed in connection with Kline's work, my comments on their reviews will be relatively brief.

The Fisher and Greenberg Reviews

Fisher and Greenberg (1977, 1985) review many of the same studies as Kline (1981), but they also rely partly on unpublished doctoral dissertations. As I noted at the beginning of this chapter, Kline (1981, 44) omits the latter group of studies from his discussion on the grounds that almost all competent research of this sort appears later in published papers. Because I want to focus on the stronger studies, I will follow Kline's practice and discuss only those that have been published.

Fisher and Greenberg (1977, 414) sum up their work by first explaining their major reservations about Freud's ideas and then listing those items they affirm to be basically sound. There are seven items in the latter category: I discuss each in turn, omitting a review of evidence examined in the first section of this chapter.

The Oral and Anal Character Concepts as Meaningful Dimensions for Understanding Important Aspects of Behavior

Fisher and Greenberg (1977) review a large number of studies bearing on the views of Abraham ([1927] 1965) on the anal and oral characters. Although inspired by Freud's work, these are not specifically Freudian views, so I will not comment on the relevant studies, except to note the following. For many of these studies—excluding, primarily, those that purport to establish only the existence of the oral and anal syndromes—much rests on the validity of the dependent measures, such as the Blacky and Rorschach tests. Concerning the measures used in the orality studies, Fisher and Greenberg note (132) that there is "really no solid information" concerning their validity. I would make the same point about many of the measures used in the anality studies. To the extent that the validity of the measures in both sorts of studies need to be established, the scientific worth of such studies is severely limited.

On Freud's views about character types and stages of development, Fisher and Greenberg's conclusions are pretty much the same as Kline's. First, (82) there are virtually no scientific findings concerning the phallic and genital types. Second, the fundamental part of Freud's character scheme (81, 393), the idea that certain clusters of traits are traceable to early childhood events and constitutional factors, has been neither empirically confirmed nor disconfirmed. Third, the existence of the oral and anal syndromes has been confirmed. I agree with these conclusions, but would again note that the last hypothesis is neither theoretical (no reference to unobservables) nor distinctively Freudian.

The Oedipal and Castration Factors in Male Personality Development

Fisher and Greenberg (1977) discuss at least nine hypotheses in this category, but what we really know, they say (219) can be reduced to three propositions.

The first proposition, despite the use of the term "pre-Oedipal," is not theoretical and is relatively trivial, that both males and females are closer to mother than father in the pre-Oedipal phase (i.e., before the age of 3 and 4 years). It would not be surprising if this proposition were true of most children given the child rearing practices of our culture.

The second proposition, that at some later point each sex identifies more with the same-sex parent than with the opposite-sex parent, is also non-theoretical. It should also be noted that not all of the studies cited by Fisher and Greenberg support this hypothesis. For example, Krieger and Worchel (1959) found no consistent pattern of same-sex parent identification in their subjects.

The third proposition is that there are defensive attitudes detectable in persons beyond the oedipal phase that suggest that they have had to cope with erotic feelings and hostility toward the same-sex parent. Someone might object that even this proposition is not distinctively Freudian. It might be true for non-Freudian reasons of some females who have had an incestuous sexual relationship with their father. However, Fisher and Greenberg make clear (p. 200) that they are postulating a Freudian variable, castration anxiety, as at least a partial cause of the pattern of erotic-hostile involvements. Castration anxiety, they claim, is a common occurrence in men and has been shown to be intensified by exposure to heterosexual stimuli. The one supporting study they cite (220) apart from three unpublished doctoral dissertations, that of Sarnoff and Corwin (1959) assumes without any argument that certain responses to the so-called castration anxiety card of Blacky cartoons is evidence of castration anxiety. I have already criticized this study above. The remaining published studies of castration anxiety cited by Fisher and Greenberg (Friedman 1952; Hall and Van de Castle 1963; Schwartz 1956) were also discussed earlier (see also Eysenck and Wilson, 1973). The basic difficulty with these studies is their reliance on an unwarranted assumption about what measures castration anxiety.

The Relative Importance of Concern About Loss of Love in the Woman's as Compared with the Man's Personality Economy

That all or most women in our society have been more concerned about loss of love than men is not a theoretical proposition; if it is true, that would not be surprising given the greater pressures on women to be married. Whether it is true or not, however, cannot be decided on the basis of the evidence cited by Fisher and Greenberg. Apart from two unpublished doctoral dissertations, they rely on two studies. One study (Gleser, Gottschalk and Springer 1961) found for 11 males and 13 females significantly higher scores for separation anxiety for the females. Given that these clients were all psychiatric patients, however, it would be rash to generalize from this small sample to groups of normal clients. For a much larger sample (N = 90) of subjects who were not psychiatric patients, the difference between males and females in separation anxiety was not statistically significant. The second study (Manosevitz and Lanyon 1965) did not directly study fear or loss of love. Forty-nine college females and 64 college males were asked to complete the Fear Survey Schedule. Although females reported more fears than men, the authors point out that it is possible that the former were simply more honest in reporting their fears. The women, on average, did score higher than men on "Feeling rejected by others," but it is not clear that this reflects a fear or loss of love. On another item, which arguably better reflects such a fear ("Being rejected by a potential spouse"), the men scored slightly higher than the women. In sum, neither study provides unequivocal evidence for the hypothesis; each could be interpreted as providing counterevidence if the validity of the measures could be assumed.

The Etiology of Homosexuality

Fisher and Greenberg (1977, 247) point out that Freud's ideas about male homosexuality have been only partially tested. They contend, however, that the available empirical data support his core concept about the kind of parents who are likely to shape a homosexual son. They are more cautious about the etiology of female homosexuality; they conclude (253) only that the empirical findings are more supportive of, than opposed to, Freud's formulation.

The studies that Fisher and Greenberg rely on are, in my view, too weak to warrant acceptance of Freud's view about the etiology of either male or female homosexuality. There is no need to review these studies here; they are effectively criticized by Kline (1981, 342–353). Kline concludes (353) that there is no sound evidence in support of the psychoanalytic theory of the etiology of homosexuality except perhaps for evidence provided by Silverman et al. (1973). Silverman's work is discussed in chapter 5.

The Influence of Anxiety About Homosexual Impulses upon
Paranoid Delusion Formation

Fisher and Greenberg (1977, 257–258) derive two testable propositions from Freud's theory of the etiology of paranoid delusions. (1)
The paranoid delusion represents a defensive attempt to control and
repress unacceptable homosexual wishes by projecting them. (2)
The persecutor in the paranoid's delusion would (in terms of its
homosexual equation) be of the same sex as the paranoid. Fisher
and Greenberg contend (269) that the second hypothesis has been
disconfirmed, but that the first has received "rather good experimental verification." They interpret the first hypothesis, however, as
not implying that repressed homosexuality is the major cause of
paranoia; they take the evidence to show merely that paranoids are,
for whatever reason, repressed homosexuals.

Attempts to confirm hypothesis (1) generate a tricky epistemological problem, as I noted in the first section of this chapter. As Fisher
and Greenberg stress (259), according to Freudian theory, unconscious impulses that are disturbing are presumably repressed and
contained so as to prevent their overt expression. So the authors take
the position (259), I think correctly, that the appearance of either
overt displays of homosexuality or of conscious homosexual imagery
by a paranoid person would contradict rather than confirm Freud's
theory of paranoia. To confirm the theory, then, investigators have
been forced to rely on indirect evidence of repressed homosexuality
in paranoids and this raises a major issue about the quality of such
evidence.

In three of the studies cited by Fisher and Greenberg a Rorschach
test was used to establish the presence of homosexuality. Aronson
(1952) and Meketon et al. (1962) found supporting data for hypothesis (1); Grauer (1954) obtained negative results. A fourth study
(Zeichner 1955) used both the Rorschach test and the *TAT* and
found mixed but generally supporting data. However, none of these
four studies qualifies as providing strong evidence either for or
against hypothesis (1) without solid evidence for the assumption that
the projective tests that were used did detect the presence of homo-

sexuality. In another study Daston (1956) studied recognition times for words judged to have homosexual, heterosexual, and nonsexual meaning; the words were presented tachistoscopically. For reasons given earlier (see above), his results were neither confirmatory nor disconfirmatory. In another study, Wolowitz (1965) tested for the presence of homosexuality in 35 paranoid and 24 nonparanoid male schizophrenic subjects by asking each subject to move a sequence of photographs along a tunnel toward himself until he found the place where it looked best. It was assumed that placing the male photos closer to oneself was evidence of homosexuality. Because the paranoid subjects did not do this, Wolowitz took his findings to disconfirm Freud's hypothesis. Fisher and Greenberg point out (264) that the paranoid subjects might have acted defensively: their fear of having their homosexuality detected might have caused them to place the photos of males farther from themselves than those of neutral objects. Fisher and Greenberg add that what is impressive is that the paranoid and nonparanoid subjects reacted differently. However, unless we have evidence that reacting differently in this situation, or placing the photos of males closer to oneself or farther from oneself, is evidence of homosexuality, Wolowitz's study yields evidence neither for nor against hypothesis (1).

Watson (1965) used three tests to measure homosexuality. First, he assumed that repressed homosexuals would have a higher mean score than a control on the Minnesota Multiphasic Personality Inventory (MMPI) Masculinity-Femininity Scale. Because the paranoid subjects in the study did just the opposite compared with nonparanoid schizophrenic subjects, Watson took this result to run counter to Freud's paranoia–repressed homosexuality hypothesis. A second assumption was that repressed homosexuals would obtain a lower mean score than controls on the Homosexuality Awareness Scale. The paranoid subjects did score lower than the controls. One might conjecture that this occurred because the paranoid subjects were homosexual but were repressing their homosexuality and thus acting defensively; however, this is only a conjecture. No evidence was provided for the second assumption that those scoring lower on the scale were repressing their homosexuality. A third assumption was that repressed homosexuals would respond less quickly than controls to a TAT-like picture having a high level of homosexual content than to a neutral picture. Again, no evidence was provided for that assumption. In addition, the only evidence that the "homosexual card" had a high level of homosexual content and that the "neutral card" did not was that five student nurses believed that this was so; they were not asked for evidence to support this belief.

One additional published study on paranoia is Zamansky's (1958) study. I discussed this work extensively above and need not repeat the criticisms here.

The Soundness of the Train of Interlocking Ideas About the Anal Character, Homosexuality, and Paranoid Delusion Formation

Fisher and Greenberg provide no independent support for this hypothesis; they rely on the arguments they give for their hypotheses on oral and anal character concepts, the etiology of homosexuality, and the influence of anxiety about homosexuality on paranoid delusion formation. Because I have already criticized the arguments for these hypotheses, this hypothesis requires no separate discussion.

The Possible Venting Function of the Dream

The authors' chapter on Freudian dream theory is, in my judgment, one of the most interesting sections of their book. They argue for certain revisions of the theory, but they also hold to one key assumption, that the dream is a vehicle for expressing (or venting) drives and impulses from the unconscious sector of the "psychic apparatus" (47). Concerning this hypothesis, they argue that the evidence shows that (a) when people are deprived of dream time they show signs of psychological disturbance; and (b) conditions that produce psychological disequilibrium result in increased signs of tension and concern about specific themes in subsequent dreams (63). They do not claim, however, that these findings confirm Freud's idea that dreams serve to vent either wishes or drives from the unconscious: "One can say these findings are *congruent* with Freud's venting model. But it should be added that they do not specifically document the model" (63; Fisher and Greenberg's italics). The key difficulty in establishing that the venting model applies to any dream is this: Even if it can be shown that a dream expresses a certain impulse, how do we know that the impulse originates in the unconscious? Fisher and Greenberg take the position (47) that presently there is no reliable scientific way of answering this question.

Kline's Replies

In commenting on earlier criticisms of mine of Freudian experiments (Erwin 1986a), Kline contends (1986, 231) that I have demonstrated two things, each of which he accepts: (1) that alternative explanations are almost always possible; (2) that there can never be full agreement concerning the formulation of Freudian theory. I have not argued for either (1) or (2), but if I have shown no more than these twin conclusions, then I have accomplished *nothing* of value. Both conclusions are uninteresting and are, of course, compatible with the view that much of Freudian theory has received strong experimental support. Before stating the conclusions that I have actually tried to establish, I need to address the conceptual and epistemological points raised by Kline's reply.

First, the conceptual point. Kline (230) notes that there is an element of value judgment in deciding, at least in certain cases, whether a hypothesis is or is not part of Freudian theory. He raises this issue because I have objected to his interpretation of the Freudian concept of repression, despite the fact that his quotation from Freud (Kline 1981, 195) seems to support his interpretation. I objected on the grounds that in Freudian theory, the concept of repression is linked to the mental apparatus posited by Freud. Perhaps a Freudian can dispense with the assumption that the id, ego, and superego exist, but at least a dynamic unconscious must exist if "repression" in the Freudian sense is to occur. If this is right, then the fact that something is "rejected or kept out of consciousness" (Kline 1981, 195) is no guarantee that Freudian repression has occurred. Otherwise, whenever I shut my eyes to avoid a bright light or deliberately try to forget some unpleasant experience, then repression has occurred. If we use "repression" in this wide sense, then nothing distinctively Freudian is being asserted when one says that repression exists. Furthermore, we do not need the Freudian experimental literature to establish the existence of repression (in this wide sense).

So I do not agree that Kline's first example illustrates an unresolvable disagreement about how to interpret Freudian theory. As I indicated, good reasons can be given for questioning his interpretation of "repression." Nor, do I agree with his other example, which concerns the work of Kragh. My objection to Kragh's work is *not* that the hypotheses tested are not distinctively Freudian, but that his dependent measures were not validated. As pointed out earlier, Kline (1987) now appears to agree with this criticism. So I will not discuss this case any further.

Even though I disagree with his two illustrations, I agree with Kline's general point. Except where it is perfectly obvious, reasons must be given for the judgment that something is or is not distinctively Freudian. In some cases, the reasons on both sides may be inconclusive. In such cases, it is better to decide about the empirical support for the hypothesis and leave open the issue of its classification as a Freudian hypothesis. Still, the presence of some hard cases does not mean that we should abandon all attempts to distinguish distinctively Freudian hypotheses from those that are not. Two extremes, it seems to me, need to be avoided. On the one hand, critics of Freudian theory can try to eliminate all of its support by the following maneuver: Identify all those hypotheses that are said both to be Freudian and to have empirical support; then, for each such hypothesis, try to find its anticipation in the writings of one of Freud's predecessors. Finally, conclude that every such hypothesis that has been anticipated by a non-Freudian is not distinctively Freudian. This procedure might not be objectionable if one were trying to judge the originality of Freudian thought, but neither Kline nor I am trying to do that. Rather, we are trying to assess the evidence for Freudian theory. So, for example, if all dreams are instigated by repressed wishes or if all psychoneuroses have a sexual origin, then both Kline and I would agree: at least one distinctively Freudian hypothesis is true, even if someone in the early 19th century had asserted both hypotheses.

The other extreme to be avoided is the labeling of commonsense hypotheses as "Freudian" if they are implied by Freudian theory *even* if they are implied by other theories as well, or if they bear only a superficial resemblance to genuine Freudian hypotheses. For example, if someone kicks a chair instead of striking out at his boss, one can say that *displacement* has occurred, even if the person is conscious of the real target of his or her anger. If one makes a verbal slip and says "breast" instead of "best," call it a "Freudian slip" even if the verbal similarity rather than a repressed wish caused the mistake. On this usage of "Freudian," some Freudian hypotheses have clearly been confirmed. Two points, however, should be noted. First, this commonsensible or "watered-down" (Crews 1986) version of Freudian theory is not what is being questioned by critics of Freudianism, such as Grünbaum (1984), Eysenck (1985), and Crews (1987). Second, we do not need sophisticated experimental designs and fancy statistical techniques to confirm such commonsense assumptions. They have, in most cases, already been amply warranted by commonsense observations. The conceptual point I want to make, then, is this: Of course, contentious claims about what is or is not "distinctively Freudian" are fallible and need to be backed by good reasons; and, of course, owing to the vagueness of the notion, some hypotheses will be difficult, perhaps even impossible, to classify. Nevertheless, some such attempt at classification is needed to avoid the complete trivialization of claims about the experimental confirmation of Freudian theory.

Kline (1986, 231) also raises certain epistemological points. In assessing the Freudian experimental evidence, much depends on the standards of evaluation that are employed. If intuition or the appeal to Freudian expertise is sufficient for confirmation (Taylor 1979), then strong support for Freudian theory can be found in the experimental literature. One could also argue (e.g., Fine and Forbes 1986) that confirmation, even strong confirmation, can occur although equally credible rivals are not ruled out. As Fine and Forbes say (1986, 238), it is a "methodological myth" that support accrues only in the absence of rivals. Another possibility is to argue that if Freudian theory provides the best available explanation of some phenomenon, that is sufficient for confirmation. If any of these standards is used, then a good case can be made for Freudian theory by appealing to the experimental literature. I argued against the use of these weaker standards in part 1, and am now taking for granted more stringent requirements. For example, for confirmation to occur, credible rivals must be ruled out. Fisher and Greenberg sometimes write as if they do not accept this more stringent standard, although I am uncertain about whether they do or not. Kline, however, clearly takes seriously the need to discredit credible rivals. In some cases, we disagree about the credibility of a non-Freudian rival, as in the Zamansky study, but this may reflect a different assessment of relevant background evidence. However, there are also two other epistemological issues which appear to divide us. First, Kline appears to place a restriction on the need to discount rival hypotheses. He seems to hold that if hypothesis H_1 predicts certain results and is part of some systematic theory, then there is no need to rule out a rival H_2, if H_2 is not part of a systematic theory. Thus, he complains (1986, 231) of the non-Freudian rival in the Zamansky case that not only does it fail to be instinctively plausible but also that it is not embedded in any theory. Elsewhere (1972, 114), he contends that it would be more parsimonious to accept Freudian theory if it predicts the results of certain studies and if the alternative is to employ a large number of ad hoc hypotheses. *If* I am reading Kline correctly, then I disagree: A plausible rival to a Freudian hypothesis needs to be discounted whether or not it is part of any systematic theory and even if it is simpler to accept the Freudian hypothesis. My grounds for this judgment are given in chapter 2 (see the section on simplicity, pp. 54–60) and need not be repeated here. (I am not denying, incidentally, that an appeal to simplicity might sometimes tip the balance in favor of the Freudian hypothesis; again, see chapter 2.)

The second point of disagreement about epistemology concerns cases where there is no plausible rival to a Freudian hypothesis. The one case that Kline cites (1986, 230) is the Friedman study (1952) in which loss of tails in a story is taken as a sign of a castration complex. Kline agrees that there is no direct evidence for the validity of Friedman's index, but makes two defenses. The first is that the notion of a castration complex includes inter alia that children "with it" would make such drawings. Thus, in this sense evidence for validity is not necessary; the test responses, Kline says, are part of the complex. In reply, I doubt that the responses really are part of the complex. Is it really self-contradictory to say: This child has a castration complex but has failed to give the specified test response? It *would be* a contradiction if part of the meaning of castration complex is that the specified test responses will be given by any child having the complex. Let us waive this objection, however, and assume that Kline is right; the test responses are *part* of the meaning of the concept. Still, it does not follow that evidence of validity is not needed. For, we can still ask: Is whatever else that is included in the concept, such as an unconscious fear of castration, present whenever the test responses are forthcoming? We could just stipulate that there is nothing else, that castration complex means no more than the disposition to give the specified test responses, but then that is not the Freudian concept. In Freudian theory, the concept of castration complex applies only if there is an unconscious fear of castration; a disposition to give certain test responses is not sufficient.

Kline, however, has a second defense. Assume that Friedman's measure needs to be validated and that this has not been done. Nevertheless, Friedman has presented a Freudian explanation of his findings. I, however, have failed to provide a non-Freudian alternative. Kline concludes: "In this case, a sensible or even plausible one [i.e. a non-Freudian rival hypothesis] is extremely hard. It is up to the opposition to provide it" (Kline 1986, 230). Here, Kline is relying on an "only game in town" sort of argument which I criticized in chapter 2. For my response to Kline's second defense, then, see that chapter.

Conclusion

In an earlier discussion (Erwin, 1986a), I examined most of Kline's exemplar studies on the supposition that they are the strongest among those that he appeals to, but I conceded that studies that I did not examine might yet yield strong supportive evidence. I now claim that this is quite unlikely. In the present discussion, I have criticized virtually all of the stronger studies appealed to by either Kline (1981) or Fisher and Greenberg (1985). If strong support for Freudian theory cannot be found in the large body of evidence that I have looked at, then citing a few additional studies here and there will make no appreciable difference to the outcome. That outcome is as follows: No distinctively Freudian theoretical hypothesis receives strong support from the pre-1980 experimental literature. This represents a massive failure of attempts at experimental confirmation, a failure that would be of great magnitude even if one or two counterexamples to my conclusion were found. We are talking about, after all, a very large number of studies. Kline (1986, 205) points out that there are 1500 references cited by Fisher and Greenberg and that he deals with only slightly fewer. In addition, we do not know how many other attempts at experimental confirmation of Freudian theory were not published because the results were negative.

How do we explain this massive failure at confirmation? Nonrealists may see it as part of a more general problem associated with attempts at confirmation of any theory. If we take this line, then we may be further encouraged to judge a theory solely by its heuristic value or by its ability to save the appearances (whether or not the theory is true). Some critics of Freudian theory will suggest a second explanation: so many attempts at experimental confirmation have failed because Freudian theory is false. Whether or not most or all of Freudian theory is false, I do not think we are entitled to infer its falsity from the failures of confirmation discussed here. I do not deny that some legitimate disconfirmations can be found among the pre-1980 experimental studies, but I agree with Kline that generally where there is a lack of confirmation this can plausibly be explained in terms of methodological problems. Someone might develop a counterargument and try to support a judgment of falsity, but I, at least, see no good grounds so far for that conclusion *if* it is based solely on the experimental failures discussed here.

There are two other explanations that deserve comment. First, some who believe in the confirmability of other theories will argue that this particular one is not confirmable even if it is true. Second, some Freudians who believe in the primacy of the clinical evidence will argue that the theory is confirmable, but not by *experimental* evidence. In forming a judgment about either of these theses, it would be helpful to have an analysis of what methodological problems have been inherent in the experimental literature and to what extent they are correctable.

One problem has been the widespread failure to provide necessary replications. Even a well-designed experiment is unlikely to produce powerful evidence for a universal hypothesis unless the experimental effect is replicated. In some areas, replications have been attempted. Silverman's work, to be discussed in chapter 5, certainly has this feature. As a general rule, however, the Freudian experimental literature consists of interesting results here and there with very few or no attempted replications. This failure to attempt replications, which is present in other areas in psychology, cannot be blamed on either the conceptual or structural features of Freudian theory. It is a defect that is clearly remediable.

A second problem has been the over reliance on unvalidated projective tests, such as the Rorschach test. In some cases, such tests have been used because of the difficulty of otherwise confirming the existence of unconscious feelings, such as castration anxiety or latent homosexual urges. Here there is a serious practical epistemological problem, but there may be ways to overcome it, in some cases by developing new measures that have more credibility. Novel uses of tachistoscopes might be examples. In other cases, such as those in which a Rorschach test has been used to identify schizophrenia, we already have better measures available.

A third experimental problem has been that in some cases the hypothesis tested has not been truly Freudian. Sometimes an investigator will give an operational definition of what is said to be a Freudian concept, but one that drains it of all Freudian content. This is one reason why some Freudians are generally skeptical of experimental studies of their theory, and argue for the epistemological primacy of the clinical evidence. This defect is clearly not present, however, in all Freudian experimental studies; furthermore, it is one that can be eliminated in practice.

A fourth problem (in a sense the most general problem) has been the failure to rule out credible rival hypotheses. In some cases, the attempt has been made, but the experimenter was unsuccessful for reasons having to do with the subject matter. It is often quite difficult to eliminate rivals when one's hypothesis talks about events alleged to have occurred in infancy or about what is presently unconscious. In other cases, however, the attempt to eliminate rivals was minimal or was not made at all. In such cases, better-designed experiments are likely to yield better-grounded outcomes.

Given, then, the practical eliminability of some of the defects of previous Freudian experiments, the failure of confirmation so far can be plausibly explained without concluding that no part of Freudian theory is experimentally confirmable in practice. Owing to the peculiar nature of the structure of the theory and some of its concepts, some parts of the theory may well be untestable in practice by experimental means, but I see no argument here for a wholesale dismissal of the view that Freudian experimentation is worthwhile. Finally, two additional points need to be stressed. One is that what is testable in practice depends to some extent on our current empirical evidence and on what research designs are now available. As new evidence is discovered and potentially useful auxiliary assumptions are confirmed and new experimental designs are developed, what is presently untestable in practice may become testable. Second, there is a point that does not touch skepticism about the testing of Freudian theory, but which is relevant to the claim that clinical investigations are preferable. In those cases where intractable epistemological problems are a bar to experimental testing, adequate clinical testing is likely to be even less feasible. It is difficult enough to rule out credible rivals to Freud's theoretical hypotheses, but eliminating experimental controls generally worsens the problems.

Chapter 5

Recent Research Programs: The Cognitive Turn in Freudian Psychology

Some of the research to be considered in this chapter is interesting in its own right. To the degree that it is, and also has a cognitive character, it is and ought to be of interest to cognitive scientists. Some of it, furthermore, has been inspired by Freudian theory. Insofar as that portion of it is worthwhile, then it illustrates the heuristic value of Freud's theory. My main concern, however, is the bearing the research has on the truth of Freudian theory.

One problem with the pre-1980 Freudian experimental studies discussed in chapter 4 is the lack of systematic followthrough. With some notable exceptions, one finds mainly an interesting study here and there on Freud's views about dreams, or defense mechanisms, or whatever, but only rarely is the study replicated. That leaves room for doubt apart from questions about any specific design flaws. What would the results be if an independent investigator tried to repeat the same experiment? However, even with replication, it is unlikely that any one type of experiment will provide substantial confirmation for a major Freudian theoretical hypothesis. The results of any single experiment, no matter how often replicated and well designed, will often leave open many doors to alternative, non-Freudian explanations. To close these doors, we need a *research* program, one that systematically pursues the issues generated by any single type of experiment. In this chapter, I look at some of the more important recent Freudian research programs beginning with one that began in the 1970s but is still being pursued today despite the tragic, accidental death of its progenitor, Lloyd Silverman.

Silverman's work, like much of the Freudian research of the 1980s, reflects a turn toward cognitive psychology. The key experimental tool of him and his colleagues, the use of a tachistoscope, has been employed quite often by cognitive psychologists who study perception. The focus of many of Silverman's experiments, moreover, was on oedipal fantasies, which is arguably a form of cognition. In other Freudian work to be discussed later, the cognitive turn becomes more pronounced: the investigators study the unconscious cognition of their subjects (Weiss, Sampson, et al. 1986) or make a direct appeal to evidence unearthed by cognitive psychologists (Erdelyi 1985). I begin with Silverman's work.

Some Recent Research Programs

The Silverman Studies

In 1976, Silverman reported on the use of his subliminal psychodynamic activation method in a paper with the intriguing title, "Psychoanalytic Theory: 'The Reports of My Death Are Greatly Exaggerated.'" The procedure involves the tachistoscopic presentation of pictorial or verbal stimuli that are designed to either enhance or diminish unconscious conflicts. Where the conflicts were enhanced, it was predicted that psychopathology would be increased, where diminished, that it would decrease.

In the enhancement experiments, subjects are initially administered tasks so that their psychopathology can be assessed. They are then told that they will be asked to view flickers of light through the eyepiece of a machine (a tachistoscope) and that they will be informed later about the purpose that this serves.

A baseline measure is then obtained of the subject's propensity for whatever pathological manifestations are being studied. The subjects are then asked to look into the tachistoscope and to describe the flickers of light that appear. In the experimental sessions, four exposures follow, each for a 4-msec duration, of a stimulus with content related to libidinal or aggressive wishes. On alternate days, a control session is held and the same subjects are shown neutral stimuli under the same conditions. Later, there is a reassessment of the pathological manifestations to determine how the subject has been affected by the particular stimulus that had been subliminally presented. To insure that the subjects were not conscious of the stimuli, a "discrimination task" is given at the end of the experiment to determine if they can distinguish between the different stimuli. The experimenter who works the tachistoscope is also kept "blind" as to the stimuli being presented, as are the other researchers who evaluate the material for pathological manifestations.

Four sorts of symptoms have been studied: depression, homosexuality, stuttering, and what Silverman calls "primary process ego pathology," which refers to disturbances in thinking and nonverbal behavior associated, in their severe form, with schizophrenia. Some of the experimental stimuli include verbal messages, such as "DESTROY MOTHER," "FUCK MOMMY," and "GO SHIT." Others include pictures of: a man defecating, a person with teeth bared about to stab an elderly woman, and a man and a woman in a sexually suggestive pose. Control (or "neutral") stimuli also consist of verbal messages (such as, "PEOPLE THINKING") and pictures (e.g., of two people facing each other with bland-looking expressions).

In his 1976 review, Silverman refers to 16 experiments (N 400) with schizophrenic subjects. In each experiment, the subliminal exposure of stimuli designed to stir aggressive wishes, when contrasted with the subliminal exposure of neutral stimuli, led to an intensification of pathological manifestations on a variety of psychological tests. A similar enhancement of pathological manifestations was found in three experiments of depression (Rutstein and Goldberger 1973; Varga 1973; Miller 1973); one on homosexuality (Silverman et al., 1973); and one on stuttering (Silverman et al., 1972).

One issue not directly relevant to the present discussion concerns Silverman's classification of homosexuality as a "pathology." Although his argument does commit him to a psychoanalytic etiological account, I do not think that he needs to take a stand on whether or not homosexuality is pathological. Being wrong on this issue, as far as I can ascertain, would not weaken his overall argument.

As noted earlier, Silverman's method has also been used to decrease pathology. Silverman (1976) refers to 10 studies in which this was attempted by reducing conflict through the activation of an unconscious fantasy of symbiotic gratification. Seven of these studies used schizophrenic as subjects. One type of stimulus, the verbal message, "MOMMY AND I ARE ONE" (and its close variant "MY GIRL AND I ARE ONE"), was found to have pathology-reducing effects.

Among other things, Silverman (1976, 630) takes his findings as evidence for a central psychoanalytic proposition: that psychopathology is rooted in unconscious conflict. He also claims an "abundant amount of clear-cut direct support" (634) for the hypothesis that the stimulation of libidinal and aggressive mental contents can intensify psychopathology, and weak support for other hypotheses, for example, that there is an inverse relationship between the adequacy of a person's defenses against the emergence of libidinal and aggressive mental contents and the appearance of psychopathology.

In some of his later writings (Silverman and Weinberger 1985; Weinberger and Silverman 1987), Silverman stresses a hypothesis that is not part of Freudian theory. Whether or not it would be considered part of *any* version of psychoanalytic theory is unclear, and perhaps unimportant. As Weinberger and Silverman (1987) point out, some psychoanalysts have endorsed it; but others have rejected it. The hypothesis has two parts (Silverman and Weinberger 1985, 1296–1297): (1) There are powerful wishes, typically unconscious, in many adults for a state of oneness with another person; and (2) when these oneness (or "symbiotic") wishes are gratified, adaptation can be enhanced if simultaneously a sense of self is preserved. Much of the research cited in support of this hypothesis has been done with schizophrenic subjects. A reduction in pathology was found in more "differentiated" schizophrenics, but not for the less differentiated ones (Silverman and Weinberger 1985, 1299). The more "differentiated" subjects were identified in the following manner: each subject filled out two rating scales, one of which bore on how he perceived himself, the other on how he perceived a picture of an older woman intended as a mother figure. The greater the extent to which the two sets of ratings coincided (the schizophrenic subject experiencing himself as similar to the mother figure), the less differentiated he was judged to be.

Non-schizophrenics were also found to benefit from the subliminal presentation of the symbiotic message, "MOMMY AND I ARE ONE." For example, Silverman, Frank, and Dachinger (1974) used the message to enhance the beneficial effects of systematic desensitization and Palmatier and Bornstein (1980) used it to enhance a "rapid smoking" behavioral treatment for reducing cigarette smoking.

Silverman's research program has several fascinating features. If he and his colleagues are right, the subliminal psychodynamic activation method has the power to stir up unconscious oedipal fantasies and to produce observable results that support some central psychoanalytic hypotheses. Even apart from supporting psychoanalysis, the method can apparently be used to produce at least transient improvement in schizophrenics, stutterers, and others, and to enhance the therapeutic powers of certain behavioral treatments. Despite the very interesting features of the program, however, it has received only modest amounts of discussion by psychologists. One reason for this relative neglect, I suspect, is that many psychologists familiar with Silverman's work are skeptical either about his results or his interpretation of them.

One reason for skepticism concerns the experimental controls used to insure that the studies are double blind. Are proper precautions typically taken to insure that the subjects are not consciously aware of the stimuli presented to them? In one paper, Silverman (1976, 624) says that his evidence in support of psychoanalytically dynamic propositions is not dependent on the belief that subliminal registration, in the strictest sense, has been demonstrated. He does not explain, however, what he means by "the strictest sense," nor does he argue for his claim. There are two reasons to doubt it. First, if the subjects are consciously aware of the experimental stimuli, then this weakens the case for invoking a psychoanalytic explanation of the results. Second, and more fundamentally, an appeal to demand characteristics of the experiment is not ruled out. Silverman himself (1976, 633–634) argues, citing Orne (1970), that without a double blind procedure, it is not possible to eliminate as a source of variance demand characteristics that come from the subject himself, based on his preconceptions and expectations of how subjects are supposed to respond. He faults "the great majority" of psychological experiments for not ruling out this possibility, but claims that the subliminal nature of the stimuli in his experiments avoids this problem.

Assuming that the issue is important, then, we need to ask: Are Silverman's controls sufficient for insuring subliminal effects? There is reason to doubt that they are. Holender (1986) has recently reviewed some of the methodological difficulties involved in studies of subliminal perception. He argues that to insure subliminal effects, evidence must be provided for the subject's lack of conscious awareness of the stimuli at the time of presentation. It is not sufficient to test the subject after a trial has been run, and certainly not at the end of an experiment, to see if at that later time he either remembers seeing the stimulus or can identify it; otherwise, it is impossible to ascertain whether the later absence of evidence of conscious awareness is due to unavailability to consciousness at the time of presentation or to forgetting during the retention interval. As Holender also argues, and almost all of his commentators agree with him, the control required to insure satisfaction of the preceding criterion is that of pattern masking. In using this procedure (see studies by Marcel 1978, 1983), the visual experimental stimulus is masked by another visual stimulus that prevents not only its conscious identification but even detection of its presence. Because the Silverman studies did not use a masking procedure and relied on tests of awareness taken at the end of the experiments, they do not provide adequate evidence of subliminal phenomena. Many investigators of semantic priming (see Holender, 1986) and other subliminal phenomena would consider this lack of control a fatal flaw in the Silverman research program.

A second issue concern the effects that are claimed to occur in Silverman's experiments. These include both increases and decreases in psychopathology. These effects, however, are not directly observed by the experimenters; rather, at least in the studies of schizophrenics, they are inferred from the observed results of certain psychological tests. We need to know, then, if there is adequate evidence that these tests measure what they are designed to measure.

In the studies of schizophrenics, Silverman has used the Rorschach, word association and story recall tests; each of these lacks independent evidence in support of its validity. Kline (1981, 384) is generally supportive of Silverman's research, but comments that his use of dubious tests to measure psychopathology constitutes the weakest aspect of the program.

The problem of test validity is far less important or altogether absent in some of Silverman's studies of nonschizophrenics. For example, in Silverman et al. (1972), increases in stuttering were "blindly" judged to have occurred after raters listened to successive samples of the subject's speech. In Silverman et al. (1978), the dependent variable was "competitive performance" as measured by scores in a darts tournament, something that obviously can be determined by direct observation. It is doubtful, however, that an increase in stuttering constitutes an increase in psychopathology; it is even more obvious that getting better at darts does necessarily reflect a decrease in psychopathology. These two experiments, then, are of dubious relevance to claims about increases or decreases in psychopathology. The dart-throwing experiment, moreover, raises a third issue that may be the most important of all. Given the surprising nature of the Silverman findings and the fact that the overwhelming majority of the studies were either performed by Silverman and his colleagues or were part of unpublished doctoral dissertations, it is important that the results be replicated and published by independent researchers. Three such replications of the dart-throwing experiment were attempted by Heilbrun (1980): all three failed. In his reply to Heilbrun, Silverman (1982) mentions six other attempted replications, with four having positive and two having negative results. All four of the sets of positive results, however, were reported in unpublished doctoral studies. In another study, Emmelkamp and Straatman (1976) tried to replicate the finding of Silverman et al. (1974) that the use of the subliminal psychodynamic activation method enhances the effects of systematic desensitization. Again, the attempt failed. Oliver and Burkham (1982) used Silverman's method and included as one of their two experimental agents the "MOMMY AND I ARE ONE" stimulus. They found a failure to decrease symptomatology in depressed women, and describe their results as a "failure to replicate Silverman's (1976)" study. Other attempts at replication by independent investigators (Haspel and Harris 1982; Porterfield and Golding 1985; and Fisher, Glenwick, and Blumenthal 1986) have also failed.

The preceding attempts at replication are not all alike; some of them raise different issues. For example, Silverman (1985a) objects to the Porterfield and Golding (1985) study on the grounds that it did not include a measure of nonverbal pathology that has been included in his previous studies of schizophrenics. He also claims (Silverman 1985b) in a reply to Porterfield and Golding (1985) that the test in question includes categories of behavior that are typically linked to schizophrenia and that these categories are given more weight than the more numerous ones that are not directly linked to the disorder. The latter categories, including scratching, cleaning one's throat, coughing, and taking a cigarette, are considered by Silverman to be "anxiety equivalents" to psychotic behavior (despite the fact that they are often exhibited by non-psychotics). Silverman does not supply any empirical evidence, however, that the test as a whole can reliably distinguish between schizophrenics and nonschizophrenics. A test may weight relevant categories more heavily than those that are not relevant, but if the latter are more numerous the test might still classify subjects incorrectly. Furthermore, even if there were firm evidence that the nonverbal test measures pathology, Porterfield and Golding did include two measures of thought disorders in schizophrenics. If there is evidence of their validity, something Silverman (1985a, 1985b) does not question, then the study did test Silverman's hypothesis that the use of his procedure affects the disordered thinking of schizophrenics in specific ways. The results, as noted earlier, were negative. Unfortunately, the significance of the results is unclear to the extent that there is not solid evidence that the Porterfield and Golding dependent measures are valid.

Silverman (1985a, 1985b) also takes issue with Oliver and Burkham's (1982) claim that their results constitute a failure to replicate "Silverman's technique." He objects on the ground that they used a "MOMMY AND I ARE ONE" stimulus with depressed female patients, but that this particular stimulus has been shown not to affect women the way it does men. Silverman has raised specific issues about failures to replicate (e.g., see Silverman 1982, and the reply by Allen and Condor 1982), but has not discredited all such studies. In a more recent paper, he relies on a more general argument: that the ratio of studies with positive results compared to those with negative results is about 3 to 1 (Weinberger and Silverman 1987). That reply, however, does not dispose of the epistemological problem. Simply adding studies with positive results, without regard to their quality or the independence of the investigators, does not necessarily provide an accurate picture of the overall evidence. Virtually all of the published studies done by independent investigators have reported negative results. This negative counterevidence cannot be wiped out merely by pointing out that such studies are outnumbered by other studies that are either unpublished or not independent. Weinberger and Silverman (1987) also point out that a meta-analysis being prepared by an independent investigator shows that the results obtained in studies by Silverman and his students and those by independent investigators are comparable (the effect sizes being, respectively, .41 and .50). The use of meta-analysis, a controversial statistical technique, is discussed in some detail in chapter 6, but one point should be stressed here: averaging effect sizes for studies of very different quality can yield misleading results. In the case being discussed here, it would be misleading to group together as "independent studies" both published and unpublished studies and then to average the effect sizes. If that were not done, then it is unclear how the average effect sizes for independent studies of the Silverman technique could be approximately .51, given that almost all such published studies have had negative results.

To sum up: Even if there were no problem at all with the subliminal nature of Silverman's experimental stimuli or with his test measures, the many failures at attempted replication by independent investigators tends to undermine his evidence. Even if, contrary to fact, all of the attempted failures were to be explained away, we would still be left with a virtual absence of independent replications with positive results. Given the very controversial nature of Silverman's hypotheses, this lack of independent corroboration would itself be reason for suspending judgment until more solid evidence becomes available.

One final issue concerns the psychodynamic hypotheses that Silverman invokes to explain his results. Suppose that we set aside the objections made so far and assume that the subliminal psychodynamic activation method can be used to increase and decrease psychopathology. Still, Silverman provides no evidence that his subliminal stimuli stir up unconscious fantasies. Without such evidence, what is, at most, demonstrated is that certain types of subliminal stimuli produce certain sorts of interesting effects. Whether this would have any bearing on psychoanalytic theory would still be unclear. Silverman's response to this sort of criticism is to say that his experiments yield results in line with psychoanalytic expectations, while ruling out rivals that seemed plausible. Thus, it is now up to his critics to provide satisfactory non-psychoanalytic explanations of his results (Weinberger and Silverman 1987, 24). I agree that the critics should propose alternative explanations, but I doubt that the absence of alternatives warrants the inference that Silverman's explanations are correct. As argued in chapter 2, the fact that one's theory provides the only available explanation of the data is not sufficient for confirmation. There are, of course, many such cases where people infer that hypotheses about religion, flying saucers, extrasensory perception, and so forth are true merely because no rival explanations are yet available. In such cases, the move from "*H* provides the best available explanation of the data" to "There is evidence that *H* is true, or approximately true" is illegitimate if *H* is sufficiently implausible and if the reason why no alternative hypothesis is yet available gives us no reason to think that an alternative cannot be found. In many cases, novel data are discovered, but scientists have not had the time or the motivation to develop alternative explanations. The lone explanation in the field thus wins by default; it is the best currently available, yet it may not be good enough to warrant our believing it. We need to look, then, at the details of Silverman's psychodynamic hypothesis.

The hypothesis stressed in Silverman and Weinberger (1985) is not, as noted earlier, part of Freud's theory; it may be classifiable as "post-Freudian psychoanalytic," but even that is unclear. It has two parts: (1) There are powerful wishes, typically unconscious, in many adults for a state of oneness with another person; and (2) when these oneness (or "symbiotic") wishes are gratified, adaptation can be enhanced if simultaneously a sense of self is preserved. The first part of this hypothesis is unclear in that it fails to specify even approximately how many of us have such wishes. Consequently, it is unclear whether the hypothesis would receive much support even if we could independently establish that most of Silverman's subjects had such wishes. If, for example, almost everyone is said to have these wishes, little support might results from the finding that schizophrenics have them. Part (*1*) is also unclear in a more radical way: What does it mean to say that I wish for a state of oneness with another person? Do I want to be literally identical with someone else, to be physically conjoined with the person, to be very much like the person, or is it a wish for something else?

A similar unclarity appears in the "MOMMY AND I ARE ONE" stimulus. This sentence can be interpreted as expressing a number of different propositions, including (*a*) "Mommy and I are the same person" (*b*) "Mommy and I have bodies that are joined together"; (*c*) "Mommy and I have a spiritual bond"; (*d*) "Mommy and I have sexual intercourse"; (*e*) "Mommy and I agree on everything." Silverman hypothesizes that the subliminal presentation of the "MOMMY AND I ARE ONE" stimulus gratifies the unconscious desire for oneness in his subjects, at least in the male schizophrenic subjects. How can this be, however, if the subjects do not know what the sentence means? Well, they might just associate a certain meaning with the sentence. For example, they might assign to it reading (*d*). If so, we have to assume that the interpretation they give in each case corresponds with their symbiotic wish. If, for example, this wish was to *be* their mother, then it is unclear why the subliminal presentation of a proposition about sex would cause the effects that we are assuming to occur. Furthermore, even if the subject's interpretation of the stimulus does correspond with his symbiotic wish, how does this explain why the subject's wish is gratified? If I wish to have sex with my mother, I am not getting what I want if I am given only a subliminal message that I interpret as "I have sex with my mother." It is also unclear how gratifying symbiotic wishes would help to improve schizophrenia, especially if, as the current evidence indicates, the disorder has a genetic and biochemical cause. I conclude, then, that even if we waive all other problems, Silverman's symbiotic hypothesis does not provide a satisfactory explanation of the alleged effects. The hypothesis is unclear in crucial respects and it does not explain how the stimulus produces the effects.

We could ignore the symbiotic hypothesis and assert merely that the Silverman method stimulates unconscious fantasies of some sort or other. It would then be equally unclear, or even more unclear, how the stimulation of the fantasies would cause either a remedial or deleterious effect on schizophrenia. Finally, if I understand Silverman's argument, he infers from the proposition that the stimulation of unconscious fantasies enhances or diminishes psychopathology in schizophrenics the additional proposition that psychopathology is rooted in unconscious conflict. That inference, however, is unwarranted. The fact that a certain sort of treatment affects a certain type of disorder is not by itself good evidence that the disorder has a certain type of cause. Drugs can favorably affect certain types of depression and anxiety states, as can cognitive and behavioral therapy, but successful treatment is not necessarily evidence that the depression or anxiety had a biological (as opposed to an environmental or cognitive) cause. In the case of schizophrenia, the effects of psychotropic drugs are often taken as evidence for a certain type of etiology, but here there is a chain of inferences with each assumption supported by specific evidence.

In sum, although I do not want to place too much stress on this, I think there is reason to question the move from "Silverman's hypotheses provide the only available explanation of his data" to "Silverman's hypotheses are warranted." His dynamic hypotheses are unsatisfactory in crucial respects: some are unclear, others are antecedently implausible, and some are both. The main problems with his interpretation of his research, however, are those discussed earlier. These include doubts about the evidence of subliminal phenomena, questions about his measures of psychopathology, and, most of all, the doubts raised by failures at attempted replications. I think it would be premature, then, to conclude that Silverman's experiments have corroborated certain Freudian hypotheses. Future results, of course, might yield a different verdict. It should also be noted that Silverman poses a problem for philosophers who claim, without qualification, that the psychoanalytic enterprise is pseudoscientific. He tried to obtain empirical evidence for psychoanalytic hypotheses through a long series of experiments and he made an honest effort to reply to many of his critics.

The Connection Principle

The research to be considered later concerns subliminal perception and the so-called cognitive unconscious. Before looking at the empirical and conceptual details, I want to consider a question about the nature of the independent variables needed to explain the phenomena: Are they mental? If they are generally not, then the connection between the experimental results and Freudian theory becomes tenuous. For example, Dixon (1971) proposes a physiological explanation for subliminal perception; if that explanation were the best one for all subliminal perception experiments, that would appear to render superfluous the postulation of unconscious mental events, at least in explaining the results of these experiments. Dixon's account would appear to be challenged by subsequent research, such as the work on semantic priming (Marcel 1983). However, the interpretation of these and other cognitivist experiments has been thrown in doubt by an ontological argument developed by John Searle.

Searle (1992) discusses the question of what distinguishes within the class of unconscious states the mental from the non-mental. This is an old issue in American psychology. See, for example, Fuller's discussion (1986, 59) of the early American functionalists. One, James Angell, is quoted as saying in his 1904 textbook, that the unconscious is "practically synonymous with the physiological." Freud also implicitly raises the issue when he discusses the origin of anxiety: "If we go further and enquire into the origin of that anxiety—and of affects in general—we shall be leaving the realm of pure psychology and entering the borderland of physiology" (1926, *S.E.* 10:93).

How do we identify the border and referred to by Freud? Searle's initial proposal (but not the one he ends up with) is that unconscious intentional mental states, besides being intrinsically mental, must have what he calls "aspectual shape" (1992, 155). What this means is not entirely clear, but it seems clear enough in simple cases of conscious mental states. Suppose that I consciously desire a glass of water. Although I know that water is H_2O, I am not desiring a glass of H_2O. I am not consciously thinking of water in that way. I see a friend coming down the street. I may believe that he is my best friend, that he is the smartest person I know, and that he has proved an important theorem. Yet, if none of these things occur to me while I watch him, I may see him simply as a man walking down the street. In seeing him in this way, and not in some other way, we might say: I am seeing him "under an aspect." To use Searle's terminology, my seeing has "aspectual shape." In the same way, my desiring, hoping, believing, and fearing something also have aspectual shape.

What about pains? I have a pain in my left shoulder. What is its aspectual shape? If it has none, then we need a different criterion for deciding whether pains are mental. However, this added bit of complexity does not affect Searle's argument, which concerns only "intentional" mental states or processes. These include only those directed at something, such as my believing that the rain will stop, or my hoping or fearing that it will.

When such states are conscious, they have aspectual shape, but, Searle argues (1990, 633), when a state is completely unconscious, there is no aspectual shape that is manifest, so to speak, then and there. However, most of my beliefs, desires, etc. are unconscious most of the time (or, in Freudian terminology, they are in the pre-conscious). I have long believed, for example, that Denver is in Colorado, but I have been consciously aware of this thought only rarely. It looks, then, that on the aspectual shape criterion, most of my so-called mental states will not qualify as being mental. Searle, however, does not draw this conclusion. Instead, he asks: What sense are we attaching to the notion of the unconscious in such cases as my belief about Denver when the belief is not in consciousness?

Searle's answer is that we can attach to it the following "perfectly adequate sense" (1990, 634): The attribution of unconscious intentionality to the neurophysiology is the attribution of a capacity to cause that state in a conscious form. There is one qualification, however, and that is that the unconscious intentionality might have the capacity to cause an unconscious action without causing a conscious mental event.

Searle concludes, then, with what he calls the "connection principle": All unconscious intentional mental states are in principle accessible to consciousness(1992, 156). In this view, there can be "shallow" unconscious mental states (including most of my beliefs and desires that are only occasionally conscious), but there can be no "deep unconscious." How does this affect Freudian theory?

In defense of Freud, we could challenge Searle's claim that at the unconscious level there is only the neurophysiological architecture and purely neurophysiological events. We could try to argue, instead, that there are both mental and neurophysiological events occurring at the unconscious level. Searle interprets (1990, 634) Freud as saying exactly that, but dismisses this position as postulating an unacceptable dualism. Whether or not this was Freud's position, a contemporary Freudian can reject it without rejecting the rest of Freudian theory. Such a Freudian might or might not adopt materialism. He or she could hold that *conscious* mental events have irreducible mentalistic properties, so at the conscious level, there would still be a dualism of properties. There remains, however, the problem that the connection principle apparently poses for the postulation of a deep unconscious, assuming that Searle is correct in rejecting what he takes to be Freud's position.

The most obvious way to defend Freud is to argue that the sorts of unconscious states and events that his theory postulates *are* in principle accessible to consciousness. One can speak here of a "blockage" in exactly the way Searle himself does (1992, 163). Even if psychoanalysis were utterly incapable of making repressed wishes conscious, we could still say that such wishes could enter consciousness if they were not stifled by anxiety. Searle, moreover, does not disagree. He agrees (1992, 172–173) that repressed desires are cases of a "shallow unconscious." In this respect, he holds, the Freudian notion of the unconscious is quite unlike the cognitive science notion.

The conflict between Freudian theory and the connection principle, then, is only apparent. Once "in principle" is explained in the way Searle explains it, a Freudian can consistently postulate an unconscious that is in some sense "deep," and yet allow that it is in principle accessible to consciousness. Still, trouble may lie ahead if a Freudian tries to incorporate into Freudian theory certain elements from current cognitive science. See, for example, Edelson's (1988) discussion of transformational grammar and Freud's theory of dreams. It might be useful, then, to ask about the implications of the connection principle for future Freudian cognitive research and for current cognitive science results that are alleged to support Freud.

One could reply to Searle that he is merely making a terminological suggestion about how to use the term "mental" (Chomsky 1990; Editorial Commentary 1990). Cognitivists who postulate a deep unconscious, then, would merely have to refrain from applying the term "mental" in Searle's new sense. Why would this terminological restriction matter?

Searle's reply to the charge of making a verbal recommendation (1990, 634) is that he could make his point without using the term "mental" at all. His point is that there is a certain apparatus of intentionalistic causal explanation employed in cognitive science. If you give up on this apparatus, then in specifying "rules" (such as rules of universal grammar), you are not specifying a cause of cognitions. You are merely specifying an association pattern.

This reply is not adequate as it stands. Why are cognitive psychologists giving up on the intentionalistic causal apparatus when they posit a deep unconscious? Searle's answer appears to be (1990, 633) that the apparatus presupposes aspectual shape, and there is no aspectual shape at the level of the deep unconscious. However, there is no aspectual shape at the shallow unconscious level either. So why are we not prohibited from specifying shallow unconscious mentalistic causes? There is a difference between the two levels: states at the shallow unconscious level have the capacity in principle to enter consciousness; states at the deep level lack this capacity. This is not a difference, however, of aspectual shape.

To focus the issue, consider the research on semantic priming (Marcel 1983) alluded to earlier. Research has shown that when color words are presented supraliminally, the color-naming reaction time decreases when the preceding word is congruent and increases when it is incongruent. For example, the color word is "congruent" when the color presented is blue and the preceding word is "blue," and incongruent when the same color is preceded by the word "red." There is, then, a priming effect when the preceding color word is congruent. In the Marcel (1983) study, this same priming effect occurred when the congruent color terms were masked and presented subliminally.

Suppose that Marcel's subjects are not suffering from any blockage, and yet cannot even in principle become aware of the process by which they recognized the meaning of the words presented subliminally. As far as we know, this inability in principle would not prevent the process from affecting the reaction time of the subjects. We might say that even though the process was causal, it was not mental. But that seems arbitrary. As Eagle (1987, 159) notes, even though the subjects were not consciously aware of the priming words, they processed the information presented "up to the semantic level." Thus, one could argue as follows: Assuming that mental events occur when we recognize the meaning of words that we are conscious of, there is reason to believe that they also occur when we unconsciously process information about the meaning of color terms presented subliminally. Postulating mental events in the latter case permits us to give the same kind of explanation of the priming effect when the congruent terms are masked as when they are presented supraliminally.

Searle might say that even if we call the process "mental," it is not intentional. So we do not have here a case of intentional causation. However, it would then appear that he is stipulatively defining "intentional." If the process is one that in principle we could become aware of, call it "intentional"; otherwise, withhold the term "intentional." There appears to be no substantive issue here.

Perhaps Marcel's experiments are not so clearly applicable here, given that they involve a process rather than an idea or the following of a rule. However, the same issues can be raised about following grammatical rules unconsciously. Suppose that I unconsciously follow two rules: one about avoiding split infinitives and one that is part of universal grammar. Searle says (1990, 633) that the first rule is not deep unconscious, but the rules of universal grammar are.

There is a difference between the two rules in that (we are assuming) only the first can enter consciousness, but that is not a difference in the capacity of either type of rule following to affect my behavior. So what is the basis for saying that following the first rule alone can make a difference to my linguistic behavior? Searle does not cite any. Perhaps the point is merely that only in the first case is there *mentalistic* or *intentional* causation. In that case, the point looks arbitrary, unless Searle is using either or both of these notions in a stipulative fashion. In the latter event, no substantive issue is raised.

Searle also points out (1992, 154) that there are two states within him: his belief that the Eiffel Tower is in Paris and axon myelination. Both have something to do with the brain, and neither is conscious (at least, the former is not conscious most of the time). What makes the one mental and the other not? Searle cannot say that only the belief has aspectual shape, for outside of consciousness, in his view, lies only the neurological. His answer, once again, is that only the belief can in principle enter consciousness. There is, however, an alternative answer. His axon myelination is a different sort of thing than a belief. Whereas beliefs that can in principle enter consciousness, those that cannot because of a blockage, and those that cannot for some other reason are still beliefs, axon myelination is not, nor is it a pain, a thought, a motive, etc. Of course, Searle can still ask: But, why do we ordinarily classify beliefs, motives, thoughts, emotions, pains, etc. as mental states? Philosophers have proposed various answers to this question, and perhaps none are satisfactory. The important point in this context is that adopting a criterion that eliminates some of the above from the category of the mental does not deprive them of their existence or their causal capacities. We can stipulate, for example, that beliefs that lack manifest aspectual shape are not "mental" (it does not matter whether this is the ordinary sense or a new, technical sense). In that case, preconscious beliefs, such as Searle's belief about the Eiffel Tower, will be non-mental. Or we can include these, but exclude those that cannot in principle enter consciousness. On either criterion, however, the proposition that an item is non-mental does not imply that it is not a belief, or that it does not exist, or that it does not play a causal role.

Putting aside issues about the implications of the connection principle, is there not good reason to have doubts about some of the items postulated by cognitive scientists, say the language of thought or implicit knowledge of a universal grammar? I think there are, although I am taking no stand on which are the dubious items. As Searle would agree, however, the empirical reasons for being skeptical, as well as the epistemological reasons (insofar as Searle's critics rely on a dubious use of inference to the best explanation), are separate from doubts generated by the connection principle.

Subliminal Perception and the Cognitive Unconscious

The next so-called research program is really a set of such programs. What they have in common is the study of the so-called "cognitive unconscious." With a few exceptions (e.g., Blum 1954), the authors of these studies were not trying to test Freudian hypotheses; however, some of the experimental results, it is argued (Erdelyi 1985), support Freud's views about the unconscious and repression. The studies include those from the perceptual defense, subliminal perception, and semantic priming paradigms. In a broad sense, most or all of these involve what is alleged to be subliminal perception.

In a typical perceptual defense experiment, stimulus words are presented to the subjects in a tachistoscope. A word is said to have a higher threshold if recognition required a greater number of tachistoscopic exposures. For example, a subject might require more exposures before recognizing a negative word, such as "raped" or "whore." As Postman (1953) notes, the term "perceptual defense" was introduced to refer to the results of such experiments, whether or not the subjects unconsciously defended against negative stimuli. Some investigators (e.g., Postman, Bronson, and Gropper 1953) explicitly challenged the idea that any sort of defense on the part of the subjects had to be postulated to account for the experimental results. Furthermore, in an early review, Brown (1961) canvassed 10 different explanations of perceptual defense, and noted that additional explanations were available in the literature. The Freudian explanation, then, was but one of a number of competing explanations.

In the 1960s new methodological difficulties were uncovered in perceptual defense research: an important one was that of separating perceptual from response factors. Dixon (1971) reviews this issue and others; he concludes that in later research the main problems had been overcome and that the existence of subliminal perception had been demonstrated.

In the 1980s, Marcel (1983) and others who study semantic priming have used a masking procedure, as noted earlier, to insure that their experimental stimuli are indeed subliminal. Some of these studies are quite rigorous and appear to provide additional evidence of subliminal perception. Nevertheless, there is still controversy about which, if any, of the vast number of subliminal perception experiments provide firm evidence that the phenomenon occurs (Holender, 1986). If the skeptics are right, then the experiments in question provide no evidence for a Freudian unconscious. However, because I doubt that the anti-Freudian can win on this issue (e.g. see the response of Dixon 1986 and others to Holender, 1986), I propose to bracket the entire question. Let us ask: *If* some experiments have shown the existence of subliminal perception, do they also support Freud's views about the unconscious? That depends on exactly what a Freudian unconscious is said to be.

Many non-Freudian theories imply the existence of mental events, states, or processes that are in some sense "unconscious." Freudian theory, however, postulates a *dynamic* unconscious: it links mental items, such as urges, wishes and desires, to both the mental apparatus postulated by Freud (the id, the ego, and the superego) and to repression. In the Freudian view, instinctual urges and wishes of the id persist in the unconscious from infancy and continually strive to force their way into consciousness. What generally prevents their emergence is the operation of repression or some other defense mechanism. One could argue that it is unnecessary to link the Freudian unconscious to the mental apparatus; after all, Freud talked about unconscious mental phenomena before he developed his structural theory. Even so, as Eagle (1987) cogently argues, there still are substantial differences between the sort of unconscious postulated by cognitive psychologists and a Freudian unconscious. One difference concerns the sort of items said to be unconscious. In the

Freudian view, it is instinctual urges, wishes, and desires; in the cognitive view, it is thought processes and ideas. Related to this difference is a second one: the Freudian items are characterized by such primary processes as irrationality, symbolization, condensation, and displacement; the cognitive items are thought of as intelligent and rational. A third difference is that the Freudian items are kept out of consciousness because of repression or the operation of other defenses. A fourth difference is that psychoanalytic therapy is generally needed to recover the Freudian unconscious contents but not, in most cognitive theories, for items in the cognitive unconscious. A fifth difference is that the Freudian items are recoverable, that is, they can emerge into consciousness if psychoanalytic therapy is successful; items in the cognitive unconscious are generally not recoverable.

Some of these contrasts can be challenged. Eagle himself (1987, 165) notes that recoverability may not mark an important difference if, as some psychologists hold, what "emerges" into consciousness in the Freudian view is not really identical with the original repressed contents. Also, the first contrast needs to be qualified. In the Freudian view, there are in the unconscious instinctual urges, but there are also repressed wishes, and these items have content. In this respect, they are like the unconscious ideas postulated by cognitive psychologists. Moreover, the unconscious ideas of the cognitive psychologists are only rational in a narrow sense. Because they are not recoverable, the subject cannot reflect on them and modify or discard them if the evidence warrants. Nevertheless, there remain the other aforementioned, important differences between the Freudian dynamic unconscious and the unconscious talked about by cognitive psychologists. It is also true, as Eagle notes, that more recent psychoanalytic formulations which talk about unconscious rules or "grim beliefs" are closer to cognitive formulations, but to that extent they also differ from Freudian theory.

One could narrow the differences between the Freudian and cognitive unconscious if, as Erdelyi (1985) suggests, the former is separated not only from the Freudian mental apparatus and psychoanalytic therapy but also from repression. Erdelyi (61) points out that Freud used the term "unconscious" in three distinct senses:

the descriptive, dynamic, and systemic senses. In the first sense, the term refers to anything psychoanalytic that is not in consciousness. For example, if I remember where I placed my keys but am not now thinking of their location, the memory is currently unconscious. Almost all of my beliefs are "unconscious" in this sense. There is, however, nothing distinctively Freudian or especially controversial about postulating the existence of the unconscious in this descriptive sense.

In the third sense (the systemic sense), the unconscious is said to be a system (structure, organization) of the mind. Some writers use the "unconscious" in this sense to refer to an entity, or part of an entity. Erdelyi (1985, 64–65) takes the position that the systemic unconscious is, in effect, abolished by Freud in *The Ego and the Id* (1923, *S.E.*, 19:12–59.) and is incorporated into his structural model as the id. Its existence need not be demonstrated in order to demonstrate Freudian unconscious mentation. What *is* at issue is the existence of the "unconscious" in Freud's second sense, the dynamic sense (or the unconscious proper). Unfortunately, Erdelyi notes, Freud defines the "dynamic unconscious" in two senses (we now have four senses).

In the second (dynamic) sense, there is a dynamic unconscious exactly if there are normal events or states that are not only outside of consciousness but also relatively inaccessible. In the second and stronger sense, the dynamic unconscious is not only relatively inaccessible; it is also *repressed* from consciousness. Erdelyi (1985, 63–64) holds that (*a*) the Freudian texts do not allow a clear choice between the weaker and stronger senses of "dynamic unconscious" and (*b*) we should separate the issue of the existence of the unconscious (the inaccessible) from the issue of why something is unconscious. Consequently, he adopts the weaker definition, the one that does not require that inaccessible mental events be repressed. If we use this definition, then, subject to several qualifications, the experiments of Marcel (1980, 1983) and others provide evidence that there is a dynamic unconscious. Two qualifications have already been mentioned: assuming that (1) the stimuli presented in the experiments are subliminal and (2) that the subjects are experiencing *mental* events that are not in consciousness. A third qualification is that the experimental results be replicated. Assuming that these three conditions are met, we would appear to have good reason to postulate a "dynamic" unconscious. What, however, are we postulating? It is not being said or implied that the Freudian mental apparatus, the id, ego, and superego, exists, or that there are items that were once in consciousness but are now repressed. Nor are we hypothesizing that there are mental contents that can be brought to consciousness only with the aid of psychoanalytic therapy. We are saying merely that there are mental events outside of consciousness that have an effect on behavior or other mental events—Erdelyi (1985, 64) includes being "active" as part of the definition of "dynamic"—and that such events are not readily accessible. So if optical rules of scaling or deep syntactic structures, to take two of Erdelyi's examples (63), are inaccessible psychic contents and make some causal difference, then there is a dynamic unconscious.

There is, then, nothing distinctively Freudian about postulating a "dynamic unconscious" in this sense. Even if one of the non-Freudian theories discussed by Brown (1961) correctly explains some of the perceptual defense effects, the inaccessible mental events of the subjects would qualify as constituting a dynamic unconscious. In fact, there is no need to appeal to any experimental results. People often have long term memories that influence their behavior but are relatively inaccessible. That alone appears sufficient for the existence of a "dynamic unconscious" as defined by Erdelyi. I am not saying, incidentally, that he is misreading Freud; rather, if Freud used the concept as defined by Erdelyi, then so, too, have non-Freudian theorists even if they used different terms. Merely asserting the existence of active mental events that are relatively inaccessible is not to assert any thing peculiar to Freudian theory. Erdelyi appears to agree with this point. He notes that Freud's contribution was not the discovery of the unconscious, but what could be done with it (1985, 57). Freud developed various hypotheses, of course, about the causal role of the unconscious in the etiology of neurosis, in producing slips, and in generating dreams. These hypotheses, however, are generally not tested by experiments in subliminal perception. I conclude, then, that even if the results of subliminal perception experiments confirm the existence of a "dynamic unconscious" in Erdelyi's sense, that fact does not support Freudian theory.

Some writers (e.g., Kline 1981; Farrell 1981) have also argued that perceptual defense experiments demonstrate the existence of re-pression. Whether that is true depends partly on how we use the term "repression." As I pointed out in Erwin (1984a), Freud intro-duced the term "defense" in 1894 to describe the ego's struggle against painful ideas or affects. He later substituted the term "repres-sion" for that of "defense." Later still, in 1926, Freud reverted to his earlier use of the concept of defense to cover all processes that serve the same purpose: the protection of the ego against instinctual de-mands. The term "repression" was then used in a narrower sense to cover only one of these definitive processes. In *Inhibitions, Symptoms and Anxiety* (1926, *S.E.*, 20:87–174), Freud notes his earlier usage, but recommends using "repression" henceforth to cover only one of the defenses. As to the wider category, Freud makes it clear in the same essay (164) that the concept of defense applies to those processes having a particular purpose: the protection of the ego against the instinctual demands of the id. The concept of defense is thus linked by Freud to his concept of the mental apparatus.

If we retain this linkage, then, as I argued in Erwin (1984a), perceptual defense experiments, and subliminal perception experi-ments in general, fail to demonstrate the existence of Freudian defenses (including that of repression).

Erdelyi (1985, 220), however, recommends breaking this linkage; he notes that the structural model was not introduced until 1923, but that the concepts of defenses and repression were used by Freud much earlier. Erdelyi also notes that Freud did not consistently fol-low his own recommendation of using "repression" to designate just one of the defenses. So Erdelyi generally uses "repression" to mean "defense." How, then, are we to interpret "repression ("defense") in this wider sense? Erdelyi (220) notes that contemporary analysts (e.g. Brenner 1973) include four elements in the concept of repres-sion (defense). The first is, distorting or outrightly rejecting from consciousness some feature of reality; the second is, that the distortion occur for the purpose of avoiding the unbearable psychological pain it would provoke in consciousness; the third is, defense mechanisms are often conceived of as ego devices; and the fourth is, the devices are prototypically unconscious. Erdelyi (220) judges that the second two components are not crucial and so he recommends deleting them as well as the linkage to the Freudian mental apparatus. Repression (defense) can occur, then, even if there is no id, ego, and superego and even if the person is conscious of the repression. All that is needed is that the person deliberately keep something out of consciousness for the purpose of avoiding psychological pain. If we use the repression concept in this way, does it apply to what is studied in perceptual defense experiments? After a subtle and complex discussion of the issues, Erdelyi concludes (258) that, although it is plausible to think that the mechanisms used by subjects in perceptual defense experiments are deployed in order to defend against averse stimuli, this fact has not been demonstrated experimentally. What is in doubt (256) is whether the perception of emotional stimuli is disrupted *because* of intentional rejection by the perceiver.

Despite this doubt, Erdelyi concludes that there is nonexperimental evidence of repression. Clearly, people sometimes forget traumatic events and later remember not only the events but the defensive intention to forget. Even here, a doubt can be raised, as Erdelyi notes (259). In explaining their own behavior, people often theorize incorrectly about why they did something, as shown in numerous studies reviewed by Nisbett and Ross (1980). When a person seems to remember that he or she intentionally kept something out of unconsciousness, then, the person may be misremembering. Still, is it really plausible to dismiss every single such seeming memory of intentional forgetting? It seems to me that it is not, so I agree with Erdelyi's conclusion: "repression" in his sense does occur. In fact, the case for its occurrence need not rely on fallible memories. For the present, I decide to turn my head from an unpleasant scene; I read a book to forget about a failed love affair; or I think about something pleasant in order to avoid thinking about my current problems. All such cases qualify as "repression" in Erdelyi's sense: I intentionally keep something out of consciousness in order to avoid psychological pain. There is, then, obviously nothing distinctively Freudian about this process.

If Erdelyi strips too much from the concept of repression to leave its Freudian identity intact, we can add back in some other element. For example, David Holmes (1990) contends, on the basis of a review of 60 years of published research, that the Freudian concept of repression has three elements: (1) repression is the selective forgetting of materials that cause the individual pain; (2) it is not under voluntary control; and (3) repressed material is not lost but is stored in the unconscious and can be returned to consciousness if the anxiety that is associated with the memory is removed (1915, *S.E.*, 14:141–158).

Here we have a concept that *is* distinctively Freudian. It does not, for example, apply to activities such as reading a book to forget a failed love affair. These activities are voluntary and, consequently, do not meet condition (*2*). It is also true, however, that the concept does not automatically apply to cases commonly interpreted as instances of repression. If I forget something unpleasant that occurred many years ago and later recall it without any negative affect, that does not necessarily mean I repressed the memory of the event. As Holmes (1990, 88–89) notes, such cases are not even evidence of repression; they are more plausibly explained in terms of the normal differential decline of affect associated with pleasant and unpleasant experiences and the effects those declines have on recall.

There is a long history of experimental attempts to establish the existence of Freudian repression. Most have concerned "repression proper"—the individual consciously recognizes something as threatening (anxiety-provoking) and then represses the thought to avoid the anxiety; some have also dealt with "primary repression"—the threatening material is relegated to the unconscious before it is consciously recognized as stressful. Some of these studies were reviewed in chapter 4, pp. 159–165. In many of the studies, the experimenters acted as if they were employing the evidential standard I referred to (in chapter 3) as "inference to the best explanation" (or Lycan's version of the rule). They generated experimental data consistent with a repression interpretation; they then reasoned that the

Freudian explanation was the only one available; and they concluded that they had provided evidence of repression. For example, in early experiments (Jerslid 1931; Meltzer 1931; Stagner 1931), investigators compared recall of unpleasant and pleasant experiences. Where the former were found to be less likely to be recalled, the finding was consistent with a Freudian interpretation, but no attempt was made to show that repression actually caused the recall differentials. Subsequent studies (e.g., Menzies 1936) found that nonrepression factors, such as the intensity of the affect, were at least as likely, if not more likely, to have caused the differentials.

In certain other experiments, non-Freudian explanations were known to the experimenters, but no attempt was made to rule them out. In short, the differential standard defended in chapter 2 was not met.

Holmes (1990) has an excellent review of the history of the experimental attempts to establish the existence of Freudian repression. As he persuasively argues, these attempts have all failed. As of now there is no experimental evidence that Freudian repression exists if we include within the concept the three elements identified by Holmes. Nor is there persuasive nonexperimental evidence that these three conditions are met.

We might still try to steer between the account of repression given by Holmes (1990) and the weaker version given by Erdelyi (1985). However, it is difficult to find any such middle account such that (1) the concept of repression is distinctively Freudian and (2) it has been shown either experimentally or through clinical observation to apply to something real.

Conclusion

In some sense, there is a convergence between research in cognitive psychology and research by Freudians. After all, cognitivists who work in the area of subliminal perception invoke not only conscious mental events but also ones that are unconscious. Even among some behavior therapists, there is an increasing appeal to mental events that in some sense are "unconscious." Do the results of cognitive and behavior therapy experiments, however, *confirm* any part of Freudian theory? There will remain uncertainty about this issue so long as there is uncertainty about exactly which elements are to be included in the Freudian concepts of the unconscious and repression. Despite this uncertainty, I am inclined to argue, as Eagle (1987) does, that there are important disanalogies between the unconscious postulated by Freudian theory and that postulated by cognitivists and behavior therapists. If one diminishes the disanalogies, as Erdelyi does (1985), by deleting some of the important characteristics that Freudians attribute to unconscious mentation, then what is left is a concept of the unconscious that is not distinctively Freudian. As I argued earlier, the exact same point applies to Erdelyi's concept of repression. If one uses the distinctively Freudian concept of repression employed by Holmes (1990), then there is no firm evidence that repression occurs. Finally, even if cognitivists or behavior therapists were to have confirmed the existence of a distinctively Freudian unconscious or Freudian repression, that would be very far from establishing that the unconscious or repression plays the causal role laid out by Freudian theory concerning the etiology of neuroses, slips and dreams.

Pathogenic Beliefs

The final research program to be considered is both Freudian and cognitive. As Weiss, et al. (1986, chapter 2), point out, Freud, in his early writings, theorizes that the unconscious mental life of an individual is regulated by *automatic* processes. For example, the id has impulses that are regulated by the pleasure principle and automatically seeks immediate gratification for them. In his later writings (e.g., the *Outlines of Psychoanalysis,* unfinished), Freud departs from this idea of automatic functioning and conjectures that a person is able unconsciously to exert some control over his behavior in accordance with his unconscious thoughts, beliefs, and assessments of current reality. This second view, although it appeals to unconscious mental processes, oedipal urges, and the like, is a cognitive theory of sorts insofar as it refers to beliefs, plans, and thoughts.

Weiss et al. (1986, 5) refers to the early Freudian view as "the hypothesis of automatic functioning": it holds that all or almost all unconscious mental activity is derived from the dynamic interplay of psychic forces beyond the patient's control and without regard for his or her thoughts, beliefs, or assessments of current reality. A rival hypothesis, referred to as "the higher mental functioning hypothesis" (26), does not rule out all automatic functioning of the unconscious, but does hold that a significant part of the patient's unconscious mental life is not determined automatically but rather is controlled by unconscious thoughts and decisions. Weiss and his colleagues refer (340) to their theory as a version of the Higher Mental Functioning Hypothesis. In fact, their theory includes far more than this one hypothesis and, as the authors note, although it draws on suggestions of Freud, it also goes beyond even later Freudian theory. Because the theory was originally formulated by Weiss, I shall refer to it as "Weissian theory" even though his colleagues helped to develop and test it.

As Weiss et al. note (4), the theory is both Freudian and new. The part that is new, although it has a cognitive component (it makes reference to beliefs, plans, etc.), is at least partly psychoanalytic in nature. One part of the theory concerns etiology: all kinds of psychopathology are said to be rooted in pathogenic beliefs that are unconscious (325). Such beliefs are the essential element, the sine qua non of psychopathology, and variations in psychopathology reflect variations in pathogenic beliefs (325).

The theory assumes, further, that pathogenic beliefs play a crucial role in the maintenance, not merely the origin, of all psychopathology, and not just of neuroses and perversion. Such beliefs might be about dangers thought to be connected to oedipal urges, but they might also be about many other things not specifically mentioned by Freud. A specifically Freudian example (Weiss et al. 1986, 6) is the male's belief that if he maintains a sexual interest in his mother, he will be castrated by his father. Another example, attributed to a client, Miss P., is that she does not deserve her parents' care and attention, and that if she were to seek more than minimal care from them, she would endanger herself either by burdening them or by provoking further rejection from them (13). A person acquires his or her pathogenic beliefs in early childhood by inference from experience, although the inferences are not necessarily warranted (7). These beliefs are "warded off," that is, repressed, and typically make an analytic patient miserable; therefore the patient unconsciously wishes to disconfirm them even though he or she is not conscious of them.

Another component of Weissian theory concerns the control which we exercise over our unconscious mental processes. In contrast to the automatic functioning hypothesis, the theory holds that we do have a high degree of control over our unconscious urges and beliefs. Each of us has an unconscious plan for getting rid of our pathogenic beliefs. The patient who comes to psychoanalysis tries to eliminate the beliefs by testing them against the reactions of the analyst. If the analyst says or does certain types of things, the belief will appear (to the patient) to be disconfirmed; other types of responses will fail to have that effect and may even "confirm" the patient's unconscious beliefs. In an analysis that is progressing well, the patient changes his or her pathogenic beliefs and so becomes less frightened of the dangers they foretell (172). Consequently, the patient may decide that he or she can safely experience certain previously repressed contents and so lifts the repressions that had kept such contents in the unconscious. One prediction derived from the theory is that such "lifting of repressions" often occurs even in the absence of interpretation by the analyst. Another is that the patient will experience only a little anxiety about a content as it becomes conscious (172). Both of these predictions are incompatible with the automatic functioning hypothesis.

Weissian theory is also about the therapeutic process and has implications for treatment. The therapeutic process is said to be in essence one in which the patient becomes aware of his or her pathogenic beliefs. It is also a process by which the patient works to change the beliefs in two ways: (1) by testing them unconsciously in relation to the analyst, and (2) by assimilating insight into them conveyed by the analysts' interpretations (329). The lesson for the analyst is that, at various points in the treatment, he or she should infer the patient's unconscious plans and help him or her to carry them out (333). For example, if a patient is working unconsciously to overcome his irrational worries about his wife, the analyst should help him to understand and overcome these worries.

The aforementioned description covers most of the essentials of Weissian theory, but it leaves out many details that enrich the theory (for a more complete description, see part I of Weiss et al. 1986).

In certain places, Weiss et al. (1986) suggest a commitment to belief in the Freudian mental apparatus. For example, they say that pathogenic beliefs, in the language of Freud's structural model, are part of the unconscious ego (7). However, it appears that most or all of Weissian theory might be true even if there is no id, ego, and superego. Suppose, then, that we separate Freud's structural model and the idea of a pathogenic belief. In that case, there is an important similarity between part of Weissian theory and theories put forth by rational emotive therapists (Ellis 1993), cognitive therapists (e.g., Beck 1976) and cognitive behavior therapists (e.g., Meichenbaum 1977). These other theorists typically agree that beliefs that are "unconscious" in the minimal sense of our not being easily able to become aware of them play a role in the maintenance of certain psychological disorders. So the hypothesis that there are "pathogenic beliefs" in this minimal sense is not peculiar to either Freudian or Weissian theory; indeed, it would seem a platitude to many clinical psychologists. There is, however, much more to Weissian theory than the claim that unconscious beliefs play a role in the development of psychopathology. As indicated earlier, some of these beliefs are held by Weiss et al. to concern oedipal urges. Furthermore, pathogenic beliefs are said to develop in childhood and to play an essential role in the development of *all* types of psychopathology. These ideas, as well as the Weissian hypotheses about unconscious plans and the nature of the therapeutic process, are not typically put forth by cognitivists, rational emotive therapists, or cognitive behaviorists.

Before discussing the evidence for Weissian theory, there are two issues that I will mention but not pursue. Assuming that I sometimes have free choice, I can often control my actions if they are a function of my conscious beliefs and motives. However, if Weiss et al. are right in holding that some of my actions are caused by beliefs and motives that I have never been conscious of, or least not conscious of since early childhood, do I have control over *these* sorts of actions? Does not the fact that the determining beliefs and motives are repressed remove them and the associated actions from my control? According to standard Freudian theory, I gain control by undergoing psychoanalysis and having my repressed wishes made conscious. At least if all goes well, I gain control *after* the repressions are lifted. Weiss, et al., however, postulates a high degree of control before the lifting of repressions. I suppose that Weiss et al. would reply that my having an unconscious plan gives me control over my unconscious beliefs and desires. However, I have no access to that plan either. So I am unclear how its existence gives me control over my repressed wishes.

The second issue concerns the motivation to disconfirm pathogenic beliefs. Weiss et al. note (8) that the analytic patient is made miserable by his or her pathogenic beliefs and "therefore" unconsciously wishes to disconfirm them. There appears to be a gap in the argument here. I have a number of conscious beliefs that distress me, for example, that I and other people will eventually die, that AIDS and cancer persist, that poverty taints the lives of millions of people, etc. Yet, I have no motivation whatsoever to disconfirm these beliefs. If I could, I would change the world so that, for example, my death would not be inevitable, but given the evidence now available to me, I have no desire to stop believing in my mortality. Why should I want to cease believing a proposition that I think is amply confirmed by empirical evidence? Perhaps what is crucial about pathogenic belief is that I do not, even unconsciously, think that they are supported by good evidence. Why, however, do I persist, then, in holding these beliefs? Why not suspend judgment about their truth or falsity? Moreover, what is the connection between my being made miserable by my pathogenic beliefs and my desire to disconfirm them? I think that Weiss et al. (341) hold that the typical patient realizes that there is a causal connection between having such beliefs and the development of his or her psychopathology. If that is what they hold, then I think that this is an implausible element at the core of their theory. Psychologists disagree about what causes neuroses and other psychological problems. However, if Weiss et al. are right, then everyone agrees with *their* etiologic theory, although unconsciously, insofar as it applies to their own case. That is, each of us not only has pathogenic beliefs (if we have any sort of psychopathology), but we also believe unconsciously that these beliefs are the root cause of our psychological troubles. We all duplicate at the unconscious level part of the theory that Weiss et al. hold consciously. I may misunderstand what they hold here, but if they do not hold the aforementioned view, then I do not see how they propose to explain the alleged widespread motivation to disconfirm pathogenic beliefs.

I am not certain that either of the above two points poses a serious objection to Weissian theory, but the issues raised do need clarification. I turn now to the evidence for the theory.

1. Weiss et al. (11) refer to "informal evidence" from process notes concerning case studies of analytic patients. As argued briefly in chapter 3, and in more detail in Grünbaum (1984), it is generally very difficult to confirm Freudian etiologic hypotheses by appealing to data taken from uncontrolled case studies. Apart from these general epistemological considerations, there is reason to doubt that any of the case studies described by Weiss et al. yield firm evidence for their theory. To illustrate, consider the case of Mrs. G. (17). Weiss et al. claim that the patient brought forth an important previously repressed beating fantasy without its being interpreted by the analyst. Their evidence for this claim is as follows. Toward the end of her second year of treatment, Mrs. G. remembered a short dream in which the analyst "does something to her." In a therapy session, in associating to the dream, she thought of several things that the analyst might do to her and mentioned this to the analyst. After a pause, the analyst asked: "Do you have any other ideas about what I might do to you?" The patient answered, with a laugh, "Well, you might turn me over your knee and spank me." How do Weiss et al. know that a preexisting unconscious fantasy about being beaten provoked this remark? It may be that Mrs. G. never had any such fantasy, but in free associating to the idea of her analyst "doing something to her" began to think of sexual activities, and eventually of being spanked. She might also have thought that the analyst himself would think of this possibility given his psychoanalytic views. Then, too, the tone in which the analyst's question was asked might have been (unwittingly) sexually suggestive. Any number of other things said during the first year of the analysis might also have prompted the remark. In short, the mere fact that Mrs. G. made the

comment in question gives us no reason to believe that prior to the session she had any unconscious beating fantasy.

In this case and the others that Weiss et al. describe, the inferences that they make about unconscious beliefs or desires may seem plausible if one is already committed to Freudian theory, but without a background of supporting evidence for that theory, they are merely conjectural; the inferences are not supported by any firm evidence. I will not try to show this for each case because I believe that Weiss et al. agree that the best evidence for their theories comes from the research findings reported in part 2 of Weiss et al. (1986). If the latter evidence is not firm, then it is unlikely that the less rigorous informal case studies will yield evidence of probative worth. I make no judgment, however, about a more modest claim: that the case studies have heuristic value and are sufficiently intriguing to justify the pursuance of the more rigorous research.

2. Weissian theory makes *general* claims about the behavior of patients in psychoanalysis, about the causes of *all* types of psychopathology (Weiss et al. 1986, 325) and about the motivation of *all* of us to change our pathogenic beliefs (341). It is imperative to ask, then, what was the number of people studied by Weiss and his fellow investigators? The answer: one. All of the empirical work reported in Weiss et al. was carried out on the psychoanalysis of a single patient, Mrs. C. (147). Even if there are no flaws in their procedures, then, their research does not provide strong support for any part of Weissian theory or any Freudian hypothesis. There may be areas in science, perhaps in investigations of the structure of a cell, where our background evidence licenses broad generalizations based on an N of 1. That kind of background evidence is lacking in this area. What, then, is the argument for concluding that what is true of Mrs. C. concerning the cause of her problems and her behavior in the therapy sessions is likely to be true of most of us? There is no such argument that is rationally compelling. At least none is presented in Sampson et al. (1986).

3. The analysis of Mrs. C was conducted entirely independently of the authors' research, which was based on process notes and verbatim transcripts taken from the completed analysis. One advantage of this procedure, as the authors note (150), is that the behavior of the subject was clearly not influenced by the theoretical expectations of

the investigators. (Neither the analysts nor the patient was familiar with Weissian theory.) One serious disadvantage, however, is that none of the various studies reported by Weiss et al. qualify as experimental, if we use the standards of, say, Campbell and Stanley (1963). There was, for example, no manipulation by the investigators of an independent variable; rather, the events being studied were already complete when the investigation began. I do not claim automatic disqualification of all causal inferences in such a retrospective study, but I have argued (see chapter 3) that confirmation of Freudian theoretical claims are especially difficult where the research is non-experimental. This point is independent of the previous one about the number of subjects studied. Still, I simply record the fact that the research was retrospective; I do not use this fact as the basis of any objections.

4. Weiss et al. were particularly interested in testing one psychoanalytic hypothesis (the automatic functioning hypothesis) against a rival psychoanalytic hypothesis (the higher mental functioning hypothesis). They may well have succeeded in their aim, that is, in showing that the latter fits their data better than the former. However, they also claim "strong support" (340) for their particular version of the higher mental functioning hypothesis and varying degrees of support for other components of Weissian theory (341). In any event, it is claims of confirmation, and not mere elevation of one Freudian hypothesis over another, that is of interest here. As argued in chapter 2, pp. 44–54, however, confirmation requires defeat of plausible rivals to the hypothesis being tested. Consequently, even if the authors' research were repeatedly replicated and had no additional flaws, confirmation would still not be forthcoming without the elimination of various non-Freudian rival clinical hypotheses about the origin and maintenance of certain types of psychological problems and others about the effectiveness of treatment. Such theories as Eysenck's (1983a) conditioning theory of etiology and treatment, Bandura's self-efficacy theory (1982), and Beck's (1976) account of the maintenance of depression are among those that would have to be considered.

5. As Weiss et al. note (238), it is crucial for their research project that they be able to discern the patient's therapeutic plan. There is a problem here because the plan is supposedly unconscious; hence,

they cannot obtain it merely by asking the patient. The authors purport to solve the problem by using the following method. First, the plan is divided into four components: (*a*) the patient's unconscious therapeutic goals; (*b*) obstructions; (*c*) test and test power (i.e., those trial actions unconsciously carried out by the patient to confirm or disconfirm his or her beliefs; and (*d*) test outcome and the plan compatibility of the intervention (i.e., the patient will either advance or retreat in certain ways depending on whether the analyst tends to confirm or disconfirm the pathogenic beliefs). The term "obstructions" in (*c*) refers to those unconscious pathogenic beliefs that the patient has repressed and is trying to reject (427, n. 4). In stage 2, clinical statements pertinent to each of the four components were developed by proposition-generating judges. In the case of Mrs. C., a highly experienced psychoanalyst generated plausible propositions for each component after reviewing the detailed process notes of the first 5 hours of her therapy. In the third and final stage, the array of generated propositions were presented to four judges who were advanced psychoanalytic candidates (251). The authors argue (238) that a high degree of reliability (as measured by the degree of agreement among the judges) demonstrates that the patient's plans may be inferred with "satisfactory objectivity" and that a high degree of reliability was found in the case of Mrs. C. and in a previous case, that of Miss K. There are several problems, however, with their argument.

(a) Establishing the presence of Mrs. C's pathogenic beliefs was of crucial importance for the overall research project. Yet the reliability coefficient for the four judges for this component of the alleged plan was remarkably low (14). The authors note (253) that if the ratings of two judges are excluded, the reliability coefficient for the remaining two judges rises to .80. No doubt. One can often finish with a high level of rates of agreement if one excludes the ratings of those who disagree.

It might seem unfair to stress the low reliability coefficient for the rating of pathogenic beliefs given that coefficients were high for the rest of the plan components. However, as previously noted, establishing the presence of Mrs. C's pathogenic beliefs is crucial for the entire research project. If there is no basis for attributing such unconscious beliefs to her, the hypotheses about the other plan components are placed in jeopardy.

(b) Even where the reliability coefficients were high, one or two cases are very weak evidence that the concepts in question can be reliably employed in a wide range of cases. The psychological literature is full of instances where rates of agreement were high for the application of diagnostic concepts in several cases, but later sank to miserably low levels.

(c) Even the repeated replications of the authors' findings would not necessarily strengthen their evidence for reliability. Consider the raters' unanimous agreement about the subject's overall goal. This unanimity looks impressive, but the raters were given five summary goal statements and were asked to choose one of them. What would have been the degree of agreement if they had been given, say, 25 goal statements? What would have been the results if they were merely given the process notes and were asked to formulate their own description of the patient's goals? Furthermore, the raters were all psychoanalytic candidates. How high would the degree of agreement have been if several critics of Freudian theory were added to the pool of judges?

(d) Even if all of the above problems are put aside, a serious one remains. The fact that the raters agreed about (most of) the components of Mrs. C's alleged plan is not evidence for the correctness of their opinions. Suppose, contrary to fact, that all four raters showed unanimous agreement about the presence of Mrs. C's pathogenic beliefs. Each would then have the same hypotheses about the presence of certain unconscious beliefs, but that is hardly evidence that the hypotheses in question are true.

(e) One of the pathogenic beliefs attributed to Mrs. C (258) is that she could devastate her father and cause him to lose control if she disagreed with him, criticized him, or held values different from his. The authors claim (265) that she tried to test this belief and other unconscious beliefs by eliciting responses from the analyst. They also claim (265) that these were demonstrable, immediate effects of a "passed" test, that is, one in which the analyst's response tended to disconfirm a pathogenic belief. A question could be raised about the occurrence of these short-term effects absent solid evidence of the validity (not merely the reliability) of the various tests used to measure the effects. I will not pursue this issue, but will inquire about the hypothesized antecedent causes, that is, the passing or failing of the tests. How did the authors determine when the analyst passed or failed the test being put to him (unconsciously) by Mrs. C.? As before, they relied on the ratings of judges. First, nine graduate students in psychology read verbatim transcripts of the first 100 sessions of Mrs. C's analysis and were instructed to identify segments in which she seemed to be pulling some response from the analyst. Eighty-seven incidents were considered by one or more rater to be of this type. In addition, 15 interchanges not selected were added for control purposes. Next, three psychoanalytically trained judges read a description of Mrs. C's case and were asked to identify which of the pool of 87 incidents (plus the 15 control segments) represented attempts by the patient to carry out central or key tests (258–259). A sample of 46 segments were selected by all three judges as key tests. Finally, four other psychoanalysts were asked to rate on a 7 point scale the extent to which the analyst passed the 46 key tests.

The authors give two examples (260–261) of the analyst's responses to the patient's tests. In the first instance, the judges rated him as passing the test and in the second as failing. In example 1, the patient expresses concern that the analyst may be impatient or may disapprove when she has nothing to say. The analyst responds by asking her what she imagines could happen if he were impatient or did disapprove. In example 2, the patient asks if it is better to force yourself to say something that you are not ready to say. The analyst responds: "Well, what was the rule I told you? Or what did I say was your job?" (261). These examples, the authors claim (261), can be understood as instances in which Mrs. C tests whether the analyst will be upset if she questions his authority. Well, they could be understood in this way, but another—and more straightforward—interpretation is that Mrs. C was not challenging the analyst's authority, but was merely seeking answers to the two questions that occurred to her. The reason given by the authors for preferring the first interpretation is that Mrs. C. had the unconscious belief that she would devastate her father if she disagreed with him. Even though I earlier questioned the evidence for this attribution, let us assume that she had the belief. Why is this assumption a reason for thinking that Mrs. C. had a similar unconscious belief about the analyst. After all, she did not, as far as is known, hold such a belief about people in general. Furthermore, even if she did have such a belief about the analyst, how do we know that she perceived his first response as neutral or disconfirmatory? Perhaps she perceived it as an implicit threat ("What do you imagine could happen then?") I have similar doubts about the second response. Depending on how she remembered or interpreted the rule given to her by the analyst, she could have interpreted his response as either confirming her belief about the effects of questioning his authority, or as being disconfirmatory or neutral.

I conclude that in neither case does the transcript provide evidence that Mrs. C. was trying to disconfirm a pathogenic belief about her father, even if we concede that she had the belief, nor does it provide evidence in either case that she perceived the analyst as passing her test in case 1 or failing it in case 2. The raters may have agreed in their opinions about these matters, but, once again, that is not a good reason to think that their opinions are correct.

(f) Finally, even if Mrs. C. had the unconscious beliefs attributed to her by the raters, several additional, crucial questions remain. First, how do we know that she repressed the beliefs, as opposed to her merely not being aware of them? Second, how do we know that they all originated in childhood? Third, how do we know that they were "pathogenic," that is, that they played an important causal role in either the origin or maintenance of Mrs. C's psychological problems? The only evidence offered to answer each of these questions is the agreement of the raters, who were guided by psychoanalytic theory. That is insufficient evidence, if it is any evidence at all.

Summary
The research of Weiss et al. (1986), as interesting and rigorous as it is in certain respects, does not confirm any part of Freudian theory. The main (but not only) problems are the reliance on the study of only one subject, the dependence on judges' ratings that have no independent confirmation, and the failure to rule out other theories of equal or greater plausibility.

The experimental research surveyed in this chapter and in chapter 4 have yielded very little support, if any, for Freudian theory. The implications of this finding are discussed in chapter 7, pp. 281–292. but first I want to consider (in chapter 6) the effectiveness of Freudian therapy.

Chapter 6
The Effectiveness of Psychoanalytic Therapy

Standard Psychoanalysis

Conceptual Questions

In evaluating Freudian therapy, we are venturing into an intellectual wilderness where empirical questions are often intertwined with complex conceptual, epistemological, and evaluative issues: the field of psychotherapy outcome research. Viewed from certain angles, a great deal of progress seems to have been made here in the last decade, at least if consensus is a reliable sign of progress. There are a lot of important issues about which almost everyone now agrees. Yet, it is disturbing to see that leading researchers in this area have fundamental disagreements about such basic items as the evaluation of research designs, the suitability of certain statistical techniques, and the very criteria for judging therapeutic success. To illustrate the great swings in opinions, Kazdin (1986, 61) points out that the study of Sloane et al (1975) has been frequently said to be one of the best, if not the best, psychotherapy outcome study ever produced, yet it has also been said to be one of the worst (Bandura 1978; Rachman and Wilson 1980). To take one more example, many reviewers (e.g. Lambert, Shapiro, and Bergin, 1986) have praised the meta-analyses of Smith, Glass, and Miller (1980); some (e.g., Fiske 1983) have even characterized the development of meta-analysis as "revolutionary." In contrast, Eysenck (1978) characterizes meta-analysis as an exercise in "mega-silliness" and (1988) refers to one facet of the meta-analytic argument of Smith, Glass, and Miller as indicative of the low state to which the whole field of psychotherapy research has sunk. When confronted with such deep disagreements, it is wise to proceed slowly and carefully.

The first thing that needs to be done is to specify the kind of therapy under discussion. In addition to "standard" (or "orthodox") psychoanalytic therapy, there are a number of related techniques typically referred to as "psychoanalytically, or psychodynamically oriented, psychotherapy," or sometimes just "dynamic therapy." I begin by discussing only standard psychoanalysis, and adopt, with one qualification, a characterization of it provided by White (1956, 322). He counts a therapy as "standard psychoanalysis" only if it has the following characteristics: (a) it involves the systematic use of free association, interpretation, and transference neurosis, and (b) it has the goal of uncovering and resolving the major emotional problems of the patient's childhood. White regards these conditions as both necessary and sufficient, but I think a time element needs to be added to distinguish standard psychoanalysis from the short term version. So I stipulate that a therapy qualifies as standard psychoanalysis if and only if it meets White's two conditions and also typically lasts 2 years or more. This definition will probably not fit some cases that others call "standard" psychoanalysis, but this problem is likely to arise for any precise definition of the concept. It is enough that the definition I am adopting marks off at least roughly the subject matter I want to discuss.

The next problem is to define "effectiveness." Here, I will be brief, ignoring certain subtleties. Let us say that a therapy was "effective" on a particular occasion if and only if it produced at least one therapeutic benefit, or at least contributed to that outcome. So, if a therapy made the client worse, or if it caused effects all of which were neither harmful nor beneficial, then it was ineffective. I assume, although this is a little oversimplified, that we are interested in therapeutic benefits for the person undergoing the therapy, even if someone else is paying for the treatment. I will say, then, that a therapy is "generally effective" if it typically produces one or more therapeutic benefits for certain types of clients. A therapy might have the capacity to produce good effects but typically fail to do so because it is generally used by inexperienced therapists, or in the case of psychoanalysis, because it is used with clients not suitable for analysis. Still, having such a capacity is not sufficient for being generally effective; it must also work in actual cases. Of course, we could also add, if the evidence warranted, the following comment: although the therapy is generally not effective, it very well might be if it were used properly. Finally, in speaking of a therapy being "generally effective," I do not mean effective for all or most clinical disorders. Rather, I mean that over a range of clients and circumstances, it tends to contribute to the production of at least one type of therapeutic benefit. As the point is sometimes put, we want to know if therapy X typically produces a certain type of benefit for a certain type of client when it is provided by a certain type of therapist in a certain type of clinical setting. There is room here for more clarification and precision, but I want to move quickly to the first substantive issue: Is there any objective way to determine whether an outcome really is beneficial? Many philosophers and psychotherapy researchers will say no; other will say yes but only if the standards for judging outcomes are relativized in some way.

Skepticism, Relativism, and Therapeutic Benefits

One way to approach this issue is to start with the goals of psychoanalysis and then to judge outcomes in terms of whether they have been met. What, however, about the starting point, the goals themselves? Can their "correctness" be established empirically? A common response is that this cannot be done. For example, Woolfolk (1992, 220) replies as follows to Hawkins' contention that the scientific question underlying every clinical assessment is what optimizes adjustment, adaptation, competence, or habilitation: "What Hawkins seems not to realize is that no experiment can establish the legitimacy or desirability of a *fundamental* goal, such as adjustment, adaption, competence, habilitation, or even happiness, for that matter." Woolfolk concludes that some aspect of psychotherapy must always be nonempirical. One could agree and still argue that ultimate choices about therapeutic goals can be defended in an a priori fashion, but many commentators appear to rule out that possibility as well. As Garfield and Bergin(1986) put it, "Recent progress in developing new and more effective techniques of psychotherapy has obscured the fact that subjective value decisions underlie the choice of techniques, the goals of change, and the assessment of what is a 'good' outcome" (16).

One reason for concluding that decisions about therapeutic goals and outcomes are subjective is the lack of agreement about standards for assessing outcome. For example, cognitive behavior therapists often use symptom remission without relapse as the main criterion of success. Psychoanalytic therapists, however, often conceptualize clinical problems, such as depression or anxiety, as symptoms of unconscious emotional conflicts. If the conflicts are not resolved, it is often held, then the patient may have not improved very much as a consequence of symptom remission and, in fact, may have become worse. The patient is likely to be worse off if, as Freudians theorize, symptoms are the most *economical* resolution of unconscious conflicts. For, if we take away the best available way to resolve an unconscious conflict that is left intact, then an even worse symptom is likely to appear (if the theory is true).

Even those who agree that symptom remission is generally good do not necessarily agree that it provides a proper standard for measuring effectiveness. Some hold that the proper goal of therapy is the achievement of some deeper result. For example, Anthony Ryle writes (1982): "The central aim and value of psychotherapy, as I see it (and this will become clearer in the course of the book) is that of enlarging people's ability to live their lives by choice" (3). A similar goal is stressed by Carl Rogers in his symposium with B. F. Skinner (Rogers and Skinner 1956), although he also recommends other goals, such as helping the client to be more self-directing and less rigid, more open to the evidence of his or her senses, and better organized and integrated. Many other therapists, especially those in the psychoanalytic tradition, advocate as the main goal of therapy the achievement of etiologic insight, or the lifting of repressions, or character change (or some combination of these). Other therapists stress the need to "get in touch with one's feelings."

Given the wide variety of opinions about criteria for judging outcomes, disagreements about therapeutic effectiveness are likely to persist even if clarity and consensus are achieved concerning empirical questions about the effects of psychotherapy.

One reaction to the diversity of standards for judging outcomes is to retreat to what may be termed "paradigm relativism." For example, in their review of the psychoanalytic outcome evidence, Bachrach et al. (1991) conclude that patients suitable for psychoanalysis derive substantial therapeutic benefits from their therapy, but stress (873) that they (the reviewers of the evidence) maintain a specifically *psychoanalytic* perspective. Thus, the authors accept without comment psychoanalytically based outcome criteria that would not be acceptable to most behavior therapists. If questioned, the authors would probably respond that nonacceptance by behavior therapists is irrelevant; they make it clear that they are recommending that each therapy be judged by the criteria appropriate to its respective paradigm (873). Other therapists (Kazdin 1986; Malan 1976) have also recommended such a relativization of outcome criteria.

One problem with paradigm relativism is that even within a single paradigm, criteria of outcome evaluations can vary considerably. The problem that the appeal to relativism was designed to solve—the problem of diverse and conflicting criteria—can reappear even after relativism (at least of this type) is accepted. Thus, in the outcome studies assessed by Bachrach et al. (1991), a wide variety of psychoanalytic criteria are used to judge outcomes. These include insight into core conflicts (883), global improvement (883), transference resolution (883), change in ego strength (883), circumstances of termination of therapy (887), change in test scores (887), changes in reality testing, object relations and affect availability (896), and many other criteria.

Even if there were not conflicting evaluative criteria within a single paradigm, there would be a second problem: guaranteeing that a paradigm-generated outcome criterion is appropriate. For any outcome criterion internal to a paradigm, we can always ask: Why is satisfaction of that criterion guarantee of a *successful* outcome? For example, in one case reported by Bachrach et al. (880), a client who came to treatment because of insecurity and difficulties in maintaining relations with women was judged "moderately improved" despite no indication in the report that either of his two problems had diminished. The basis for the verdict of improvement was that he had acquired "helpful intellectual insights." One could question, however, whether that is a satisfactory basis for saying he had improved. Legitimate doubts can also be raised about the other psychoanalytic criteria mentioned earlier, such as change in ego strength or transference resolution. Yes, the client's ego strength has increased, but has his therapy been successful to any degree? A relativist might reply that "therapeutic success" simply means *therapeutic success relative* to one or more criteria of a particular paradigm. However, we can then ask why a "therapeutic success" in this sense is valuable? The relativist might, of course, also claim that "therapeutic benefit" is also to be defined relativistically, but there is no way to demonstrate this. Some relativists are likely to reply that if outcome criteria are not relativized to a paradigm, then there is no way to determine whether there has been a successful outcome. Even if this were true, it would be no justification for relativism; rather, it would provide grounds for skepticism about the evaluation of therapies. Before being forced toward a skeptical conclusion, however, I want to examine some other approaches.

Another standard approach is to judge a therapy in terms of how well it meets the goals of individual therapists. This, too, constitutes a kind of relativism: a single outcome can be both good and bad relative to conflicting therapeutic aims. However, there are two advantages that this sort of relativism has over paradigm relativism. First, it does not matter that within the same paradigm different outcome criteria are used, as long as therapists in the paradigm have different goals. Second, for many therapies, there is nothing that is recognizable as a full-blown paradigm, so paradigm relativism is not easily applied to them. Nevertheless, goal-related relativism encounters the second problem mentioned earlier: even if a therapist does exactly what he or she aims to do, we can still ask if the outcome was valuable. Suppose that the client entered therapy to eliminate his problem drinking but now drinks just as much as before. Perhaps the therapist's goal was to increase his ego strength, or to help him get in touch with his feelings, and the goal was achieved. Still, there *may* have been no therapeutic benefit or, at best, a rather minor one. Thus, appealing to the aims of the therapist does not by itself resolve the problem of how one decides if a therapy has been successful.

Perhaps we should look to the client's goals rather than those of the therapist. After all, if a client enters therapy with a particular aim in mind, and the aim is met as a consequence of the therapy, has not a result occurred that is good to some degree? Not necessarily, although the point may be too obvious to pursue very far. A client may undergo therapy so he can drink with less anxiety, but if his problem is alcoholism the result may not be good at all. If a client is depressed about her extramarital affair, and rational emotive therapy facilitates her continuing in the affair without depression, she may achieve her therapeutic aim but be worse off than before, even from her point of view.

Another problem with appealing to client aims in assessing therapy is that clients often are confused about the nature of their problems when they enter therapy. Even if the outcome they hope to achieve is a good one, it may be peripheral to their real problem and provide, at best, a superficial test for judging the therapeutic outcome. Furthermore, there is research suggesting that clients often adopt the values of their therapists (Tjeltveit 1986; Jensen and Bergin 1988). So, even if they value the outcome (the test shows that ego strength has increased), they may simply be mirroring the theory-determined values of the therapists, and the outcome may not be beneficial. There are other standard views about judging outcomes, but they all encounter problems. For that reason, I want to argue for a different approach.

We can begin by distinguishing a normative and meta-ethical question. The first question, the one that concerns me here is: By what criterion (or criteria) should we judge that a therapeutic outcome has been beneficial to the client? Suppose we find a criterion that is intuitively plausible. We can go on to ask the meta-ethical question: How ultimately do we prove that the criterion is correct? Can intuition itself serve as a kind of proof, at least under certain conditions? Philosophers disagree about this issue, and indeed about whether any type of value judgment, even of a non-moral kind, can be justified. I will say nothing about these meta-ethical issues except this: If a total skepticism about value judgments is correct, then the psychoanalyst is no worse off than his or her counterpart in physical medicine. Yes, the operation saved the client's life or eliminated unspeakable pain, but, the skeptic will ask, how does one prove that either outcome is good for the client? I will put to one side such a general skepticism, making no judgment about whether it is true or not, and ask: *If* we can sometimes know whether an outcome in psychotherapy is good, by what criterion can we determine this?

A commonsensible approach is to appeal to the preferences and goals of the client, but for reasons given earlier, there are problems with this idea. The client may prefer a certain outcome, but be unduly influenced by the underlying clinical theory and mistakenly judge a neutral outcome to be good. The alcoholic client may want to learn to drink with less anxiety, but if he or she succeeds, the client may be worse off. So we need to ask if there is any objective way to distinguish between cases where the client's preferences are a suitable criterion and those where they are not.

There is a long philosophical tradition according to which that distinction cannot be drawn. I have my own goals, desires, likes, and dislikes, so the arguments goes, and they determine what is good or bad for me. I like opera and philosophy; you like neither. You enjoy reading romantic poetry, gambling and drinking alcohol in large quantities. I like none of these things. That is all there is to say; there is no objective, rational way to criticize our respective preferences, aversions and goals. So if we rely on client preferences, we introduce an uneliminable subjective element in the determination of therapeutic effectiveness. Whatever results *seem* good to the client will be good.

There is something correct embedded in the aforementioned view, but it goes too far. Suppose my client is 6 years old or psychotic. Cannot the client's evaluation of his or her own welfare be simply mistaken? Even the non-psychotic adult may value a therapeutic outcome because of a false belief. The client agrees with the therapist, say, that the therapy has been partly successful given an increase in ego strength, but he or she may value this only because the person mistakenly believes it to correlate with something else that is valuable. Some clients determine that they are now improved because they are in better touch with their feelings, but they may simply, and temporarily, have embraced a therapeutic value of the therapist. If they were to discover that the outcome in no way makes them happier or improves the quality of their lives, they might soon decide that it was of no value.

Is there, then, a way to use client preferences as a criterion but sift out those that are rationally unacceptable? Richard Brandt, in his theory of the good (1979), provides an answer. His theory is attractive for several reasons. First, it has an initial plausibility. Second, it provides an *empirical* way to criticize even ultimate preferences and goals. We do not have to appeal to our own values, in his view, to object to the value preferences of others. Third, because of its therapeutic element, Brandt's theory seems particularly well suited to analyzing therapeutic issues. Even if it is not satisfactory as a general theory of the good, it might serve the more limited function of aiding in the evaluation of therapeutic outcomes.

Brandt's key idea is that a "good" thing is one that it is *rational* to desire in the sense that one would desire it after undergoing "cognitive psychotherapy." This therapy, which is not identical to any standard form of cognitive therapy, involves the use of logic, the science of today, and propositions supported by publicly accessible evidence in examining one's desires. Roughly, those desires that would survive such critical examinations are rational. There need be no circularity in employing Brandt's definition of the "good" and talking of cognitive therapy results. That is, we need not first judge whether "cognitive therapy" (in his sense) generally produces *good* outcomes and then appeal to such outcomes in order to determine whether they are good. Rather, we merely try to figure out which desires would be likely to survive such therapy: these are rational and their objects are good. So if people generally desire to be free from depression, phobias, and anxieties, then being free from these conditions is generally good provided that people would retain their desires even after sustained cognitive therapy.

To see how Brandt's theory may be used, consider its application to some controversial cases. Suppose that a client is satisfied with his therapy because of his improvement on a Rorschach test. If the evidence, unknown to him, indicates that the test fails to measure anything of value, then his liking the outcome would presumably not survive cognitive therapy and can be criticized. Or consider a client of a behavior therapist who reduces her problem drinking, but does not like the result because her reading of Freud convinces her that symptom substitution is inevitable. If the evidence tells against this conviction, then the dislike is not likely to survive cognitive therapy. These sorts of cases do not involve judgments of intrinsic value and raise primarily empirical issues. However, consider an actual case of a heterosexual accused of having sex with children. With his consent, his therapist trained him to enjoy homosexual sex. Commentators on the case disagreed strongly as to whether this was a good outcome (Davison 1976). A similar question can be raised by efforts to "cure" homosexuals of their homosexuality (see Feldman and MacCulloch 1971). In questioning such outcomes, one might be raising a moral issue of what ought to be done rather than one about the value of the result. The moral question is: Whether or not the outcome is beneficial to the client, should the therapist try to produce it? That is not the question of interest here. I am asking only about the value of the outcome, not about the morality of pursuing that outcome. Once again, according to Brandt's theory, if the client desires the outcome and that desire would not be extinguished by cognitive therapy (in Brandt's sense) if the client were to undergo it, then the outcome is good for that client.

Consider one other type of case. Alan Bergin (1991) and others have argued for the use of religious criteria in the evaluation of outcomes. If we use Brandt's theory, that can be done, but the evidence for the related religious belief would also have to be assessed. For example, suppose that a marriage counselor encourages a client to get a divorce but the client finds that unsatisfactory because he believes that he will be condemned to hell if he follows the therapist's advice. According to Brandt's criterion, the aversion to divorce can be criticized if there is reason to believe that cognitive therapy would extinguish it. Of course, even if the client's verdict is criticizable, it might still be wrong for the therapist to urge divorce upon him.

I turn now to some problems with Brandt's approach. Some objections that have been raised in the philosophical literature (Harman 1982; Gibbard 1990) concern his attempt to construct a *general* theory of either the good or the rational. With one exception, these problems need not concern us here unless they also bear on the more limited issue of adapting his account to the study of psychotherapy outcomes. However, I will make one exception and make brief mention of the issue of the cognitive status of Brandt's criterion. How do we know that a desire that would survive cognitive therapy is either rational or good? Brandt's answer, roughly, is this (Brandt 1979, chapter 8): He is stipulating that such a desire is "rational," but whether it is also "good" in any ordinary sense is unclear, he argues, because the ordinary sense is unclear. Despite this unclarity about the ordinary sense of "good," there are some facts, Brandt argues, that will recommend rational desires to virtually everyone. I will not discuss here what these facts are or the adequacy of Brandt's defense, but if his argument does not work, we might settle for something more modest than a proof of what the good is. We can at least ask the following two questions: First, is Brandt's criterion potentially useful in therapeutic contexts?; Second, will its use square with our intuitions about what is or is not a good outcome? I am not assuming that even a perfect fit with our intuitions (where our intuitions agree) is a guarantee of correctness, but I will assume, without argument, that if an evaluative criterion is fundamental, then a lack of fit counts against it—unless there is some reasonable explanation consistent with its truth for the discrepancy.

On the first issue, that of potential usefulness, there is much in favor of Brandt's criterion. As noted, earlier, its use requires no appeal to other evaluative criteria, and subject to certain qualifications it can be applied empirically. To evaluate a client's preference, we need not actually provide cognitive therapy; we need only appeal to our background evidence to decide whether the preference is likely to be extinguishable by cognitive therapy. Given all we know, it is likely, for example, that for most clients, the desire to be free from a crippling anxiety or depression is likely to survive cognitive therapy. However, one limitation is that in some cases, we may not have enough information about a client to reach a reasonable decision about certain fundamental preferences. Another problem concerns the specification of what "cognitive therapy" is. The therapy is said to involve the confrontation of desires with relevant information by repeatedly representing it in an ideally vivid way and at an appropriate time (Brandt, 1979, 113). This is obviously rather vague. What counts as *relevant* information, an *ideally* vivid way, and an *appropriate* time? Without a more precise description of the therapy, we are likely to have a wide range of cases in which there will be no way to tell how to apply Brandt's criterion *even if* we know a great deal about the client. I turn next to some questions about the intuitive plausibility of Brandt's criterion.

One problem that analysts are likely to raise concerns the role of repressed wishes. Suppose that a client has what looks like an irrational desire to persist in a very troubling sexual relationship. Even if the desire truly is "irrational" in an ordinary sense, it might not be extinguishable by cognitive therapy if it is the product of a repressed wish. Even if there are no such things as repressed wishes, there are non-psychoanalytic types of cases that also pose a challenge to Brandt's criterion. Suppose that someone has a phobic reaction to riding on elevators. If the aversion is long standing and deeply rooted, even if it is not due to a repressed wish, Brandt's cognitive therapy might not extinguish it. In this latter sort of case, perhaps we could draw a distinction between phobias due to conditioning and those due to cognitive factors (see Wolpe, 1977). We might then modify Brandt's criterion and say that an aversion is rational if and only if (*a*) it is not due to conditioning (or perhaps a certain kind of conditioning) and (*b*) it would survive cognitive therapy. There is, however, a more general problem than that posed by phobias or repressed wishes: there may be various classes of irrational desires, aversions, and preferences that are so woven into someone's personality that cognitive therapy will not extinguish them. We may try to handle these by further complicating Brandt's criterion, but another way out is to treat his conditions for being rational as necessary but not sufficient. A desire is rational, it might be said, *only if* it would survive cognitive therapy. Of those that would survive, some may be rational and some not. So, a conscious desire resulting from a repressed wish or a phobic aversion may be irrational, according to Brandt's modified theory, even if cognitive therapy cannot eliminate it.

An opposite sort of problem is the possible extinguishability of desires that seem to be rational and good. As Gil Harman (1982, 128) argues, benevolence (i.e., the desire to be benevolent toward others) might prove to be a casualty of cognitive therapy, although as he also notes, there may be a way to modify Brandt's theory to avoid this result. The general worry, however, is that there may be various types of desires that are neither bad nor irrational but are just too fragile to survive cognitive therapy. Suppose, for example, that our cognitive therapy involves repeatedly showing the subject pictures of people around the world who are starving. It is possible that the client will infer that helping people is a hopeless task and, as a consequence, he or she may lose the desire to help. The general worry here is that some preferences in some people may be rational but fragile. Subjecting them repeatedly to certain types of information might extinguish them even if the desires are rational.

Perhaps some of the problems associated with Brandt's theory can be solved in the following way. First, banish the idea that preferences capable of surviving cognitive therapy are necessarily rational. Some preferences may be neither rational nor irrational; they just "are," so to speak. My colleague Ramon Lemos suggests the following example. A client is envious of certain people and prefers that they suffer and fail in their endeavors. Assuming that his having this preference has no bad consequences, it might survive cognitive therapy and so not be irrational, but neither is it rational (unless we stipulate that we will use "rational" in a technical sense to cover all such preferences). It is enough, for my purposes, that a client's preference not be irrational; if it is not, we need not endorse it as "rational." My second suggestion is that we adopt a proposal that Harman (1982) makes in passing but does not develop. Keep some of Brandt's ideas, but eliminate the appeal to cognitive therapy. Instead of trying to figure out if a desire would survive if confronted with information *repeatedly* represented in an *ideally* vivid fashion, develop various criteria for deciding if a desire or aversion is irrational.

One way to criticize a client's preference for a certain outcome is to demonstrate that it is causally linked to a false belief. The client, say, values a result not for its own sake but because he or she mistakenly believes that it will lead to something else of value. Even if something is valued for its own sake, say chastity or self-sacrifice, it may be valued because of a religious, moral, or political belief that is false, or at least unwarranted. A second line of criticism concerns final ends: a client may value something for its own sake, but it may be unobtainable and its pursuit may have deleterious effects. Thus, some clients reportedly want "everyone to love them" or they want to live a life of total perfection. These ends may be good from the client's point of view, but it may be unreasonable to prefer them to more modest goals if their pursuit is bound to be futile and harmful. A third form of criticism involves the comparison of competing final ends. For example, a client may value fame for its own sake, but pursuing that end may conflict with an end valued even more, such as contentment. (Strictly speaking, these last two types of criticism may be applicable not to the client's preference for certain ends but to his or her desire to pursue them.)

I conclude that it may be possible to adapt Brandt's theory of the evaluation of therapeutic outcomes, provided that the problems can be worked out. Even in the absence of a general philosophical theory, however, we can and should appeal to client preferences, purified by rational criticism, to question the widespread practice of accepting at face value the satisfaction of a paradigm's aim or the aims of an individual therapist as a criterion of therapeutic success. If a therapy's effectiveness is determined by its capacity to help a client, then the satisfaction of his or her preferences, filtering out those that are irrational, is the proper criterion for judging therapeutic success. It then becomes an empirical question as to which of the many theory-driven criteria, such as a certain score on a Rorschach test, an increase in ego strength, or getting in touch with one's feelings, are reliable indicators of satisfying this more basic criterion. In many outcome studies and reviews, the needed empirical evidence is missing. Consequently, there is no way to tell whether the therapy was effective in helping the client *even if* we have established a causal relationship between therapy and outcome.

The Need for Controlled Experiments

Are controlled experiments required to establish that psychoanalysis is generally effective in producing certain types of beneficial outcomes? Many clinicians do not think so.

One view is that psychoanalytic hypotheses should not be judged by standards appropriate to the natural sciences (Taylor 1985). I criticized this view in chapter 1, and will not discuss it here. Another view is that the analyst can just "see' that his or her therapy sometimes helps clients (Fromm 1970). The reply to this view is obvious. The analyst may be able to tell merely by looking that certain clients have improved, but how does he or she know that the therapy caused the improvement? To know that, one would have to rule out credible rival explanations, in particular, that factors outside the therapy setting caused the improvement. Unless the analyst can show how these rival hypotheses can be discounted, the claim to "see" what caused the improvement cannot be taken seriously.

A third view is that we should rely on the clinical wisdom of analysts rather than experimentation or, rather, we should do that *if* we do not have any experimental evidence. There may be something to this view. Analysts surely learn something of value after many years of clinical practice. Furthermore, if we had no better evidence, and if (which today is not true) no alternative therapy were available, then a case might be made for relying on clinical wisdom. However, if the claim is that clinical wisdom is sufficient to warrant therapeutic hypotheses, that claim is suspect for the reasons just mentioned. Without using experimental controls, how does the analyst discount plausible rivals to his or her therapeutic hypothesis? If the analyst cannot do this, then it is implausible to say that he or she has learned through clinical experience when the therapy has worked. Still, even though this is not antecedently plausible, some skillful analysts might be able to discern that their treatment is effective. It is not that they know this it is rather that what seems to them to be true really is true. This state of affairs is possible, but we still need evidence that it is actual. To have such evidence, we would need to confirm that for some analysts there is a high correlation between two things: their judging that the therapy worked and the therapy really working. How we do we get evidence for the latter? Not by appealing to clinical wisdom; to do that would be to appeal to the very thing that we are trying to substantiate, that clinical wisdom can warrant therapeutic hypotheses. Rather, we need to do controlled experiments first if we wish to vindicate the claim that there is a high correlation between analysts' thinking their therapy has worked and its really having worked.

A fourth view appeals to a Kuhnian type of relativism, the idea that the proper epistemological standards are determined by the particular paradigm one is operating in: one set of standards for psychoanalysts, a different set for behavior therapists, etc. This point of view is embraced by the Subcommittee on Efficacy Research of the Committee on Scientific Activities of the American Psychoanalytic Association. In their report of the committee's findings (Bachrach et al., 1991), the authors list five criteria for evaluating research on treatment outcomes, such as the need to demonstrate that the treatment being evaluated is taking place, the requirement that the patient be suitable for treatment, etc. The criteria do not require, however, that a study be *experimental* (with random assignment to treatment and comparison groups, and the inclusion of at least a no treatment or wait-list control group). Furthermore, although the authors make a number of criticisms of the studies they review, they nowhere fault a study for being nonexperimental. Finally, despite their criticisms, Bachrach et al. conclude (p. 911) the studies, *none of which is experimental,* "confirm that patients suitable for analysis derive therapeutic benefit" (911). I infer from the foregoing that the authors do not agree that it is generally necessary to meet an experimental standard to confirm the efficacy of psychoanalysis.

A likely explanation for the authors' adoption of a nonexperimental standard is that they are consciously employing criteria they believe acceptable to the psychoanalytic community. Thus, they write: "For too long psychoanalytic research has been defensively toned, and analysts have failed to fully appreciate that it is both a common and legitimate strategy for scientists to work within their own disciplinary matrix (Kuhn, 1977). For this reason it is important to conduct our inquiry from a point of view native to psychoanalysis" (873). The major difficulty with this sort of relativization of epistemological standards to a psychoanalytic paradigm is the same as that raised earlier about outcome criteria. Yes, most psychoanalysts (let us assume) will agree with the Bachrach et al. criteria, but are they the *right* criteria? That is, if outcome studies satisfy all such criteria (and any others that the authors employ) will that suffice for the production of credible evidence that psychoanalysis generally causes beneficial outcomes? Merely pointing out that analysts generally accept such criteria, and, more pointedly, generally do *not* insist on the introduction of experimental controls, does nothing to answer the question. Some reply must be given to those who argue (e.g., Grünbaum 1984, 1993; Erwin 1994) that experimental controls are generally necessary in assessing claims of psychoanalytic effectiveness.

The first step in an argument for an experimental standard is the assumption that a psychoanalytic outcome hypothesis *H* is not confirmed by data *D* if a competing hypothesis is at least as credible as *H*, all things considered (i.e., given *D* and our background evidence and the appeal to any nonobservational criteria that are epistemically relevant). If this initial assumption were challenged, as it apparently is by Fine and Forbes (1986), I would appeal to philosophical arguments designed to show that all confirmation must be "differential" (see Erwin and Siegel 1989). If the initial step is conceded, the next one is well known: it is the claim that for the types of non-psychotic problems typically treated by analysts, there are generally at least two credible hypotheses that need to be defeated. First, factors external to the therapeutic situation or, second, placebo factors (or a combination of both) caused most or all of the therapeutic gains. Most psychotherapy researchers agree about the need to discount the first rival, but not everyone agrees about the placebo hypothesis. There are various doubts that have been raised about placebo controls, including questions about the intelligibility of the placebo concept (Kazdin 1986). I have tried to answer the doubts in Erwin (1994), but here will concentrate on one recurring issue.

One reason that some outcome reviewers are skeptical about using placebo controls is that a placebo treatment may be effective for a certain type of problem. So, the argument continues, comparing a treatment with a placebo may understate the effectiveness of the former. In fact, if it "ties" the placebo, so to speak, it may appear that the treatment had no beneficial effect at all. In reply, I do not dispute this point, but I want to argue there are nevertheless two reasons for using placebo controls, although not, of course, in every outcome study.

The first reason is epistemological. To obtain evidence that a therapeutic intervention had a beneficial effect, we need to rule out the possibility that all improvement was due to causes preceding the therapy or to factors appearing later that are not part of the therapy. In studies of placebos, it has been found that clients often improve after the initial interview but *before* the therapy begins (Frank 1983). This could be because the client's morale improves as a consequence of deciding to enter therapy or as a result of the pretherapy interview and the promise of being helped. If some combination of pretreatment factors made all of the beneficial difference, then the treatment was not effective.

This first problem may not be too serious. In many cases, our background evidence makes a causal explanation referring exclusively to pretreatment factors implausible. However, we still have the second problem. Suppose that during the course of analysis, the patient free-associates, talks about his problems, resolves the transference, and eventually gains what appears to be insight into the cause of his or her problem. If the patient improves, and improves more than he or she would have without having undergone treatment, how do we know that the treatment factors made any difference at all? For all we know, expectations of being helped made all of the difference, just as it apparently does when people are given a sugar pill and then show improvement. It could be replied that the psychoanalytic ingredients did play a causal role; they were needed for the patient to retain his or her confidence. Perhaps, but how do we know that? The decisive event, the creation of an expectation of cure, might have occurred at the beginning of the therapy. The client's confidence might have been maintained even if the analytic ingredients were dispensed with altogether. To show, then, that the *therapy*, not merely whatever went on in the analyst's office, made the therapeutic difference, we need a placebo control *or* some alternative mechanism for discounting a causal role for nontreatment factors. If this is right, it is a mistake to infer that a treatment is more effective than no treatment merely because a treatment group on average improves more than a wait-list control. To establish that the treatment was effective to any degree, we need to show that it, and not some accompanying nontreatment factors (such as expectation of cure), caused the improvement (or at least helped cause it).

It might be said that psychoanalytic therapy should include not merely such items as resolution of transference, the gaining of insight, etc., but whatever goes on in the analyst's office. We should include the therapeutic relationship, talking about one's problems, and, yes, the expectation of cure. We can no doubt, widen the notion of psychoanalysis in this way, but then to say that the therapy is generally effective in producing benefit B, we do not mean what is ordinarily meant. We mean whatever goes on in the analyst's office—whether it is behavior therapy, the forming of a friendly bond, or just plain talking—that is effective.

I conclude, then, that if by "psychoanalysis" we mean the use of interpretation, free association, the resolution of transference, and the other ingredients stipulated by Freudian theory, then we need a placebo control or some alternative mechanism to show that *it* is generally effective in producing some type of beneficial result. Comparison to no treatment or to a wait list control is not enough.

Suppose that we look at effectiveness from the patient's point of view. What he or she is likely to care about is this: Will I obtain some benefit from undergoing analysis? From this point of view, it may not matter at all exactly what produces the benefit. The benefit may be a placebo effect, but that may be of no concern to the client. Yet, as I noted earlier, there is a second reason for using a placebo control, a nonepistemic reason. And this reason is likely to matter to the client. For an expensive, time-consuming therapy such as classical psychoanalysis, there is a further criterion for judging it beyond mere effectiveness. Can it outperform a simple, brief placebo treatment, such as the provision of a sugar pill? If it cannot, then it is inferior in terms of cost and efficiency. If the inferiority is substantial, it is hard to see the justification for giving the client psychoanalysis rather than the placebo, *if* the placebo would produce the same beneficial results. To justify the use of a long, expensive treatment such as psychoanalysis, then, establishing mere effectiveness is insufficient. We need evidence that it is more effective than a simple, brief inexpensive placebo.

One could reply to the above argument that even if experimentation is *generally* required in evaluating therapeutic claims, there are exceptions, such as cases where the therapeutic changes are so sudden and dramatic that spontaneous remission and placebo hypotheses can be ruled out even in the absence of experimental controls. Paul Meehl (1983) describes two such psychoanalytic cases that he finds convincing. I disagree about the interpretation of these cases, as interesting as they are (see Erwin 1988a, 206–209), but here I want to emphasize a different point. There is an extraordinary case in the placebo literature (see Kazdin 1980, 21–22) of a patient with large cancerous tumors who was treated with kreboizen, a fake cancer cure. Given the pattern of subsequent dramatic changes in the patient, it looks as if his confidence in kreboizen caused a remission of his cancer and a temporary elimination of his tumors. Yet, no one should infer from this one case that a placebo treatment is generally effective for the treatment of any type of cancer. The lesson here is clear. If our question is not, Has the use of analysis ever produced a significant therapeutic benefit?, but rather, Is analysis, when employed by a trained therapist, *generally* effective in treating a certain type of patient with a certain type of problem in a certain type of clinical setting?, then a *body* of evidence, not a few scattered cases, is needed to answer the question with assurance.

I conclude, then, that to provide firm evidence that psychoanalysis is generally effective in producing a certain type of benefit for a certain type of client, we generally need experimental evidence. There may be exceptional cases where some other type of evidence will suffice, but that there are such cases needs to be demonstrated.

The Current Psychoanalytic Outcome Evidence

In addition to the case studies of Freud and other analysts, there is a body of data obtained in systematic, formal research studies. Disagreement persists, however, even among analysts, as to what inferences can be reasonably drawn from these data.

I begin with Fisher and Greenberg's useful discussion of some of the more serious problems involved in interpreting psychoanalytic outcome research. One of these has to do with the diversity and vagueness concerning what is labeled "psychoanalysis" by many investigators. For example, as Fisher and Greenberg note (1985, 334), the therapy called "psychoanalysis" in one report may fit the definition given for "psychoanalytically oriented psychotherapy" in another investigation. In addition, there is almost always no attempt to measure whether the therapy that was given actually matches the description given by the investigator. On the outcome side, the widespread practice of relying on analysts' judgments to measure improvement is called into question by various studies. In one study, Weiss (1972) utilized two ambiguous taped therapy excerpts alternately labeled "early" and "late." Analytic therapists were found more likely than behaviorists to find positive changes where none existed. Substituting projective tests for analysts' judgments, as has been done in some studies, might appear to enhance objectivity, but the practice only raises the issue of whether there is sound evidence that the tests measure what they are supposed to measure. In short, in any study where there is reasonable doubt about the existence of either the putative cause (psychoanalytic treatment) or effect (therapeutic benefit), there will be reasonable doubt about proof of efficacy. Even where the two sorts of problems are avoided, there is the additional difficult problem of establishing a causal connection between treatment and outcome. This requires, at a minimum, some form of comparison. As Fisher and Greenberg note (312), however, many of the outcome studies of psychotherapy and psychoanalysis lack such a comparison.

Despite the widespread presence of the aforementioned difficulties, Fisher and Greenberg do reach some conclusions which they cautiously describe (309) as "tentative." One of these (334) is that the weight of the evidence suggests no major differences in outcome between therapies labeled "psychoanalysis" and other approaches. However, Fisher and Greenberg note that glaring deficiencies in methodology make a firm conclusion of this sort impossible. A second major conclusion is this: "While we cannot conclude that the studies [i.e., those they have reviewed] offer unequivocal evidence that analysis is more effective than no treatment, they do indicate with consistency that this seems probable with regard to a number of analysts and their non-psychotic, chronic patients." This conclusion is based on six studies: Schjelderup 1955; Orgel 1958; Barendregt et al. 1961; Cappon 1964; O'Connor et al. 1964; Duhrssen and Jorswieck 1965). I am not sure of the extent of my disagreement with Fisher and Greenberg about these studies. They do say (315) that the studies have a number of drawbacks or methodological flaws and that the evidence they offer is *not* unequivocal (332). However, I would go further and argue that taken together or separately, these studies fail to make it likely that psychoanalysis is generally effective in producing any sort of therapeutic benefit. For example, in the Cappon study (1964) there is no way to tell even whether standard psychoanalysis was employed; there is, in fact, some reason to think that it was not. Cappon describes his treatment as a personal modification of analysis combined with an influence of Jungian theory. The Orgel (1958) study is a retrospective report of the author's treatment of 15 peptic ulcer patients. No control group was utilized. Of the 15 patients, 10 were judged to be cured. However, peptic ulcer often responds to certain medical treatments, and the possibility is not ruled out that many of the patients who improved received such treatment either immediately before or during the 3- to 5- year period of psychoanalysis. In fact, in 6 out of 10 "improved" cases, the patient did receive such treatment, usually consisting of alkalies or a special diet or both. Given this fact, the possibility cannot be ruled out that the diet or medical treatment caused the remission of symptoms. I will not discuss the remaining four studies because they have been criticized elsewhere (e.g., Erwin 1980; Rachman and Wilson 1980).

Fisher and Greenberg's conclusion, weak and tentative as it is, only concerns the superiority of psychoanalysis to no treatment. Earlier, however, I argued for a higher standard if one wants to justify the use of psychoanalysis. Some evidence has to be provided that the therapy is more than weakly effective. To obtain such evidence, we need a well-controlled study with a placebo control group (or alternatively, some other feature that rules out certain placebo factors). How many studies of psychoanalysis are there of this sort? The answer is: none at all. It is worth mentioning here some comments by Gene Glass, who along with his colleagues (Smith, Glass, and Miller 1980) did the most exhaustive review ever attempted of the psychotherapy outcome literature. Glass points out that he is sympathetic to psychoanalytic theory, but adds that there exists in the Smith et al. database not a single experimental study that qualifies by even "the shoddiest standards" as an outcome evaluation of orthodox psychoanalysis (Glass and Kliegl 1983, 40). Other reviews (e.g., Erwin 1980; Rachman and Wilson 1980) have also noted the lack of experimental studies and have concluded that firm evidence for the efficacy of psychoanalysis still does not exist. This skepticism about the evidential support for psychoanalytic effectiveness is also shared by some who are generally sympathetic to Freudian theory. For example, Paul Kline notes in a paper (1988, 226) referring to my conclusions: "I agree with his conclusions, incidentally, that no good evidence exists that it is effective." (Kline adds [226] that he favors an alternative approach which aims to evaluate the process rather than the outcome of psychoanalysis. He claims that by using psychoanalytic theory to predict what occurs in analytic sessions, one might provide sound evidence for the theory. I do not question whether this could be done, only whether it has been done so far in a way that supports the theory. However, at this point I am discussing not Freudian theory, but Freudian therapeutic outcomes. Kline's reply is not directly relevant to this issue.)

Not all psychoanalysts agree with Kline's negative assessment. In the report of the Subcommittee on Efficacy Research, Bachrach et al.(1991) conclude (904) that patients suitable for analysis derive substantial therapeutic benefit (they clearly mean derive substantial benefit *from* their therapy). They base this conclusion on data from six systematic, clinical-quantitative studies involving 550 patients, plus two provisional studies of 139 completed analyses and studies conducted at three psychoanalytic centers involving 71 additional cases. They interpret the data on the basis of the five criteria I mentioned earlier: (1) it must be demonstrated that the treatment being evaluated is taking place; (2) the treatment is conducted by practitioners of sufficient knowledge, skill, and experience in accord with accepted standards of practice; (3) treatment can be meaningfully evaluated only in relation to clinical conditions to which they are applicable; (4) the patient must be a suitable candidate for treatment; and (5) germane variables must be adequately specified conceptually, operationally, and reliably, and studied systematically. The authors claim (909) that their second criterion, concerning analysts' knowledge and experience, is clearly not met by the majority of studies. However, the failure to meet this condition does not disqualify the studies from providing proof of efficacy. Indeed, an analyst might argue that even though the inexperienced (mostly training) analysts did reasonably well, better trained analysts would have done better. The first criterion, the authors argue (908), is met "at varying levels" by the studies and the remaining criteria are also "variously met."

Some questions need to be asked about the claim that four of the five criteria were satisfied to varying degrees. First, was there any *independent* way of determining whether psychoanalysis was actually employed? Except for the Menninger Foundation Project, the answer is no. Most of the studies are based on treatments conducted by student analysts supervised by highly qualified practitioners, but, as the reviewers note (908), the supervisory process does not guard against the introduction of systematic biases. Second, even if operational definitions were offered for such key terms as "improvement," "analytic process," and "therapeutic benefits," were these terms defined in the same ways in the various studies? Apparently not. As Bachrach et al. note (910), there was no consensus about the meaning of terms or the methods of measurement.

The main problem, however, with the reviewers' argument concerns not the satisfaction of four of five of the criteria, but the assumption that satisfying even all of them is *sufficient* for providing firm evidence of therapeutic effectiveness. Citing Kuhn (1977) here, as the authors do (873), is of no help. Even if there were no problem with Kuhn's relativistic arguments (see Siegel 1988), he nowhere argues that no matter what standards are employed in a paradigm, satisfaction of them will necessarily guarantee confirmation of causal hypotheses. We could, if we wished, embrace a paradigm that sets extremely low standards: let the therapists' unargued opinion determine whether a therapy was effective on a particular occasion. However, we could still ask: Is meeting that standard a guarantee of finding confirming evidence? It is not an adequate reply to say that it is because it is the standard of our paradigm. The standards employed by Bachrach et al. are much more sophisticated than this made-up standard but, I argue, they are still not sufficient.

First, even if all five criteria were met for *all* of the studies, the subjects might be unrepresentative. On this issue, the reviewers say the following: "It should come as no surprise that the patients in most of the studies were selected for pedagogic reasons (i.e. suitable for analysis by a candidate) and stringent efforts were made to eliminate more difficult or unsuitable cases" (907–908). However, if the more difficult cases were generally eliminated, then even if evidence of effectiveness were found, a further argument would be needed to show that the therapy works in cases typically treated by analysts.

Second, there are several problems that arise in determining patient improvement no matter what the cause. A wide variety of psychoanalytic criteria were used to judge outcomes. These include insight into core conflicts (883), change in ego strength (883), circumstances of termination of therapy (887), change in test score (887), changes in reality testing, object relations and affect availability (896), and many other criteria. It is doubtful that the satisfaction of many, if any, of these criteria would in itself constitute a good for the patient, at least not by the rational desire standard argued for earlier. Presumably, the authors would agree but claim that such psychoanalytically sanctioned outcomes as increase in ego strength correlate with something else, which in turn is beneficial to the patient. The problem then becomes one of specifying the therapeutic benefits and providing the required empirical evidence that the correlation holds. Until that is done, it cannot be assumed that the outcomes claimed to be beneficial really were. Even if it were true that the psychoanalytic outcome criteria marked genuine benefits, there would be further problems. As the reviewers note, the treating analyst was often the final arbiter of clinical outcomes; in some cases (892), the judgment was made years after the cases had terminated.

Even if there were no other problems, satisfaction of the reviewers' criteria is consistent with the complete absence of required experimental controls which is what one finds in the studies reviewed. The studies may qualify as "formal, systematic research studies," but none of them qualifies as an experimental study. But without a no-treatment or wait-list control, or firm evidence about the base rate of spontaneous remissions for the particular types of problems studied, there is no basis for inferring that the outcomes were caused by the therapy. To take but one example, one client was a housebound phobic woman with a barbiturate addiction who, after much therapy, was able to travel and give up her addiction. However, she was initially treated for more than 1300 hours and later became a "lifer" who continued in once-monthly psychotherapy. It is not clear from the review when she improved, but given the long duration of treatment, it is surely reasonable to ask: How do we know which events in her life caused her to travel and give up her addiction? Without some proper basis for comparison, there is no way of knowing.

Given that the studies were not of a proper sort to establish a causal connection between psychoanalysis and beneficial outcomes, it would be gratuitous to add that the higher standard argued for in the previous section was also not met. That is, even if causal connections had been established, justification of the use of such an expensive long term therapy would require something in addition: the demonstration that it can typically outperform a simple, cheap, brief, but credible placebo.

Conclusion

Proponents of psychoanalysis have, at various times, claimed that their treatment is effective for a large number of clinical problems. Bachrach et al. (1991, 877, table 1) list more than 30 clinical disorders treated by analysts, including anxiety, hysteria, compulsion, neurosis, depression, sexual impotence, transvestism, bronchial asthma, and character disorders. The existing evidence, however, fails to substantiate the claim that psychoanalysis is generally effective in treating any of these problems. In fact, there is little, if any, good evidence that the therapy is generally effective in producing any type of therapeutic benefit, and there is no evidence at all that if it does contribute to the production of any such benefit, its contribution is typically greater than that of a credible placebo.

Some analysts are likely to reply that the explanation for the lack of supporting evidence is that the proper experiments have not yet been done, and there is a good reason for this state of affairs. It is either impractical or unethical, or both, some analysts argue, to do experiments with a long term therapy such as psychoanalysis, especially, if we insist on employing a placebo control. Some of the same ethical obstacles arise in the testing of medical procedures (for a discussion, see Erwin, Gendin and Kleiman 1994, chapter 3) and there may be a way around them. Suppose, however, that is impossible. In that case, the relevant experiments should not be done. However, nothing follows about the epistemological need to do such experiments. I am asking if we are justified in believing without experimental evidence that psychoanalytic therapy is effective. I have argued that we are not. Whether we should take the necessary steps to obtain the required evidence is a separate issue, one that I am not going to try to resolve here.

Another issue that I will leave unresolved is whether patients should enter analysis. I have not argued that psychoanalysis is ineffective, only that there is no good evidence that it is effective. If we do not know whether or not therapy is effective, what should a patient do? The first reasonable move is to look to alternative, cheaper therapies that are supported by good evidence. However, for certain types of problems, such as re-formation of character, there may be no alternative to psychoanalysis. A patient might reasonably wish to gamble on psychoanalysis for this sort of problem even if there is no likelihood of a suitable payoff. In addition, certain patients enter therapy to explore their feelings or to talk to someone for an extended duration, or for some other reason. Whether a particular patient should undergo psychoanalysis depends on other issues besides effectiveness.

The Concept of Psychoanalytically Oriented Psychotherapy

It is estimated that of those who undergo psychological therapy, less than 10% receive orthodox psychoanalysis. In contrast, many more clients receive short term psychoanalytically oriented psychotherapy, or what is also called "psychodynamic psychotherapy." What is the difference, other than duration, between short term psychodynamic psychotherapy and orthodox psychoanalysis?

One difference is that in psychodynamic psychotherapy, the goal is often symptom remission, while in psychoanalysis deeper changes are typically sought. The orthodox analyst may also engage in what is primarily investigative therapy, while the dynamic psychotherapists may give frequent advice and generally provide what is called "supportive" therapy. However, some of these features may be found in both types of therapy.

There is also a problem in distinguishing dynamic psychotherapy from certain non-Freudian types of psychotherapy. One might have no problem in distinguishing the former from obviously non-Freudian therapies, such as behavior therapy or cognitive therapy, but in other cases classification is more difficult. Some of the more than 400 psychotherapies bear a close resemblance to classical psychoanalysis except for length of treatment, but others, such as some of the holistic therapies (Erwin 1985), developed out of psychoanalysis but contain important non-Freudian ingredients. In the face of these difficulties, I shall begin by defining "dynamic therapy" very broadly. I use the expression to refer to any therapy that contains at least some distinctively Freudian elements, such as the analysis of transference, free association, dream interpretation, or the attempt to lift repressions. As I have defined it, the category "dynamic therapy" may include too much, but that is not a problem given my purposes. If a therapy has been shown to be effective, but contains non-Freudian as well as Freudian elements, we can then go on to inquire about which characteristics of the therapy account for its effectiveness. One caution, however, should be mentioned. As just noted, to qualify as dynamic therapy, a treatment must contain at least some elements that are distinctive of traditional psychoanalysis. It is not enough that the therapies use Freudian concepts to explain how the therapy works. For example, some writers have proposed that Freudian theory explains how systematic desensitization works. A therapist who agrees with this proposal would not thereby be practicing Freudian therapy when using systematic desensitization. Rather, he or she would be using a type of behavior therapy, but using Freudian theory to explain how the various ingredients in the therapy, such as relaxation and the use of an image hierarchy, make a therapeutic difference.

Individual Studies

In contrast to (orthodox) psychoanalysis, there are a number of controlled studies of short-term psychodynamic psychotherapy (hereinafter STPP). In many respects, one of the best is the study of Sloane et al. (1975) comparing STPP to systematic desensitization in the treatment of clients with real clinical problems. Despite its virtues, however, the study has also encountered serious criticism (Rachman and Wilson 1980). In addition, the study employed a wait-list rather than a placebo control So a placebo explanation of the results was not ruled out. If these objections are temporarily waived, then the Sloane et al. study, taken in isolation, provides some evidence of modest therapeutic gains for both STPP and systematic desensitization.

A far more ambitious and expensive study is the National Institute of Mental Health (NIMH) collaborative study comparing a drug, cognitive therapy, interpersonal psychotherapy, and a pill placebo in the treatment of depression. Of these therapies, only interpersonal psychotherapy (IPT) possibly qualifies as a form of STPP. Its proponents claim to have been influenced by psychodynamic theory (although they trace their most direct line of influence to Harry Stack Sullivan rather than Freud). In some respects, it does resemble other therapies usually classified as "psychoanalytically oriented," but there are also important differences.

Most generally, in contrast to most psychodynamic therapies, the nature of IPT is the interpersonal rather than the intrapsychic, with the focus on the "here and now" instead of on the early developmental experiences. Furthermore, the overall goals of treatment are to encourage mastery of current social roles and adaptation to interpersonal situations; in addition, interpretation and personality reconstruction are not attempted. Sometimes IPT therapists do dream analysis, but as Klerman et al. point out (1984, 15), in the course of therapy, dreams are not usually asked for. If a patient does report a dream, the therapist may work on it, but only by focusing on its manifest rather than its latent content. Furthermore, although the IPT therapist may recognize the operation of defense mechanisms, he or she does not attempt to help the patient see the current situation as a manifestation of an internal conflict. There are, then, some similarities between IPT and more typical examples of STPP, but there are also important differences. Still, if one uses "psycho-analytically oriented" in a very broad fashion, then IPT qualifies if only because it sometimes involves an analysis of dreams. However one classifies the therapy, though, the results of the NIMH collaborative study were not encouraging. IPT did only slightly better than the sugar pill, and the cognitive therapy just about tied the latter in effectiveness (Elkin et al. 1989).

There are other less famous controlled studies of psychoanalytically oriented psychotherapies. Many of these are discussed in the review by Smith et al. (1980) to which I now turn.

The Meta-Analytic Argument

Smith and Glass (1977) and Smith et al. (1980) introduce what has now become a widely used statistical technique for resolving the "integration problem." This problem arises because the evidence bearing on psychotherapeutic outcome hypotheses is disparate and in some cases inconsistent. Much of the evidence concerns very different kinds of clinical problems, ranging from mild snake phobias to cases of severe schizophrenia. Also, the therapists providing the therapy often differ considerably in their training and clinical experience. The therapeutic settings are also dissimilar and the outcomes are very different for different studies. Finally, the quality of the studies varies quite a bit. Some are relatively well designed, others are of moderate quality, and others are almost impossible to interpret. Here, then, is the integration problem. If we wish to judge the effectiveness of psychotherapy in general—or, more realistically, the psychoanalytically oriented psychotherapies—we must have some way of putting together and assessing all of the relevant data, some of which are conflicting. How precisely are we to do this? Are there reliable rules to be followed? Do we rely on the unargued judgment of experts? Is there some other way? Consider one facet of the problem. How do we weigh the evidence from poor studies against that from superior ones? There are at least two standard solutions to this problem. The first is the "box score" solution used by Luborsky, Singer, and Luborsky (1975). The reviewers resolved to consider all studies that compared two or more therapies, but included only studies that were at least passably controlled. Poor and superior studies were given equal weight. Scores were then tabulated for each comparison (e.g., behavior therapy vs. psychotherapy; group vs. individual therapy) by counting the number of studies in which the treatments did significantly better or worse than their competitors, or were tied with them. Luborsky et al. also included a grading of the studies, using 12 methodological criteria to decide whether a study deserved an A, B, C, or D. They then compared the results of the superior and poorly designed tests, found no difference in their trend, and used this finding to justify giving equal weight to all of the studies.

Several reviewers have objected to the use of the box-score method. For example, Smith et al. (1980) point out that the use of this method ignores considerations of sample size. Large samples tend to produce more statistically significant findings than small samples. For example, one may find nine small studies that concern a particular clinical hypothesis, none of which quite reaches statistical significance. If one large sample study is significant, then the score is 1 for the hypothesis and 9 against (see also Rachman and Wilson 1980).

A second approach to the integration problem has been termed the "narrative" solution (Smith et al. 1980, 36). A reviewer will attempt to portray multiple findings in a verbal, nonquantitative report written like a story. To make the story intelligible, the reviewer is forced to cut the body of evidence down to size by ignoring certain studies and by "impeaching" others because of bad design or use of poor outcome measures. Smith et al. (1980) object to the narrative approach for a number of reasons.

A third solution to the integration problem, one favored by Smith et al. (1980), is to use meta-analysis. The key feature of this approach is the transformation of different measures of therapeutic effects into a single measure, the effect size (ES). ES is calculated for each study by subtracting the average score on the outcome variable for the control group from the average score for the treatment group and dividing the result by the standard deviation for the control group. Thus:

$$ES = \frac{M\,(therapy) - M\,(control)}{S\,(control)}$$

where M (therapy)= the average outcome score for the psychotherapy group; M (control)= the average outcome score for the control group; and S (control)= the standard deviation for the control group

Smith et al. (1980) calculated approximately 1760 effect sizes for 475 controlled studies of psychotherapy and found that the average effect size was .85. This result is explained as follows: subject to certain qualifications, the average person receiving psychotherapy is better off at the end of it than 80% of those persons who do not undergo psychotherapy (Glass and Kliegl 1983, 29).

Smith et al. (1980) thus claim that (*a*) the use of meta-analysis is sufficient for resolving the integration problem; (*b*) their analysis demonstrates a causal connection between psychotherapy and beneficial therapeutic effects; and (*c*) other methods of research integration are inadequate. Other writers have endorsed one or both of these claims (Glass and Kliegl 1983; Fiske 1983). In what follows, I argue that each of these claims is unwarranted.

Several objections have been raised to the Smith et al. argument (Eysenck 1983b; Erwin 1984b; Wilson 1985; Bruno and Ellett 1988). One of the more serious concerns their weighting equally studies of good and poor methodological quality. Their justification for this democratic treatment is that both types of studies tended to yield the same types of results. I question this finding because I doubt that their criteria for distinguishing good from bad studies were sufficiently rigorous (Erwin 1984b, 426–428), but even if they were, many of the studies included in Smith and Glass's (1977) original meta-analysis and incorporated in Smith et al. (1980) were too weak to warrant a causal inference (see, e.g., the criticisms of Rachman and Wilson 1980, 250–255). For those types of psychotherapy examined only in these seriously deficient studies, no firm evidence of effectiveness is presented in Smith et al. (1980). Consequently, their first major, general conclusion, that "Psychotherapy is beneficial, consistently so and in many different ways" (183) is not supported by their overall argument. The most that is shown is that certain *types* of psychotherapy are effective (and even for these, only for certain types of problems and clients). If the good studies they reviewed are primarily those of cognitive behavior therapy, the remaining studies may tell us little about the effectiveness of other types of psychotherapy. When Prioleau et al. (1983) performed a meta-analysis on the same data, but excluding studies of behavior therapy, they found that for real patients, there was no evidence that the benefits of psychotherapy exceeded those of a placebo.

In addition to the problems with the particular meta-analysis of Smith et al. (1980), there are problems (not necessarily insurmountable) that arise generally in doing a meta-analysis. Some concern the concept of an effect size. Suppose that a meta-analysis is performed on the results of 100 poorly controlled experiments with a certain type of psychotherapy. The effect size might be .90 and yet we might have no evidence that the therapy is effective in producing any beneficial outcome. In general, to say that an effect size is positive does not logically imply that there is any evidence that the outcomes were the results of the hypothesized causes. For that reason, talk of *effect* sizes can be misleading, especially where crucial epistemological requirements for causal inference have been violated. I regard this objection as terminological, but there are also substantive problems with the calculation of effect sizes.

In the analysis of Smith et al. (1980), every measure for a study is counted as a separate effect size. This violates the requirement of statistical independence and has the consequence that studies with a greater number of outcome measures are given greater weight. Hunter and Schmidt (1990, 480) reply that this criticism is "statistically correct," but in a Glassian type of meta-analysis, the purpose of research integration is more descriptive then inferential. However, as Smith et al. (1980) make quite clear, they do use their meta-analysis results in making important causal inferences about the effects of psychotherapy. Had they not made such inferences, it is doubtful that their work would have had the tremendous impact it has had on the field of psychotherapy.

Another way of treating effect sizes (Hunter and Schmidt 1990, 482) is to calculate one for each study, thus insuring statistical independence. One could select one outcome measure among many as "primary," but that would require the kind of substantive methodological judgment that meta-analysts generally want to avoid; more seriously, in the field of psychotherapy, at least, it would run counter to the generally accepted requirement that multiple outcome measures are necessary to adequately assess therapeutic effectiveness. The preferred way, consequently, is to average the effect sizes for a single study. This solution, however, generates other problems. Suppose that in a treatment of depression, treated subjects show only a marginal decrease in depression but a major change in various test scores that reflect tiny beneficial changes. Averaging the results will seriously overestimate the beneficial effects. As Paul (1985) demonstrates, the opposite problem can also occur. In one of his studies, the average effect size for his two focal scales was .45, but in the meta-analysis of Landman and Dawes (1982), an averaging of *all* the outcomes for this same study resulted in a meager effect size of only .04. Apart from underrepresentation or overrepresentation problems, some averaging of outcome measures, as Wilson (1985, 40) points out, makes no clinical sense, as in a study of obesity where we obtain a mean effect size for body fat, body weight, body image, lipoproteins, systolic and diastolic blood pressure, depressed effect, and marital satisfaction. Other problems with the concept of an effect size are raised by Bruno and Ellett (1988).

Even if some of the general difficulties with meta-analysis have not yet been resolved, that does not necessarily argue in favor of non-meta-analytic methods of research integration. All known methods have at least some problems. Furthermore, proponents of meta-analysis argue that their methods have weighty advantages over rival methods. I turn now to some of the more important of these alleged comparative virtues of meta-analysis.

One of these is that the methods are quantitative. If everything else were equal, this would make meta-analysis decidedly more attractive than standard , so-called narrative methods of data analysis. I assume that this point is acceptable even to critics of meta-analysis.

A second alleged virtue of meta-analytic reviews is that they are more complete than narrative reviews. This may be insignificant in areas of science where only a few studies are available, but very important in a field such as psychotherapy where there are hundreds of studies. However, two issues need to be separated. One is about the failure of a reviewer to consider all relevant studies and the second concerns the deliberate decision of a reviewer to dismiss certain studies because of methodological defects.

As to the first issue, there is nothing in the very nature of meta-analysis that guarantees completeness or in narrative reviews that necessitates incompleteness. The meta-analytic review of Smith et al. (1980), for example, is seriously incomplete. In assessing the effects of behavior modification and cognitive behavior therapy, for example, substantial chunks of evidence from studies having a single-subject design were ignored. Other omissions are discussed in Rachman and Wilson (1980, 251–252). A narrative review, in contrast, could cover all those studies reviewed by Smith et al. *plus* those that they failed to consider. So, a meta-analytic review need not be more comprehensive than a narrative review.

As to the question of deliberately excluding very poor studies, some proponents of meta-analysis (Hunter and Schmidt 1960, 468) complain that this tactic unjustifiably wastes much information. It is crucial to distinguish , however, between information that is evidentially relevant and information that is not. If a study of psychotherapy lacks a control group (or the subject's base rate in a single subject design), or provides no evidence that any of the outcome measures reflect any beneficial effect, then the study provides no evidence of effectiveness. Excluding such a study may "waste information," but none that has any evidential bearing on the issue of therapeutic effectiveness. Some proponents of meta-analysis are likely to respond that the rules for determining which information is evidentially relevant and which is not are subjective and arbitrary. I take up this issue next, but so far, on the assumption that studies can be impeached on objective grounds, I see no inherent advantage for meta-analysis on either of the two issues of comprehensiveness: the simple failure to even consider some studies and the considered judgment that some ought to be excluded.

A third alleged advantage of meta-analysis is that it solves the problem of how to treat studies that differ considerably in quality while avoiding the subjectivity of narrative reviews. In traditional, nonquantitative reviews, reviewers often disqualify studies that fall below a certain epistemological standard, but some proponents of meta-analysis, including Smith et al. (1980, 48), complain that such standards are often subjective and arbitrary. Thus, Schmidt (1992, 1179) refers to traditional reviews as being based on "the narrative-subjective method," and Hunter and Schmidt (1990) write: "Glass's position—one that we agree with—is that judgments of overall methodological quality are often very subjective, and inter-evaluator agreement is often low. Therefore, the question should be decided empirically by meta-analyzing separately the studies judged methodologically strong and weak and comparing the results. If they differ, one should rely on the 'strong' studies; if they do not, then all studies should be used" (480–481).

In assessing Hunter and Schmidt's position, it is important to distinguish between an empirical claim about the behavior of reviewers of outcome literature and a philosophical claim about epistemological standards. If their claim is an empirical one, namely, that reviewers often use subjective standards in rejecting certain studies, nothing follows without additional premises about the proper treatment of allegedly weak research studies. If reviewers typically use the wrong standards, the proper remedy is to employ the correct ones. If Hunter and Schmidt, however, are making a philosophical claim, that, too, is not a reason to accept their solution. If the standards for judging psychotherapy outcome standards are inevitably subjective and arbitrary, there is no way of knowing whether any type of psychotherapy is effective. Switching to meta-analysis will do nothing to avoid this skeptical result. Indeed, the solution suggested by Smith et al. (1980) and by Hunter and Schmidt (1990) presupposes that we *can* objectively distinguish between good and bad studies; if that were not possible, we could not empirically determine if the trends of the good and bad studies differ.

Fortunately, there are at least some objective, defensible rules for impeaching poor outcome studies (for a brief discussion of some obvious ones, see Erwin 1984b, 434–435). In that case, traditional narrative reviews need not employ methods that are subjective or arbitrary. Furthermore, the solution recommended by Smith et al. (1980) and Hunter and Schmidt (1990) to the problem of integrating data from good and bad studies encounters its own problems. Assume that a meta-analysis correctly divides up psychotherapy studies into "good" and "bad" categories, finds that their trends are the same, and, consequently, weights them equally. Suppose, however, that the therapies of types T^1 and T^2 are examined only in studies lacking a placebo control, or in those having some other serious defect that prohibits a causal inference, and that the average effect sizes are comparable to those of good studies. In that case, we are not entitled to infer from a conclusion about the overall effect size that either T^1 or T^2 is effective *at all*, let alone that either therapy is as effective as the treatments examined in the superior studies.

Granted that there are some objective, defensible rules for disqualifying certain studies, something that the meta-analyst must presuppose, they might nevertheless yield no decision in certain cases of data integration. Suppose, for example, that there is *some* evidence that the "therapy integrity" problem was resolved in a study (i.e., the therapy described in the study was actually employed), and that the outcome measures were adequate, and that the placebo treatment was credible to the clients, *but* there is also some reason to doubt one or more of these things. To use Rosenthal's (1990, 126) terminology, we do not give the study a zero, but rather a 3 or 4 (out of 10). Exactly how do we weight the evidence from these studies compared with evidence from better studies? This raises complex epistemological issues for the traditional narrative reviewers, but they arise equally for the meta-analyst. There are various proposals for handling this problem, but none has won general assent. It may be that the search for a general solution will prove futile; different rules have to be devised for different areas of research and even different subareas.

This third putative advantage for meta-analysis, then, looks dubious. In cases where certain studies clearly provide no evidence to support a causal inference, a narrative reviewer can disqualify the studies on objective, defensible grounds. Where the evidence is weak but not nonexistent, the narrative reviewer may have no general solution to the problem of how to weight that evidence, but using meta-analysis does not by itself solve the problem.

I conclude, then, that Smith et al. (1980) fail to show either that psychotherapy in general or psychoanalytically oriented psychotherapies in particular are effective. They have also failed to demonstrate that meta-analysis by itself can resolve the epistemological problems of data integration, or that the traditional type of scientific review is inherently incapable of resolving the problems. A fair conclusion would be that some of the problems of data integration have not yet been resolved and meta-analysis might play a useful role in addressing some of them.

The Equivalence Thesis

In their 1975 landmark paper, Luborsky et al. argue for what is known as the equivalence thesis: all psychotherapies are effective and equally effective. If this thesis is true, then, of course, short-term dynamic therapy is effective. Indeed, so is orthodox psychoanalysis, although it would be hard to justify its use given its cost and inefficiency. In a more recent paper, Luborsky and colleagues (1993) provide additional support for the equivalence thesis, citing recent meta-analyses, including their own, of studies pertaining specifically to short term dynamic therapy. Before turning to these recent meta-analyses, a few comments should be made about the original (1975) Luborsky et al..

There are several problems with that review. One concerns the results that were reviewed: they are somewhat mixed. There were 33 comparisons of psychotherapy (excluding behavior therapy) with no treatment. In 20 of these, the psychotherapy group did better than the no treatment group, but in 13 comparisons, there was a tie (Luborsky et al, 1975, 1003). This does not constitute clear and unequivocal evidence for the equivalence thesis.

A second problem concerns the box score method of averaging results. One of these, concerning sample size, was mentioned earlier;

for others, see the penetrating critique of Rachman and Wilson (1980). Other problems (apart from the mixed results) pertain to the original studies. These problems include small sample sizes, atypical patients, problems of therapy integrity, inadequate controls, and dubious outcome measures. The last problem is particularly important. Any reasonable doubt, either about the beneficial nature of the outcome or the validity of the outcome measures, automatically translates into a reasonable doubt as to whether the therapy used in the study was effective to any degree in producing a beneficial outcome. Yet the reviews of Luborsky et al. (1975, 1993) and Smith et al. (1980) do not contain criteria for screening out studies that fail to provide firm evidence of beneficial outcomes. In the original (1975) and new (1993) Luborsky et al. reviews, only two criteria for judging a study pertain to outcomes: one requires that the outcome measures take into account the target goals of the treatment and the other requires that the treatment outcome be evaluated by independent measures. Neither of these, nor both together, guarantee exclusion of a study in which, as far as one can tell, there was no result of any benefit to the client. I turn now to the recent meta-analyses discussed in the new (1993) Luborsky et al. paper.

The results of two of them (Luborsky et al. 1993, Crits-Christoph 1992) are at least consistent with the equivalence thesis. The third, Svartberg and Stiles (1991), is partly in conflict with that thesis. Svartberg and Stiles (1991) review 19 clinically relevant comparative outcome studies of STPP published between 1978 and 1988. Nine of the studies contained a no-treatment comparison (in four studies of patients awaiting psychotherapy, and in five studies of patients not awaiting psychotherapy). In eight of the studies, STPP was compared with a form of cognitive therapy or cognitive behavior therapy (in some cases in addition to a no-treatment condition). Overall, STPP demonstrated a small but statistically significant superiority to wait-list patients at post treatment. This finding is consistent with the equal effectiveness thesis, although Svartberg and Stile note (711) that STPP shows its superiority (to no-treatment controls) predominantly in methodologically poor studies. Another finding is clearly inconsistent with the equivalence thesis: STPP showed significant but small-sized inferiority to alternative treatments at post treatment, and close to a large-sized inferiority at 1-year follow-up. Svartberg and Stile estimate (711) that patients will increase their chance of improvement (assessed at 1-year post testing) from 33% (STPP) to 67% by undergoing a form of psychotherapy other than STPP.

Luborsky et al. (1993) challenge the classification of two studies in the Svartberg and Stiles review as "psychodynamic." It is doubtful, however, that the deletion of these two studies would undermine any of the conclusions stated above. Still, Luborsky et al. raise an important point for the present discussion. Even if one sets aside doubts about methodological quality, what does averaging results of short-term "dynamic" psychotherapy tell us about psychoanalysis, even if only indirectly? Luborsky et al. (6) view short term dynamic therapy as an early "split-off" from psychoanalytic treatment, "copying the parent" in its principles but being shorter. However, there are many different types of dynamic therapy; Koss and Butcher (1986) identify more than 20 variants. Not all "copy the parent," to any great extent. Thus, apart from any other problems, recent meta-analytic reviews of dynamic therapy may be averaging the results of different types of therapies, some of which are quite unlike psychoanalysis. To take but one example, 4 of the 11 studies of "dynamic" therapy in the Crits-Christoph (1992) review employed interpersonal therapy, which, as I noted earlier, bears little resemblance to psychoanalysis. It would clearly be misleading to say of this therapy that it "copies the parent" in its principles, if the parent is said to be psychoanalysis. Crits-Christoph acknowledges the point when he writes of IPT that it "may be quite distant from the psychoanalytically oriented forms of dynamic therapy more commonly practiced" (156).

In reflecting, then, on the recent meta-analyses of dynamic psychotherapy, several points need to be considered, even after setting aside doubts about the meta-analytic method of averaging results. First, although all of the therapies in the original studies are classified by the reviewers as "dynamic," not all bear any close resemblance to psychoanalysis. Second, one of the meta-analyses (Svartberg and Stiles 1991) reached some conclusions inconsistent with the claim that all therapies are equal. Third, if we insist on a higher standard than doing better than a no-treatment group, that is, if we require outperforming a credible placebo, then the studies reviewed in these recent meta-analyses generally fail to meet this standard.

Instead of stating a general conclusion now about the recent (1993) Luborsky et al. paper, I conclude with a discussion of some pertinent theses about both orthodox psychoanalysis and those short term dynamic therapies that closely resemble the parent except for duration of treatment.

The first set of claims concerns orthodox psychoanalysis, although not all analysts would endorse all three: For certain types of clients (say, those suitable for analysis), there is some type of therapeutic benefit, B, such that standard psychoanalysis is (1) generally superior to all other standard treatments in bringing about B; (2) generally more effective than a credible placebo in bringing about B; or (3) generally more effective than no treatment in bringing about B. Given that there are so many different types of therapeutic benefits that might possibly be generated by psychoanalysis, it is difficult to conclude with much confidence that any one of these theses is false; but neither is there any good evidence that any of them is true. So, the verdict for all three should be: not proven (i.e., there is no firm empirical support for any of the three theses).

If we substitute for "psychoanalysis," "psychoanalytically oriented psychotherapy" or "dynamic therapy" (hereinafter "dynamic therapy") of a sort that closely resembles psychoanalysis except for duration, the issues become more complicated. As already noted, there is evidence from controlled studies concerning the latter type (or types) of therapy that needs to be weighed and measured. Here is my brief (perhaps overly brief) analysis of that evidence.

Concerning thesis (1) there is no solid evidence of the superiority of dynamic therapy for any type of therapeutic benefit. Luborsky et al. (1993) would also seemed committed to this verdict insofar as they accept their own equivalence thesis. (They do mention a few possible matches of "special efficacy" of type of treatment with type of patient, but none of these matches includes dynamic therapy.) Despite their embrace of the equivalence thesis, however, they conclude by asking: "Don't you feel, despite all the evidence for the nonsignificant difference effect, that dynamic therapies have some special virtues to offer that are still not well enough recognized?" (26). They answer: "definitely yes." If they mean by this that they definitely *feel* that there are such virtues, no matter what the evidence presently shows, then their sincerity is a guarantee that they are right. If, however, they mean that there now exists some good reason, that is, some evidence, for believing that there are such virtues, they fail to mention any such reason. They list some possibilities—for example, that dynamic therapies have unique long-term benefits—but they cite no evidence of any kind that these possibilities are actualities. The verdict, then, for thesis (*1*) insofar as it pertains to dynamic therapy, is again: not proven.

As to thesis (*2*), it, too, has no supporting evidence. Some will say that this does not matter. Some researchers question whether a psychotherapy should be required to do better than a credible placebo; they question this standard because placebo treatments are not inert or because they themselves count as a form of psychotherapy, or for some other reason. I have replied to these objections earlier, but will repeat one point. Even if it were true that a placebo control is not needed to establish effectiveness, there would remain an issue about degrees of effectiveness. If a particular psychotherapy cannot outperform the sort of placebo used in the collaborative study, a sugar pill plus minimal therapist contact, then it is likely to be inferior on grounds of efficacy and cost-effectiveness. This is clearly true of long term psychoanalysis, but it is also true of most short-term dynamic therapies *if* they cannot outperform a sugar pill. Where it is true, why use dynamic therapy to bring about a certain result, if a sugar pill plus minimal therapist contact will provide the same benefit at less cost and in a shorter time?

Luborsky et al. (1993) might reply that even if the evidence is not yet definitive, dynamic psychotherapies are likely eventually to prove superior to standard placebos. That could happen, but the evidence does not make this result likely. Consider the record of placebo successes.

During the early 1970s, systematic desensitization was said, on the basis of controlled studies, to be more effective than a placebo in treating certain problems. After it was pointed out, however, that the credibility of placebo treatments and systematic desensitization was not equal, new research was done, but conflicting results were obtained (Erwin 1978, 8–9). These results are not directly relevant to psychoanalysis, but they do indicate the potency of credible placebos. Moreover, in studies of dynamic therapy with patients having "real" clinical problems (e.g., Brill et al. 1964; McLean and Hakstian 1979), the clients receiving the dynamic therapy improved approximately to the same degree as those receiving the placebo treatment (see Prioleau et al. 1983, for discussion). Most disturbing of all, in the best-controlled study so far, the National Institute of Mental Health Collaborative Study (Elkin et al. 1989), neither of the two (nondynamic) psychotherapies was able to do more than marginally better than the pill placebo. It may be that dynamic therapies will someday prove to be more effective than the treatments used in the collaborative study, at least for certain types of clients or benefits, but on current evidence there is no reason to be confident that this will prove true. Given the overall record, then, thesis (2) requires a skeptical verdict.

What about thesis (3)? Is it not true, at least, that clients receiving dynamic therapy have generally fared better in controlled experiments than those in no treatment groups? The answer is yes, but that has not been uniformly true. As I noted, in the original (1975) Luborsky et al. review, in 13 of the 33 comparisons the psychotherapy did no better than no treatment. Moreover, in the studies reviewed by Svartberg and Stiles (1991), the superiority to no treatment was shown, as noted earlier, mainly in methodologically deficient studies. So the record is somewhat mixed. But even if it were not, we cannot infer, for reasons given earlier, that a therapy has been effective to any degree merely from the fact that the average improvement is greater at the end of treatment for the therapy group compared with a no-treatment or wait-list control. We would still need reason to discount the causal influence of such pretreatment factors as the client's decision to enter therapy and his or her expectations of cure that existed prior to the onset of the therapy and the pretreatment interview. Even if we can rule out these factors, there is still the problem of separating out the factors that make up the treatment package from such factors as continued expectation of cure, the therapist's warmth, talking about one's problems and other factors common to most therapeutic situations. If we count all of these factors as part of the therapy, and if we can reasonably discount the pretreatment factors, then there may be good evidence that dynamic therapy is more effective than nothing at all in producing certain types of benefits.

We still are not entitled to infer, however, that the ingredients in the therapeutic package that make an important difference are those deemed to be efficacious by psychoanalytic theory. To justify the latter inference, we need more than a comparison with a no-treatment or wait-list control. So, the verdict on thesis (*3*) depends partly on what it means. If it implies merely that when dynamic therapy is used with certain types of clients, some types of benefits generally result from what occurs in the therapeutic situation, then the thesis is probably true (assuming that pretherapy factors cannot plausibly explain all of the gains found in experiments with dynamic therapy). If, however, thesis (*3*) is interpreted to mean that the ingredients that constitute dynamic therapy (according to psychoanalytic theory) generally make an important causal contribution to some type of beneficial change, then the verdict should be, once again: not proven. (For a brief summary, see the beginning of chapter 7, pp. 281–282.)

Chapter 7

A Summing-Up

What, then, does the evidence show concerning Freud's theories and therapy?

Freudian Therapy

Although Freud believed at the time of his 1917 lectures that psychoanalysis was uniquely effective in treating the psychoneuroses, he later expressed doubts. Most contemporary analysts would share those doubts: Few would now argue that *only* analysis is effective, say, in treating depression, phobias, obsessive compulsive disorders, anxiety, and other typical clinical problems. Most would be content with more modest claims, such as one or more of the following:

For certain types of clients (say, those suitable for analysis), there is some type of therapeutic benefit *B* (not necessarily the elimination of some symptom) such that standard psychoanalysis is: (1) generally superior to other treatments in bringing about *B;* (2) generally more effective than a credible placebo in bringing about *B;* (3) generally more effective than no treatment in bringing about *B.* My verdict in chapter 6 (pp. 256–263) on all three propositions was: not proven (where this means not merely not certain but *not supported by any credible evidence*).

Some might be content with even more modest contentions. For example, an analyst might claim to help some patients without contending that it is psychoanalysis that causes the improvement.

Perhaps it is the analyst's skill, intelligence, or warmth that makes the difference. A patient might also say:"Whatever the effects of psychoanalysis, I find it valuable to explore my problems with a trained professional." I have no reason to dispute such claims, but neither implies anything about the effectiveness of psychoanalysis.

Suppose that we change the subject and replace "standard psychoanalysis" with "short-term psychoanalytically oriented psychoanalysis" (or "dynamic psychotherapy") in propositions (*1*), (*2*), and (*3*). The verdicts, then, would be mixed. As I argued in chapter 6 (pp. 277–280), the first two propositions are not supported by current evidence, but the third may be, depending on how it is interpreted. It has empirical support if it implies nothing about the contributions made by the ingredients constituting dynamic therapy as specified by psychoanalytic theory. If, however, we take thesis (*3*) to mean that those psychoanalytic ingredients generally make a significant causal contribution in producing some type of benefit for a certain type of patient, then the verdict is again: not proven.

Freudian Theory

In chapter 1 (pp. 3–8), I collected many of Freud's more important theoretical hypotheses under the following headings.

1. The mental apparatus
2. The theory of dreams
3. Personality types and stages of sexual development
4. The oedipal phase and castration complex
5. The defense mechanisms
6. The etiology of psychoneuroses and slips
7. Paranoia

How many of these hypotheses are we now warranted in believing are true or approximately true? My answer is: virtually none. The verdict is the same, moreover, whether one appeals to experimental or nonexperimental evidence. However, here are some possible exceptions.

(a) Fisher and Greenberg (1985) and Kline (1981) cite evidence for the existence of the anal and oral syndromes. I do not question their evidence, but, as I noted in chapter 5, to assert merely the existence of the syndromes is not to make any theoretical claim (there is no reference here to anything unobservable). Kline does not disagree with this point (1981, 46). I also question whether the claim that the syndromes exist is distinctively Freudian. What are both distinctively Freudian and theoretical are Freud's claims about the etiology and causal consequences of the syndromes, but none of these has been confirmed. Nevertheless, one might argue that even if we subtract the etiological element, Freud should be credited for his observation that certain personality factors, such as orderliness, parsimony, and obstinacy, sometimes come in clusters. I have no quarrel with that point.

(b) Of more potential importance are Freudian claims about the unconscious. As Ellenberger (1970) and others have noted, Freud was hardly the first to talk about the unconscious. Today, it is relatively uncontroversial even among non-Freudians that unconscious mental events occur. There is nothing distinctively Freudian about this claim. Of more interest are Freud's claims about the causal role played by the unconscious, via the operation of defense mechanisms, in the etiology of psychoneuroses, dreams, and parapraxes. These causal claims, however, have not been empirically confirmed.

What about the hypothesis that a specifically Freudian (or dynamic) unconscious exists? Some writers use the following criterion to identify this type of unconscious. They do not mean to refer to an entity, but rather to mental events or states that are inaccessible to consciousness unless the subject is psychoanalyzed. If this is interpreted as implying a causal connection between accessibility and undergoing psychoanalysis, there is no evidence of the unconscious in this sense. Some writers (e.g., Erdelyi 1985), however, use a different criterion: there is a dynamic unconscious if there are mental events outside of consciousness that have an effect on behavior or other mental events and the events are not *readily* accessible and perhaps not accessible at all. I agree that there is evidence of a "dynamic unconscious" in this sense, but not that the mere existence of such events qualifies as distinctively Freudian. As I noted in chapter 5, unconscious mental events studied in semantic priming experiments (Marcel 1983) would qualify as part of the dynamic unconscious according to the criterion just mentioned, as would optical rules of scaling, to take one of Erdelyi's own examples (1985, 63); but both of these are postulated by theories in cognitive psychology and neither is distinctively Freudian.

Because there are clear and important disanalogies between a Freudian and so-called cognitive unconscious (see Eagle 1987), I concluded in chapter 5 that recent experimental work in cognitive psychology fails to support the existence of a specifically Freudian unconscious. However, there are continuing attempts to draw analogies of one sort or another between Freud's concept and that employed by non-Freudian cognitivists (see, for example, Greenwald's 1992 discussion of whether the unconscious is "smart or dumb," and various replies, including Bruner 1992; Kihlstrom, Barnhardt, and Tataryn 1992; Erdelyi 1992; and Merikle, 1992). Without some way to tell which analogies and disanalogies are crucial, there is bound to be some unclarity about what exactly is the Freudian concept of the unconscious. Given this conceptual unclarity, there is room for doubt about my conclusion (chapter 5) that the evidence fails to support the existence of a distinctively Freudian unconscious. So here is one possible case of a confirmed Freudian theoretical hypothesis: that a Freudian unconscious exists.

(c) Finally, there is the much-discussed issue of the existence of repression, and of other Freudian defense mechanisms (if these are distinguished from repression). Freud's theory of repression, which postulates a certain causal role for repression, in the etiology of slips, dreams, and psychoneuroses, has not been empirically confirmed. But what of the mere existence of repression? Some writers detach the concept of repression from talk of the Freudian mental apparatus and of any distinctively Freudian unconscious. What appears to be left, however, is something very much like Erdelyi's (1985) account: we repress something if we intentionally keep something out of consciousness in order to avoid psychological pain. Repression in this sense does occur; it occurs, for example, when people succeed in blocking out of consciousness the fact that they are dying or when they deliberately do things to cause the forgetting of a failed love affair. Repression in this sense is not distinctively Freudian. In the sense defined by Holmes (1990), in contrast, it is distinctively Freudian, but even its existence, let alone its causal role, has not been established.

Still, as with Freud's concept of the unconscious, there can be reasonable disagreement as to what to include within the concept. So, here is another possible instance of a confirmed Freudian hypothesis: that Freudian repression does occur. As noted before, that is far different, of course, from saying that the theory of repression has been confirmed.

The points made about repression also apply to the other defense mechanisms. Freud sometimes ties them conceptually to his postulated mental apparatus, as when their operation is said to involve the ego's acting to protect against the id or superego. Their very existence, then, is as doubtful as the existence of the Freudian mental apparatus. One can certainly break this connection, but then it is unclear that the mere claim that they exist is distinctively Freudian. Freudian theory also makes causal claims about certain defense mechanisms and clinical disorders. For example, projection and reaction formation are said to play a crucial role in the development of paranoia; isolation is said to be important in the development of obsessional neurosis. None of these etiological claims, however, has been confirmed.

In sum, none of the aforementioned cases constitutes a clear example of a well confirmed, distinctively Freudian hypothesis. Because of vagueness and other unclarities in the concepts of repression, a Freudian unconscious, or the idea of a distinctively Freudian hypothesis, the existence of a Freudian unconscious *or* repression *or* other defense mechanisms *might* qualify. Still, without support for the etiology postulated by Freudian theory (in the case of the personality syndromes, repression, and the other defense mechanisms) or the theorized causal role of the unconscious, confirmation merely of the existence of these items would constitute vindication of a relatively minor part of Freudian theory.

The seven Freudian categories listed earlier were intended to include distinctively Freudian theoretical hypotheses that have been studied experimentally. What of those that do not have any even seeming experimental support, such as Freudian claims about penis envy, the pleasure principle, the death instinct, the inheritance of our ancestors' experiences, or the origin of religion? Based on the arguments of part I, it is reasonable to infer that none of the ones just mentioned are well supported if the putative support is entirely nonexperimental. I leave open whether there might be other parts of Freudian theory not discussed here that have firm support of a nonexperimental kind, but I am skeptical.

There is one other part of Freudian theory that should be mentioned. It is considered by some analysts as being extremely important and as having empirical support. I am referring to Freud's transference hypothesis. In *An Outline of Psychoanalysis,* Freud says the following about the patient's typical reaction to the analyst:

On the contrary, the patient sees in him the return, the reincarnation, of some important figure out of his childhood or past, and consequently transfers on to him feelings and reactions which undoubtedly applied to this prototype. This fact of transference soon proves to be a factor of undreamt-of importance, on the one hand an instrument of Irreplaceable value and on the other hand a source of serious dangers. This transference is *ambivalent:* it comprises positive (affectionate) as well as negative (hostile) attitudes towards the analyst, who as a rule is put in the place of one or other of the patient's parents, his father or mother. (Freud's emphasis, 1940, *S.E.,* 23:174–175)

The key theoretical claim here is that in the course of an analysis, the patient sees the analyst as the reincarnation of some important figure of the patient's childhood or past, and as a consequence transfers toward the analyst positive or negative feelings that were formerly directed toward the figure from the past. As Laplanche and Pontalis (1974, 455) succinctly phrase the thesis, "In the transference, infantile prototypes re-emerge and are experienced with a strong sensation of immediacy."

In their respective reviews of Freudian experimental literature, nether Fisher and Greenberg (1985) nor Kline (1981) claim that there is any experimental support for the transference hypothesis. Without such support (and the more recent literature also fails to provide any), this particular theoretical proposition is still speculative.

As Laplance and Pontalis point out (1974), 456), however, the term "transference" is also used to refer to *observable* aspects of the patient-analyst relationship, regardless of what causes them. The proposition describing these observable phenomena are not part of Freudian theory; nor are they distinctively Freudian, whether or not Freud was the first to state them. Even a critic of Freudian theory, such as Hans Eysenck (1994, 480), can agree, for example, that an observable dependence relationship sometimes develops between the therapist and client, but he can offer a non-Freudian explanation of such occurrences.

The ambiguity in the use of the term "transference" is reflected in the title of a paper by Lester Luborsky and his colleagues, "A Verification of Freud's Grandest Clinical Hypothesis: The Transference" (Luborsky et al. 1985). One might read this as suggesting that Freud's theory about the reemergence of infantile prototypes has been verified. In fact, the research that is reported, which is systematic but nonexperimental, provides no confirmation at all of this hypothesis. What Luborsky and his colleagues attempt to support is a series of hypotheses that for the most part describe observable behavioral patterns of the patient in analysis. There are two exceptions, but neither is distinctively Freudian. One says that the patient is aware of some of his or her libidinal impulses, but is unaware of others. The second says that the so-called "transference" pattern of behavior is "derived from" the patient's innate disposition and the influences brought to bear on him during his early years.

As Morris Eagle points out (1986, 77–78), if "derived from" is interpreted in causal terms, Luborsky's data fail to support the proposition. If, as Luborsky apparently intends (see Luborsky et al. 1985, 242),. what is being claimed is merely that there are *similarities* between the patient's current attitudes toward the therapist and past attitudes toward his or her parents, the proposition is not distinctively Freudian, and as Eagle notes (77), is not especially startling.

I have argued for an agnostic verdict concerning most of Freudian theory, but some of Freud's opponents are unlikely to be satisfied. Hans Eysenck (1985), for example, concludes that what is new in Freudian theory is not true and what is true is now new. This implies that everything that is new is false, no merely not known to be true.

If this is what Eysenck intends, then I believe that his verdict is too extreme. There are too many parts of Freudian theory that have been neither confirmed no disconfirmed. I would agree, however, that in some cases it is reasonable to go beyond a "not supported" verdict.

One example concerns Freud's claim about the etiology and maintenance of the psychoneuroses. If that claim were generally true, we should expect to find that symptom substitution or relapse would *generally* (perhaps not invariably) follow successful so called symptomatic treatments (i.e., treatments not aimed at rooting out repressed wishes). Indeed, many Freudians did make this prediction on the basis of Freudian theory when behavioral treatments first became popular. That prediction has been disconfirmed by numerous studies of behavioral and cognitive-behavioral therapies that included relatively long term follow-ups. One could try to explain away these negative results by claiming, for example, that symptomatic treatments generally *do* eliminate repressed wishes, even though the therapists using the treatments make no attempt to do so. Such a claim, however, is not supported by any evidence and is implausible. Without any plausible way to explain away the findings, a reasonable conclusion is that Freud's claim about the origin and maintenance of the psychoneuroses is false. (One might still try to salvage his etiologic claim by postulating "ghost symptoms," as Rhoads and Feather [1974] do. Their hypothesis, however, has no independent support. Furthermore, if it were confirmed, it would undermine completely the rationale for using Freudian therapy in treating the ghost symptoms (see Erwin [1978, 161] and Grünbaum [1984, 165]).

A second major example of a disconfirmation concerns Freud's theory of dreams. Although Freud revised his theory more than once, a central component of what is now called "Freud's dream theory" is the thesis that all dreams are wish fulfillments, or attempts at wish fulfillments. Counterwish dreams, where the dreamer dreams of events running directly counter to his or her wishes, are quite common and provide an apparent disconfirmation of Freud's theory. Freud agreed, and asked of one such dream, as Grünbaum notes (1993, 361), "was not this the sharpest possible contradiction of my theory that in dreams wishes are fulfilled?" He tried, however, to save the theory by attributing to the dreamer the wish to refute him or her. However, as Grünbaum shows (360–370), Freud's attempt fails. On the plausible assumption that in some, indeed many, cases of counterwish dreams, there is no wish to refute, or any other such wish consistent with Freudian theory, or any masochistic disposition on the part of the dreamer, such dreams count as some evidence that Freud's theory is false. Of course, it would be too strong to say this with certitude. It is possible that in all cases of counterwish dreams, there is a hidden wish that no one has unearthed. It would also be too weak, however, to say merely that Freud's dream theory is unsupported; it is more plausible than not, for reasons given by Grünbaum, to conclude that the theory is wrong.

Grünbaum (1993, 370–376) also develops a second objection to Freudian dream theory. He argues that if long term psychoanalytic treatment succeeds in lifting the client's repressions, then the cured patients will experience a significant reduction in the frequency of their dreams if the dream theory is true. Assuming, as is likely, that such a reduction in the frequency of dreaming generally does not occur, the dream theory is false. It is not adequate to reply here, as David Sachs does (1989, 371), that Freud himself did not believe that patients cured by analysts will dream less. Grünbaum's point is not about what Freud believed on this issue; it is about what Freudian theory says about the role of repressed wishes in instigating dreams and about what the theory plus plausible assumptions implies about reduction of the frequency of dreaming. A better reply, as Grünbaum is aware, is to challenge the supposition that analysts typically eliminate repressed wishes in those cases where the patient is cured. There is no evidence that this assumption is true. Now, however, we must choose: either the dream theory or the assumption about the lifting of repressions is false. I am inclined to reject the second disjunct because of the evidence alluded to earlier about symptom substitution. That evidence makes it likely that neurotic symptoms, whatever their original cause, are not maintained by repressed wishes. One could argue that perhaps analysts typically eliminate other repressed wishes, ones that do not cause the symptoms. But how likely is that? And of what use would this be? It is more plausible to infer that even when the patient is cured, the analyst does not typically lift repressions. We might, then, try to save the dream theory by denying the second disjunct of the dilemma that I stated (i.e., that analysts typically lift repressions). However, as I noted earlier, counterwish dreams provide independent evidence against Freudian dream theory.

Findings in the neurosciences may also tell against other parts of Freud's dream theory. However, I shall not argue the case here (see Hobson 1988; Porte 1988).

A third example of a disconfirmation is the Freudian hypothesis that repressed homosexuality is causally implicated in all cases of paranoia. This hypothesis is disconfirmed by the finding that some paranoids are consciously homosexual (Klaf and Davis 1960). Freud's hypothesis about the etiology of paranoia, however, is not so central to his overall theory compared to the first two examples. Moreover, it is still possible to hold that in a certain unknown percentage of cases of paranoia, repressed wishes are an important causal factor. This weaker claim is unsupported but not refuted.

Even when experiments fail either to confirm or disconfirm a Freudian hypothesis, the proper verdict may not be merely "not proven," or even "not supported to any degree." The proper verdict may be that there is some reason to think the hypothesis is false. Failure to confirm by itself does not provide such a reason, but it may do so in conjunction with other evidence. If a hypothesis is antecedently implausible given our background evidence, and we fail to confirm it, then we have some reason to believe the hypothesis false. When Wilhelm Reich went to see Einstein about his alleged discovery of orgone energy, he believed that the energy could be measured using a Geiger-Müller counter (Boadella 1973). The failure to register any such measurement was not merely reason for Einstein to suspend judgment; given his overall background evidence, it was reason to believe that the existence of orgone energy was unlikely.

Many distinctively Freudian hypotheses are like Reich's theory in that they have an initial implausibility. As I pointed out in an earlier paper (Erwin 1986b, 236), that is one reason why they are interesting. Of course, not all are equally implausible, and some may have indirect support. But for those that are implausible, all things considered, are we not entitled to say, although tentatively, that there is some reason to think them false?

Marshall Edelson (1988, 316) has replied to the above point, but he has not answered it. Contrary to what he suggests, I am *not* assuming that indirect evidence is not evidence, or that the absence of evidence is by itself equivalent to no evidence, or that clinical data cannot count as evidence (whether it is likely to be confirmatory of Freudian theory in particular is a separate issue).

The present point is actually quite trivial: if hypothesis H is rendered implausible by background evidence, and we fail to confirm it to any degree, then of course we have reason to believe it false. The background evidence either supplies such a reason or it fails to make the hypothesis implausible. The only reason I stress such a modest point is that it is often overlooked in the discussion of Freudian evidence. Commentators often note that certain experiments fail to confirm a certain hypothesis, but then point out that the design was defective. So they conclude that the hypothesis is neither confirmed nor disconfirmed. This overlooks, in some cases, the fact that the hypothesis was implausible from the outset. Which distinctively Freudian hypotheses fall into this category is not always easy to determine. Here, without offering any supporting arguments, are what I conjecture to be some likely candidates: that the therapy is generally more effective than a credible placebo in treating psychoneurotic patients suitable for analysis; that the mind consists of an id, ego, and superego; parts of the theory of dreams besides the thesis that dreams are wish fulfillments; the theory of the Oedipus and castration complexes; the theory of psychosexual development (minus the claim that some of the personality syndromes exist); and the causal role of repressed wishes, as postulated by the repression theory, in explaining the etiology and maintenance of the psychoneuroses, or the etiology of dreams, or slips of the tongue. To argue for the implausibility of all of these claims would take some time and work. In some cases, it would require reviewing vast amounts of evidence and counterevidence concerning theories that rival Freud's. I am not going to attempt such an undertaking here. I conclude only that some of Freud's distinctive hypotheses are implausible if unsupported. I am not going to argue that this is so for any particular hypothesis. Instead, I rest with the earlier verdict: Most of Freudian theory, including all of those parts identified earlier (some possible exceptions were noted), are unsupported by good evidence; a few parts that I named earlier, and possibly others, have been disconfirmed.

A Final Accounting?

I return now to the question I asked in the introduction: Is it now possible to give a final accounting of Freud's work?

Freudian Therapy

I doubt that any final verdict is possible now on the effectiveness of the various kinds of short-term dynamic psychotherapies that resemble standard psychoanalysis in varying degrees. Research on these therapies is continuing and better evidence is likely to be discovered in the future. That is not likely, in contrast, for standard psychoanalysis. Because of perceived ethical problems and the expense of conducting a series of experimental studies of such a long term therapy (the past record indicates that *one* experimental study would not be enough), the needed experiments are unlikely to be performed. Consequently, the current verdict is not likely to change even 50 years from now. We may not know that the therapy is generally ineffective (I omit here the necessary caveats), but neither are we ever likely to be justified in believing that it is effective. The verdict given earlier—that for any type of therapeutic benefit, there is no evidence that standard, long term psychoanalysis is generally more effective in producing it than a credible, inexpensive placebo—is likely to remain the final verdict.

Freudian Theory

First, I need to explain what I am not saying. I am not saying that discussions of Freudian theory are likely to end in the near future, nor that they should stop. Many issues are still unresolved. In addition, Freudian theory can sometimes play a useful heuristic role in guiding experiments. Doing the experiments may be worthwhile even if what is confirmed is only marginally relevant to traditional Freudian theory. Whether the likely payoff is sufficient to justify the time, money, and effort is a complicated issue; some may be worth doing and others not.

I am also not saying that the two verdicts that I am about to give are the only ones that can be given. One could, for example, evaluate Freudian theory from a nonrealist perspective, and inquire about its fertility in generating useful research.

I also do not mean to suggest, of course, that my account is unassailable. One could attack some of the underlying epistemic principles, or some of the empirical arguments, or some of my interpretations of Freud; or one could argue that some of the empirical evidence left undiscussed would make a significant difference if considered. I believe that in the end none of these things will radically alter the picture, but this raises a different issue than the hypothetical one I am about to raise. The claim that my account is basically right rests, of course, on the preceding arguments, but *if* it is right, and the supporting arguments are sound, are the verdicts I am about to render likely to be final? I think the answer is yes, although my reasons are meant to be tentative.

Future confirmatory evidence for the theory will necessarily be either experimental or nonexperimental. Consider first the experimental option.

There are several factors to weigh here. One I referred to earlier is the initial implausibility of many Freudian hypotheses. Compare them to hypotheses currently neither established nor refuted but also not implausible given our total evidence. Suppose, for example, that the evidence so far is conflicting as to whether vitamin E protects certain populations against heart disease to some degree. Supporters of the hypothesis may reasonably claim that even if it is not likely it is also not unlikely that future epidemiological studies will provide confirming evidence, provided that the studies are done and are properly designed. How many Freudian hypotheses are like the vitamin E thesis in this respect? Perform the following thought experiment. Subtract out all of the evidence that has been falsely claimed to support Freud's views, and add in all of the relevant evidence amassed in the past 30 years in cognitive science, in neuroscience, and in studies of behavior therapy, cognitive therapy, dream research, personality theory, drug studies, etc.

Given this recent evidence, how many parts of Freudian theory are like the vitamin E hypothesis? Of how many can we correctly say: Agnosticism is the proper epistemic attitude about the likelihood of future experimental confirmation, assuming that the needed experiments are done? I think the answer is: very few. Because I have not argued for this answer, I will not rely on it. Nevertheless, to have a complete picture of the prospects for future experimental confirmation, we obviously would have to consider the issue of current plausibility.

Current plausibility aside, the Freudian experimental record to date also needs to be considered. The Freudian experimental tradition is more than 60 years old. More than 1500 Freudian experiments have been done during this period, many reflecting great ingenuity and immense labor. Yet the amount of confirmation of distinctively Freudian hypotheses is close to zero. Even if the tradition were to continue, how likely is it that we would do better in the next 60 years? I think it unlikely for the following reasons.

I remain unconvinced by the Popperian arguments that it is logically impossible to test Freudian theory (Erwin 1988b; Grünbaum 1993, chapter 2) or by the a priori arguments of Freudians who say, without examining the evidence, that experimental confirmation is not possible. However, both groups do have a point: devising experiments that would really test Freudian theory, and not merely some pale commonsense reflection of it, is extremely difficult. Once we look at the track record and see how little has been accomplished, despite great ingenuity and hard work, we have reason to doubt that we are likely to do significantly better in the future. Anti-Freudians may explain the poverty of the results in terms of the basic falsity of the theory, Popperians in terms of its pseudo-scientific nature, humanistic Freudians in terms of the sterility of experimental methods (at least when used in the social sciences), and experimentally minded Freudians in terms of methodological mistakes. Whatever the correct explanation, the record so far is not encouraging.

It is still possible for an experimentally minded Freudian to argue that we will do better when we correct the methodological mistakes of the past. But exactly how are we to do that? Take one example. We can repeat some of the earlier Freudian experiments but stop relying on projective tests that lack validity. However, what is to take their place? Someone who wishes to argue that the poor track record so far is primarily due to methodological errors *that are likely to be corrected* should explain how that is likely to be done.

Perhaps a new sort of experimental approach would work. Significant progress is being made in neuroscience. Should we not expect that discoveries in this area will confirm some of Freud's ideas? That is a possibility, but there is a reason why it is unlikely. Neuroscientists can find correlations or causal connections between certain brain events and mental events, but only if they can establish the occurrence of both types of events. To demonstrate that the events postulated by Freudian theory really do occur and that they have the causal significance assigned by the theory, neuroscientists would have to overcome the same sorts of obstacles faced by experimentally minded psychologists who tried, unsuccessfully, to confirm Freudian hypotheses.

A third factor to consider is whether a robust Freudian experimental tradition is likely to continue. Experiments are still being done in the areas of repression, the defense mechanisms, and the Freudian-cognitive unconscious. For most parts of Freudian theory, however, the experimental output is anemic. Experimental psychologists are much more interested in cognitive science and other matters than in confirming Freud's views. It is a conjecture, but a reasonable one, that this trend of experimentalists turning their attention away from Freudian psychology will continue.

Predicting the future of science is usually risky. Still, when the last two factors I mentioned are added together, it becomes reasonable (though hardly guaranteed) to suppose that little, if any, confirmation of distinctively Freudian hypotheses will come from future experimental studies.

Most Freudians will respond that the absence of experimental confirmation is not crucially important. Future confirmation, they will say, will come *as before* from nonexperimental sources: from the study of patients; from anthropology, history, and sociology; from art, literature, and even our dreams. Here my reply is based on the arguments of the earlier chapters concerning evidential standards, and on the arguments of Adolf Grünbaum (1984, 1993) and others who have argued for the need for experimental evidence. The cumulative result of these arguments is that the hope of confirming more than a tiny part of Freudian theory through future *nonexperimental* discoveries is one unlikely to be realized.

As the century ends, a century that some have called "the century of Freud," the evidence supports the following verdicts. Has the effectiveness of Freud's therapy been established? No. How much of his theory has been confirmed? Virtually none of it. These verdicts are likely to be final.

References

Abraham, K. [1924] 1965. Contributions to the theory of the anal character. In *Selected Papers of Karl Abraham*. London: Hogarth Press and Institute of Psychoanalysis.

Abraham, K. [1927].1965 The influence of oral erotism on character formation. In *Selected Papers of Karl Abraham*. London: Hogarth Press and Institute of Psychoanalysis.

Accord, L. D. 1962. Sexual symbolism as a correlate of age. *Journal Consulting Psychology* 26:279–281.

Achinstein, P. 1965. The problem of theoretical terms. *American Philosophical Quarterly* 2:193–203.

Achinstein, P. 1983. The concept of evidence. In *The Concept of Evidence,* edited by P. Achinstein. New York: Oxford University Press.

Achinstein, P. 1991. *Particles and Waves: Historical Essays in the Philosophy of Science.* New York: Oxford University Press.

Achinstein, P. 1992. Inference to the best explanations: Or, who won the Mill-Whewell debate? *Studies in History and Philosophy of Science* 23:349–364.

Allen, J., and T. Condor. 1982. Whither subliminal psychodynamic activation? A reply to Silverman. *Journal of Abnormal Psychology* 9:131–133.

American Psychiatric Association. 1976. *Task Report Force 11: The Psychiatrist as Psychohistorian*. Washington, D.C.: American Psychiatric Association.

Aronson, M. 1952. A study of the Freudian theory of paranoia by means of the Blackey Pictures. *Journal of Projective Techniques* 17:3–19.

Ayllon, T., and E. Haughton. 1964. Modification of symptomatic verbal behavior of mental patients. *Behaviour Research and Therapy* 2:87–97.

Ayllon, T., E. Haughton, and H. Hughes. 1965. Interpretation of symptoms: Fact or fiction? *Behaviour Research and Therapy* 3:1–7.

References

Bachrach, H., R. Galatzer-Levy, A. Skolnikoff, and S. Waldron. 1991. On the efficacy of psychoanalysis. *Journal of the American Psychoanalytic Association.* 39:871–916.

Bandura, A. 1978. On paradigms and recycled ideologies. *Cognitive Therapy and Research* 2:79–103.

Bandura, A. 1982. Self-efficacy mechanisms in human agency. *American Psychologist* 37:122–147.

Bandura, A., N. Adams, and J. Beyer. 1977. Cognitive processes mediating behavioral change. *Journal of Personality and Social Psychology* 35:125–139.

Barendregt, J., J. Bastiaans, and A. Vermeul-van Mullen. 1961. A psychological study of the effect of psychoanalysis and psychotherapy. In *Research in Psychodiagnostics,* edited by J. Barendregt. The Hague and Paris: Mouton.

Barlow, D., and M. Hersen. 1984. *Single Case Experimental Designs: Strategies for Studying Behavioral Change.* New York: Pergamon Press.

Beck, A. 1976. *Cognitive Therapy and the Emotional Disorders.* New York: International Universities Press.

Beloff, H. 1957. The structure and origin of the anal character. *Genetic Psychology Monographs* 55:141–172.

Berger, P. L. 1963. Experimental modification of dream content by meaningful verbal stimuli. *British Journal of Psychiatry* 109:722–740.

Bergin, A. 1991. Values and religious issues in psychotherapy and mental health. *American Psychologist* 46:394–403.

Binns, P. 1990. Experimental evidence and psychotherapy. *British Journal for the Philosophy of Science* 41:531–551.

Bloom, L. 1962. Further thoughts on tipping. *Psychoanalysis and the Psychoanalytic Review* 149:135–137.

Blum, G. S. 1954. An experimental reunion of psychoanalytic theory with perceptual vigilance and defence. *Journal of Abnormal and Social Psychology* 49:94–98.

Blum, G. S. 1955. Perceptual defence revisited. *Journal of Abnormal and Social Psychology* 51:24–29.

Boadella, D. 1973. *Willhelm Reich: The Evolution of His Work.* New York: Dell.

Brandt, R. 1979. *A Theory of the Good and Right.* New York: Oxford University Press.

Brenner, C. 1973. *An Elementary Textbook of Psychoanalysis,* ed. 2. Garden City, N.Y.: Doubleday.

Brewer, W. 1974. There is no convincing evidence for operant or classical conditioning in adult humans. In *Cognition and the Symbolic Processes,* edited by W. Weimer and D. Palermo. Hillsdale, N.J.: Lawrence Erlbaum.

References

Brill, N., R. Koegler, L. Epstein, and E. Forgy. 1964. Controlled study of psychiatric outpatient treatment. *Archives of General Psychiatry* 10:581–595.

Brown, W. 1961. Conceptions of perceptual defense. *British Journal of Psychology,* Monograph Supplement No. 35.

Bruner, J. 1992. Another look at new look 1. *American Psychologist* 47:780–783.

Bruno, J., F. Ellet, Jr. 1988. A core-analysis of meta-analysis. *Quality and Quantity* 22:111–126.

Cameron, P. 1967. Confirmation of the Freudian psychosexual stages utilizing sexual symbolism. *Psychological Reports* 21:1.

Campbell, D., and J. Stanley. 1963. *Experimental and Quasi-Experimental Designs for Research.* Chicago: Rand McNally.

Cappon, D. 1964. Results of psychotherapy. *British Journal of Psychiatry* 110:35–45.

Cattell, R. B., 1957. *Personality and Motivation Structure and Measurement.* Yonkers: New World.

Cattell, R. B., and K. Pawlik. 1964. Third-order factors in objective personality tests. *British Journal of Psychology* 55:1–18.

Cavell, M. 1993. *The Psychoanalytic Mind: From Freud to Philosophy.* Cambridge, Mass.: Harvard University Press.

Chomsky, N. 1990. Accessibility in principle. *Behavioral and Brain Sciences* 13:600–601.

Crews, F. 1986. *Skeptical Engagements.* New York: Oxford University Press.

Crews, F. 1993. The unknown Freud. *New York Review of Books,* November 18, pp. 55–66.

Crits-Christoph, P. 1992. The efficacy of brief psychotherapy: A meta-analysis. *The American Journal of Psychiatry* 149:151–158.

Daston, P. 1956. Perception of homosexual words in paranoid schizophrenia. *Perceptual and Motor Skills* 6:45–55.

Davison, G. 1976. Homosexuality: The ethical challenge. *Journal of Consulting and Clinical Psychology* 44:157–162.

Dixon, N. 1958. Apparatus for the continuous recording of the visual threshold by the method of "closed loop control." *Quarterly Journal of Experimental Psychology* 10:62–63.

Dixon, N. 1971. *Subliminal Perception: The Nature of a Controversy.* London: McGraw-Hill.

Dixon, N. 1986. On private events and brain events. *The Behavioral and Brain Sciences* 9:29–30.

References

Dixon, J., C. De Monchaux, and J. Sandler. 1957. Patterns of anxiety: The phobias. *British Journal of Medical Psychology* 30:34–40.

Dollard, J., L. W. Doob, N. E. Miller, O. H. Mowrer, and R. R. Sears. 1939. *Frustration and Aggression*. New Haven, Conn.: Yale University Press.

Duhrssen, A., and E. Jorswieck. 1965. Ein empirisch-statistische Untersuchung zur Leistungs-fähigkeit psychoanalytischer Behandlung [An empirical-statistical investigation into the efficacy of psychoanalytic therapy]. *Nervenarzt* 36:166–169.

Eagle, M. 1984. *Recent Developments in Psychoanalysis: A Critical Examination*. New York: McGraw-Hill.

Eagle, M. 1986. Critical notice: A. Grünbaum's *The Foundations of Psychoanalysis: A Philosophical Critique*. *Philosophy of Science* 53:65–88.

Eagle, M. 1987. The psychoanalytic and the cognitive unconscious. In *Theories of the Unconscious and Theories of the Self*, edited by S. Stern. Hillsdale, N.J.: Analytic Press.

Eagle, M. 1993. The dynamics of theory change in psychoanalysis. In *Philosophical Problems of the Internal and External Worlds: Essays on the Philosophy of Adolf Grünbaum*, edited by J. Earman, A. Janis, G. Massey, and N. Rescher. Pittsburgh: University of Pittsburgh Press.

Edelson, M. 1984. *Hypothesis and Evidence in Psychoanalysis*. Chicago: University of Chicago Press.

Edelson, M. 1988. *Psychoanalysis: A Theory in Crisis*. Chicago: University of Chicago Press.

Editorial Commentary. 1990. *Behavioral and Brain Sciences* 13:632.

Elkin, I., T. Shea, J. Watkins, S. Imber, S. Sotsky, J. Collins, D. Glass, P. Pilkonis, W. Leber, J. Docherty, A. Fiester, and M. Parloff. 1989. National Institute of Mental Health treatment of depression collaborative research program. *Archives of General Psychiatry* 46:971–982.

Ellenberger, H. F. 1970. *The Discovery of the Unconscious*. New York: Basic Books.

Ellis, A. 1993. Reflections on rational emotive therapy. *Journal of Consulting and Clinical Psychology* 61:199–201.

Emmelkamp, P., and H. Straatman. 1976. A psychoanalytic reinterpretation of the effectiveness of systematic desensitization: Fact or fiction? *Behaviour Research and Therapy* 14:245–249.

Erdelyi, M. 1985. *Psychoanalysis: Freud's Cognitive Psychology*. New York: W. H. Freeman.

Erdelyi, M. 1992. Psychodynamics and the unconscious. *American Psychologist* 47:784–787.

Erwin, E. 1978. *Behavior Therapy: Scientific, Philosophical and Moral Foundations*. New York: Cambridge University Press.

References

Erwin, E. 1980. Psychoanalytic therapy: The Eysenck argument. *American Psychologist* 35:435–443.

Erwin, E. 1984a. The standing of psychoanalysis. *British Journal for the Philosophy of Science* 35:115–128.

Erwin, E. 1984b. Establishing causal connections: meta-analysis and psychotherapy. *Midwest Studies in Philosophy* 9:421–436.

Erwin, E. 1985. Holistic psychotherapies: What works? In *Examining Holistic Medicine,* edited by D. Stalker and C. Glymour. Buffalo, N.Y.: Prometheus Books.

Erwin, E. 1986a. Psychotherapy and Freudian psychology. In *Hans Eysenck: Consensus and Controversy,* edited by S. Modgil and C. Modgil. London: Falmer Press.

Erwin, E. 1986b. Defending Freudianism. *The Behavioral and Brain Sciences* 9:235–236.

Erwin, E. 1988a. Psychoanalysis: Clinical versus experimental evidence. In *Mind, Psychoanalysis and Science,* edited by P. Clark and C. Wright. New York: Basil Blackwell.

Erwin, E. 1988b. Testing Freudian hypotheses. In *Theory and Experiment,* edited by D. Batens and J. van Bendegem. Boston: D. Reidel.

Erwin, E. 1992. Current philosophical issues in the scientific evaluation of behavior therapy theory and outcome. *Behavior Therapy* 23:151–171.

Erwin, E. 1993. Philosophers on Freudianism: An examination of replies to Grünbaum's *Foundations.* In *Philosophical Problems of the Internal and External Worlds: Essays on the Philosophy of Adolf Grünbaum,* edited by J. Earman, A. Janis, G. Massey, and N. Rescher. Pittsburgh: University of Pittsburgh Press.

Erwin, E. 1994. The Effectiveness of psychotherapy: Epistemological issues. In *Philosophical Psychopathology: A Book of Readings,* edited by G. Graham and L. Stephens. Cambridge, Mass.: MIT Press.

Erwin, E., S. Gendin, and L. Kleiman (editors). 1994. *Ethical Issues in Scientific Research: An Anthology.* New York: Garland.

Erwin, E., and H. Siegel. 1989. Is confirmation differential? *British Journal for the Philosophy of Science* 40:105–119.

Esterson, A. 1993. *Seductive Mirage: An Exploration of the Work of Sigmund Freud.* Chicago: Open Court.

Eylon, Y. 1967. Birth events, appendicitis and appendectomy. *British Journal of Medicine* 40:317.

Eysenck, H. J. 1978. An exercise in mega-silliness. *American Psychologist* 33:517.

Eysenck, H. J. 1983a. Classical conditioning and extinction: The general model for the treatment of neurotic disorders. In *Perspectives on Behavior Therapy in the Eighties,* edited by M. Rosenbaum, C. Franks, and Y. Jaffe. New York: Springer.

References

Eysenck, H. J. 1983b. The effectiveness of psychotherapy: The specter at the feast. *The Behavioral and Brain Sciences* 6:290.

Eysenck, H. J. 1985. *Decline and Fall of the Freudian Empire*. New York: Viking.

Eysenck, H. J. 1986. Consensus and controversy—Two types of science. In *Hans Eysenck: Consensus and Controversy*, edited by S. Modgil and C. Modgil. London: Falmer Press.

Eysenck, H. J. 1988. Psychoanalysis to behavior therapy: A paradigm shift. In *Paradigms in Behavior Therapy: Present and Promise*, edited by D. Fishman, F. Rotgers, and C. Franks. New York:Springer.

Eysenck, H. J. 1994. The outcome problem in psychotherapy: What have we learned? *Behavior Research and Therapy* 32:477–495.

Eysenck, H. J., and M. Soueif. 1972. An empirical test of the theory of sexual symbolism. *Perceptual and Motor Skills* 35:945–946.

Eysenck, H. J., and G. D. Wilson. 1973. *The Experimental Study of Freudian Theories*. London: Methuen.

Farrell, B. A. 1981. *The Standing of Psychoanalysis*. New York: Oxford University Press.

Feldman, M., and M. MacCulloch. 1971. *Homosexual Behavior: Therapy and Assessment*. Oxford: Pergamon Press.

Fine, A., and M. Forbes. 1986. Grünbaum on Freud: Three grounds for dissent. *The Behavioral and Brain Sciences* 9:237–238.

Fisher, C., D. Glenwick, and R. Blumenthal. 1986. Subliminal oedipal stimuli and competitive performance: An investigation of between-groups effects and mediating subject variables. *Journal of Abnormal Psychology* 95:292–294.

Fisher, S., and R. Greenberg. 1977. *The Scientific Credibility of Freud's Theories and Therapy*. New York: Basic Books.

Fisher, S., and R. Greenberg. 1985. *The Scientific Credibility of Freud's Theories and Therapy*. New York: Columbia University Press.

Fiske, D. 1983. The meta-analytic revolution in outcome research. *The Journal of Consulting and Clinical Psychology* 51:65–70.

Forster, C., and R. J. Ross. 1976. References for sexual symbols in the genital stage: A replication. *Psychological Reports* 37:1048–1050.

Frank, J. 1983. The placebo is psychotherapy. *The Behavioral and Brain Sciences* 6:291–292.

Freud, S. *S. E. The Standard Edition of the Complete Psychological Works of Sigmund Freud*, 24 vols., translated by J. Strachey. London: Hogarth Press, 1953–1974.

Friedman, S. M. 1950. An empirical study of the Oedipus complex. *American Psychology* 5:304.

References

Friedman, S. M. 1952. An empirical study of the castration and Oedipus complexes. *Genetic Psychology Monographs* 46:61–130.

Fromm, E. 1970. *The Crisis of Psychoanalysis*. Greenwich, Conn.: Fawcett.

Fuller, R. 1986. *Americans and the Unconscious* New York: Oxford University Press.

Gallo, R. 1987. The AIDS virus. *Scientific American* 256:46–55.

Gardner, S. 1993. *Irrationality and the Philosophy of Psychoanalysis*. New York: Cambridge University Press.

Garfield, S., and A. Bergin. 1986. Introduction and historical overview. In *Handbook of Psychotherapy and Behavior Change*, ed. 3, edited by S. Garfield and A. Bergin. New York: Wiley.

Gibbard, A. 1990. *Wise Choices, Apt Feelings: A Theory of Normative Judgement*. Cambridge, Mass.: Harvard University Press.

Glass, G., and R. Kliegl. 1983. An apology for research integration in the study of psychotherapy. *Journal of Consulting and Clinical Psychology* 51:28–41.

Glesser, G., L. Gottschalk, and K. Springer. 1961. An anxiety scale applicable to verbal samples. *Archives of General Psychiatry* 5:593–605.

Glymour, C. 1974. Freud, Kepler and the clinical evidence. In *Freud*, edited by R. Wollheim. New York: Anchor Books.

Glymour, C. 1983. The theory of your dreams. In *Physics, Philosophy and Psychoanalysis: Essays in Honor of Adolf Grünbaum*, edited by R. S. Cohen and L. Laudan. Boston: Reidel.

Goldman-Eisler, F. 1948. Breast-feeding and character formation—I. *Journal of Personality* 17:83–103.

Goldman-Eisler, F. 1950. Breast feeding and character formation—II: The aetiology of the oral character in psychoanalytic theory. *Journal of Personality* 19:189–196.

Goldman-Eisler, F. 1951. The problem of "orality" and its origins in early childhood. *Journal of Mental Science* 97:765–782.

Grauer, D. 1954. Homosexuality in paranoid schizophrenia as revealed by the Rorschach test. *Journal of Consulting Psychology* 18:459–462.

Greenwald, A. 1992. Unconscious cognition reclaimed. *American Psychologist* 47:766–779.

Grünbaum, A. 1980. Epistemological liabilities of the clinical appraisal of psychoanalytic theory. *Nous* 14:307–385.

Grünbaum, A. 1984. *The Foundations of Psychoanalysis: A Philosophical Critique*. Berkeley: University of California Press.

Grünbaum, A. 1986. Author's response. *The Behavioral and Brain Sciences* 9:266–281.

References

Grünbaum, A. 1988. The role of the case-study method in the foundations of psychoanalysis. *Canadian Journal of Philosophy*, 18:623–658; Nagl, L., and H. Vetter (editors), *Die Philosophen und Freud*. Vienna: Oldenbourg.

Grünbaum, A. 1990. "Meaning" connections and causal connections in the human sciences: The poverty of hermeneutic philosophy. *Journal of the American Psychoanalytic Association* 38:559–577.

Grünbaum, A. 1993. *Validation in the Clinical Theory of Psychoanalysis: A Study in the Philosophy of Psychoanalysis*. Madison, Conn.: International Universities Press.

Grünbaum, A. 1994. Freud's permanent revolution: An exchange. *New York Review of Books*, August 11, pp. 54–55.

Haack, S. 1993. *Evidence and Inquiry: Toward Reconstruction in Epistemology*. Oxford: Basil Blackwell

Hall, C. S. 1963. Strangers in dreams: An experimental confirmation of the Oedipus complex. *Journal of Personality* 3:336–345.

Hall, C. S. 1966. A comparison of the dreams of four groups of hospitalized mental patients with each other and with a normal population. *Journal of Nervous and Mental Disease*. 143:135–139.

Hall, C. S., and R. L. Van De Castle. 1963. An empirical investigation of the castration complex in dreams. *Journal of Personality* 33:20–29.

Hammer, E. F. 1953. An investigation of sexual symbolism: A study of HTPs of eugenically sterilized subjects. *Journal of Projective Techniques* 17:401–415.

Harman, G. 1982. Critical review: Richard Brandt: *A Theory of the Good and Right*. *Philosophical Studies* 42:119–139.

Harman, G. 1992. Review of Peter Lipton's *Inference to the Best Explanation*. *Mind* 101:578–580.

Haspel, K., and R. Harris. 1982. Effect of tachistoscopic stimulation to subconscious Oedipal wishes on competitive performance: A failure to replicate. *Journal of Abnormal Psychology* 91:437–444.

Heilbrun, K. 1980. Silverman's subliminal psychodynamic activation: A failure to replicate. *Journal of Abnormal Psychology* 89:560–566.

Heller, J. 1983. *Report on the Shroud of Turin*. Boston: Houghton Mifflin.

Hempel, C. 1966. *Philosophy of Natural Science*. Englewood Cliffs, N.J.: Prentice-Hall.

Hempel, C., and P. Oppenheim. 1948. Studies in the logic of explanation. *Philosophy of Science* 15:135–175.

Hesslow, G. 1976. Two notes on the probabilistic approach to causality. *Philosophy of Science* 43:290–292.

References

Hobson, A. 1988. Psychoanalytic dream theory: A critique based on modern neurophysiology. In *Mind, Psychoanalysis, and Science*, edited by P. Clark and C. Wright. New York: Basil Blackwell.

Holender, D. 1986. Semantic activation without conscious identification in dichotic listening, parafoveal vision, and visual masking: A survey and appraisal. *The Behavioral and Brain Sciences* 9:1–66.

Holmes, D. 1990. The evidence for repression: An examination of sixty years of research. In *Repression and Dissociation: Implications for Personality Theory, Psychopathology, and Health*, edited by J. Singer. Chicago: University of Chicago Press.

Holt, R. 1989. *Freud Reappraised.* New York: Guilford Press.

Hopkins, J. 1988. Epistemology and depth psychology: Critical notes on *The Foundations of Psychoanalysis.* In *Mind, Psychoanalysis and Science*, edited by P. Clark and C. Wright. New York: Basil Blackwell.

Hopkins, J. 1991. The interpretation of dreams. In *The Cambridge Companion to Freud*, edited by Jerome Neu. New York: Cambridge University Press.

Hopkins, J. 1992. Personal correspondence. May 6, 1992.

Hunter, J., and F. Schmidt. 1990. *Methods of Meta-Analysis: Correcting Bias in Research Findings.* London: Sage.

Jahoda, G. 1956. Sex-differences in preferences for shapes—A cross-cultural replication. *British Journal of Psychology* 47:126–132.

Jaspers, K. 1963. *General Psychopathology.* Chicago: University of Chicago Press.

Jensen, J., and A. Bergin. 1988. Mental health values of professional therapists: A national interdisciplinary survey. *Professional Psychology Research and Practice* 19:290–297.

Jerslid, A. 1931. Memory for the pleasant as compared with the unpleasant. *Journal of Experimental Psychology* 14:284–288.

Karacan, I., D. Goodenough, A. Shapiro, and S. Starker. 1966. Erection cycle during sleep in relation to dream anxiety. *Archives of General Psychiatry* 15:183–189.

Kazdin, A. 1980. *Research Design in Clinical Psychology.* New York: Harper & Row.

Kazdin, A. 1981. Drawing valid inferences form case studies. *Journal of Consulting and Clinical Psychology* 49:183–192.

Kazdin, A. 1986. The evaluation of psychotherapy: Research design and methodology. In *Handbook of Psychotherapy and Behavior Change*, ed. 3, edited by S. Garfield and A. Bergin. New York: Wiley.

Kettner, M. 1991. Peirce's notion of abduction and psychoanalytic interpretation. In *Semiotic Perspectives on Clinical Theory and Practice*, edited by Bonnie Litowitz and Phillip Epstein. New York: Mouton de Gruyter.

References

Kihlstrom, J., T. Barnhardt, and D. Tataryn. 1992. The psychological unconscious: Found, lost, and regained. *American Psychologist* 47:788–791.

Kitcher, P. 1992. *Freud's Dream: A Complete Interdisciplinary Science of Mind*. Cambridge, Mass.: MIT Press.

Klaf, F., and C. Davis. 1960. Homosexuality and paranoid schizophrenia: A survey of 150 cases and controls. *American Journal of Psychiatry* 116:1070–1075.

Klein, G. S. 1976. *Psychoanalytic Theory*. New York: International Universities Press.

Klerman, G., M. Weissman, B. Rounsaville, and E. Chevron. 1984. *Interpersonal Psychotherapy of Depression*. New York: Basic Books.

Kline, P. 1969. The anal character: A cross-cultural study in Ghana. *British Journal of Social and Clinical Psychology* 8:201–210.

Kline, P. [1972] 1981. *Fact and Fantasy in Freudian Theory*, ed. 2. New York: Methuen.

Kline, P. 1978. The status of the anal character: A methodological and empirical reply to Hill. *British Journal of Medical Psychology* 51:87–90.

Kline, P. 1979. Psychosexual personality traits, fixation and neuroticism. *British Journal of Medical Psychology* 52:393–395.

Kline, P. 1986. Kline replies to Erwin. In *Hans Eysenck: Consensus and Controversy*, edited by S. Modgil and C. Modgil. London: Falmer Press.

Kline, P. 1987 The scientific status of the DMT. *British Journal of Medical Psychology* 60:53–59.

Kline, P. 1988. Freudian theory and experimental evidence: A reply to Erwin. In *Mind, Psychoanalysis and Science*, edited by P. Clark and C. Wright. New York: Basil Blackwell.

Kline, P., and R. Storey. 1977. A factor-analytic study of the oral character. *British Journal of Social and Clinical Psychology* 16:317–328.

Kline, P., and R. Storey. 1980. The aetiology of the oral character. *Journal of Genetic Psychology* 136:85–94.

Koss, M., and J. Butcher. 1986. Research on brief psychotherapy. In *Handbook of Psychotherapy and Behavior Change*, edited by S. Garfield and A. Bergin. New York: Wiley.

Kragh, U. 1955. *The Actual Genetic Model of Perception Personality*. Lund, Sweden: Gleerup.

Kragh, U. 1960. The defense mechanism test: A new method for diagnosis and personnel selection. *Journal of Applied Psychology* 44:303–309.

Kragh, U., and G. Smith. 1970. *Percept-Genetic Analysis*. Lund, Sweden: Gleerup.

References

Krasner, L. 1958. A technique for investigating the relationship between the behavior cues of the examiner and the verbal behavior of the patient. *Journal of Consulting Psychology* 22:364–366.

Krieger, M., and P. Worchel. 1959. A quantitative study of the psychoanalytic hypotheses of identification. *Psychological Reports* 5:448.

Kuhn, T. 1977. *The Structure of Scientific Revolutions*. Chicago: University of Chicago Press.

Lambert, M., D. Shapiro, and A. Bergin. 1986. The effectiveness of psychotherapy. In *Handbook of Psychotherapy and Behavior Change,* edited by S. Garfield and A. Bergin. New York: Wiley.

Landman, J., and R. Dawes. 1982. Psychotherapy outcome: Smith and Glass conclusions stand up under scrutiny. *American Psychologist* 37:504–516.

Laplanche, J., and J. Pontalis. 1973. *The Language of Psycho-Analysis*. New York: Norton.

Larder, B., G. Darby, and D. Richman. 1989. HIV with reduced sensitivity to ziovudine (AZT) isolated during prolonged therapy. *Science* 243:1731–1734.

Leckie, E., and R. Withers. 1967. A test of liability to depressive illness. *British Journal of Medical Psychology* 40:273.

Lee, S. G. 1958. Social influences in Zulu dreaming. *Journal of Social Psychology.* 47:265–283.

Levinger, G., and J. Clark. 1961. Emotional factors in the forgetting of word associations. *Journal of Abnormal and Social Psychology* 62:99–105.

Levy, D. 1988. Grünbaum's Freud. *Inquiry* 31:193–215.

Levy, D. M. 1928. Finger-sucking and accessory movements in early infancy (an etiological study). *American Journal of Psychiatry* 7:881–918.

Levy, D. M. 1934. Experiments on the sucking reflex and social behaviour in dogs. *American Journal of Orthopsychiatry* 4:203–224.

Levy, G. A. 1954. Sexual symbolism: A validity study. *Journal of Consulting Psychology* 18:43–46.

Lipton, P. 1991. *Inference to the Best Explanation*. London: Routledge.

Lovaas, I., and J. Simmons. 1974. Building social behavior in autistic children by use of electric shock. In *Perspectives in Behavior Modification with Deviant Children,* edited by O. Lovaas and B. Bucher. Englewood Cliffs, N.J.: Prentice-Hall.

Luborsky, L., L. Diguer, E. Luborsky, B. Singer, D. Dickter, and K. Schmidt. 1993. The efficacy of dynamic psychotherapies—Is it true that "everyone has won and all must have prizes?" In *Dynamic Psychotherapy Research: A Handbook for Clinical Practice,* edited by N. Miller, L. Lurborsky, J. Barber, and J. Docherty. New York: Basic Books.

References

Luborsky, L., J. Mellon, P. van Ravenswaay, A. Childress, K. Cohen, A. Hole, S. Ming, P. Crits-Christoph, F. Levine, and K. Alexander. 1985. A verification of Freud's grandest clinical hypothesis: The transference. *Clinical Psychology Review* 5:231–246.

Luborsky, L., and J. Mintz. 1974. What sets off momentary forgetting during a psychoanalysis? *Psychoanalysis and Contemporary Science* 3:233–268.

Luborsky, L., B. Singer, and L. Luborsky. 1975. Comparative studies of psychotherapy: Is it true that "everyone has won and all must have prizes?" *Archives of General Psychiatry* 32:995–1008.

Lycan, W. 1988. *Judgment and Justification*. New York: Cambridge University Press.

Macmillan, M. 1991. *Freud Evaluated: The Completed Arc*. New York: North Holland.

Malan, D. 1976. *Toward the Validation of Dynamic Psychotherapy: A Replication*. New York: Plenum.

Manosevitiz, D., and R. Lanyon. 1965. Fear survey schedule: A normative study. *Psychological Reports* 17:699–703.

Marcel, A. 1978. Unconscious reading: Experiments on people who do not know they are reading. *Visible Language* 12:393–404.

Marcel, A. 1980. Conscious and preconscious recognition of polysemous words: Locating the selective effect of prior verbal context. In *Attention and Performance*, vol. 8, edited by R. Nickerson. Hillsdale, N.J.: Lawrence Erlbaum.

Marcel, A. 1983. Conscious and unconscious perception: Experiments on visual masking and word recognition. *Cognitive Psychology* 15:197–237.

Marcus, S. 1984. *Freud and the Culture of Psychoanalysis*. Boston: G. Allen & Unwin.

Marmor, J. 1970. Limitations of free association. *Archives of General Psychiatry* 22:160–165.

Masson, J. M. 1984. *The Assault on Truth: Freud's Suppression of the Seduction Theory*. New York: Farrar, Straus & Giroux.

Maxwell, G. 1962. The ontological status of theoretical entities. In *Minnesota Studies in the Philosophy of Science*, Vol. 3, edited by H. Feigel and G. Maxwell. Minneapolis: University of Minnesota Press.

Mays, D., and C. Franks (editors). 1985. *Negative Outcome in Psychotherapy and What to Do About It*. New York: Springer.

McElroy, W. A. 1954. Methods of testing the Oedipus complex hypothesis. *Quarterly Bulletin of the British Psychological Association.* 1:364–365.

McLean, P., and A. Hakstian. 1979. Clinical depression: Comparative efficacy of outpatient treatments. *Journal of Consulting and Clinical Psychology* 47:818–836.

Medawar, P. B. 1975. Review of I. S. Cooper, *The Victim Is Always the Same. New York Review of Books*, January 23, p. 17.

References

Meehl, P. 1983. Subjectivity in psychoanalytic inference: The nagging persistence of Wilhelm Fliess's Achensee question. In *Testing Scientific Theories. Minnesota Studies in the Philosophy of Science*, vol. 10, edited by J. Earman. Minneapolis: University of Minnesota Press.

Meichenbaum, D. 1977. *Cognitive-Behavior Modification: An Integrative Approach.* New York: Plenum.

Meissner, W. 1958. Affective response to psychoanalytic death symbols. *Journal of Abnormal Social Psychology* 56:295–299.

Meketon, B., R. Griffith, V. Taylor, and J. Wiedman. 1962. Rorschach homosexual signs in paranoid schizophrenics. *Journal of Abnormal and Social Psychology* 56:295–299.

Meltzer, H. 1931. Sex differences in forgetting pleasant and unpleasant experiences. *Journal of Abnormal Psychology* 25:450–464.

Menzies, R. 1936. The comparative memory value of pleasant, unpleasant, and indifferent experiences. *Journal of Experimental Psychology* 18:267–279.

Merikle, P. 1992. Perception without awareness: Critical issues. *American Psychologist* 47:792–795.

Mill, J. S. [1843] 1973. *A System of Logic.* In *Collected Works of John Stuart Mill*, edited by J. M. Robson. Toronto: University of Toronto Press.

Miller, J. 1973. The effects of aggressive stimulation upon adults who have experienced the death of a parent during childhood and adolescence, unpublished doctoral dissertation. New York University, New York.

Moore, R., and M. Selzer. 1963. Male homosexuality, paranoia and the schizophrenias. *American Journal of Psychiatry* 119:743–747.

Moos, R., and P. Mussen. 1959. Sexual symbolism, personality integration and intellectual functioning. *Journal of Consulting Psychology* 23:521–523.

Nagel, E. 1958. Methodological issues in psychoanalytic theory. In *Psychoanalysis, Scientific Method and Philosophy*, edited by S. Hook. New York: Grove Press.

Nagel, T. 1994a. Freud's permanent revolution. *New York Review of Books,* May 12, pp. 34–38.

Nagel, T. 1994b. Freud's Permanent Revolution: An exchange. *New York Review of Books,* August 11, pp. 55–56.

Nisbett, R., and L. Ross. 1980. *Human Inference: Strategies and Shortcomings of Social Judgment.* Englewood Cliffs, N.J.: Prentice Hall.

Nussbaum, C. 1991. Habermas and Grünbaum on the logic of psychoanalytic explanations. *Philosophy and Social Criticism* 17:193–216.

O'Connor, J., G. Daniels, A. Karush, L. Moses, C. Flood, and L. Stern. 1964. The effects of psychotherapy on the course of ulcerative colitis: A preliminary report. *American Journal of Psychiatry* 20:738–742.

References

Oliver, J., and R. Burkham. 1982. Subliminal psychodynamic activation in depression: A failure to replicate. *Journal of Abnormal Psychology* 9:337–342.

Orgel, S. 1958. Effect of psychoanalysis on the course of peptic ulcer. *Psychosomatic Medicine* 20:117–123.

Orne, M. 1970. Hypnosis, motivation, and the ecological validity of the psychological experiment. In *Nebraska Symposium on Motivation*, Vol. 18, edited by W. Arnold and M. Page. Lincoln: University of Nebraska Press.

Palmatier, J., and P. Bornstein. 1980. Effects of subliminal stimulation of symbiotic merging fantasies on behavioral treatment of smokers. *Journal of Nervous and Mental Disease* 168:715–720.

Paul, G. 1985. Can pregnancy be a placebo effect?: Terminology, designs and conclusions in the study of psychosocial and pharmacological treatments of behavioral disorders. In *Placebo: Theory, Research and Mechanisms*, edited by L. White, B. Tursky, and G. Schwartz. New York: Guilford Press.

Porte, H. 1988. The analogy of symptoms and dreams: Is Freud's dream theory an impostor. In *Mind, Psychoanalysis and Science*, edited by P. Clark and C. Wright. New York: Basil Blackwell.

Porterfield, A., and S. Golding. 1985. A failure to find an effect of subliminal psychodynamic activation upon cognitive measures of pathology in schizophrenia. *Journal of Abnormal Psychology* 94:630–639.

Postman, L. 1953. On the problem of perceptual defense. *Psychological Review* 60:298–306.

Postman, L., W. Bronson, and G. Gropper. 1953. Is there a mechanism of perceptual defense? *The Journal of Abnormal and Social Psychology* 48:215–224.

Prioleau, L., M. Murdock, and N. Brody. 1983. An analysis of psychotherapy versus placebo studies. *The Behavioral and Brain Sciences* 6:275–310.

Rachman, S., and G. T. Wilson. 1980. *The Effects of Psychological Therapy.* New York: Pergamon Press.

Radnitzky, G. 1985. Psychoanalysis as research, therapy, and theory. *Annals of Theoretical Psychology* 3:201–211.

Rhoads, J., and B. Feather. 1974. Application of psychodynamics to behavior therapy. *American Journal of Psychiatry* 131:17–20.

Richardson, R. 1990. The "tally argument" and the validation of psychoanalysis. *Philosophy of Science* 57:668–676.

Ricoeur, P. 1970. *Freud and Philosophy.* New Haven, Conn.: Yale University Press.

Robinson, P. *Freud and His Critics.* 1993. Berkeley: University of California Press.

Rogers, C., and B. F. Skinner. 1956. Some issues concerning the control of human behavior: A Symposium. *Science* 124:1057–1065.

References

Rosenthal, R. 1990. An evaluation of procedures and results. In *The Future of Meta-Analysis*, edited by K. Wachter and M. Straf. New York: Russell Sage Foundation.

Rutstein, E., and L. Goldberger. 1973. The effects of aggressive stimulation on suicidal patients: An experimental study of the psychoanalytic theory of suicide. In *Psychoanalysis and Contemporary Science*, Vol. 2, edited by B. Rubenstein. New York: Macmillan

Ryle, A., 1982. *Psychotherapy: A Cognitive Integration of Theory and Practice.* London: Academic Press.

Sachs, D. 1989. In fairness to Freud: A critical notice of the foundations of psychoanalysis, by Adolf Grünbaum. *The Philosophical Review* 98:349–378.

Salmon, W. 1984. *Scientific Explanation and the Causal Structure of the World.* Princeton, N.J.: Princeton University Press.

Salmon, W. 1989. *Four Decades of Scientific Explanation.* Minneapolis: University of Minnesota Press.

Salzinger, K., and S. Pisoni. 1958. Reinforcement of affect responses of schizophrenics during the clinical interview. *Journal of Abnormal and Social Psychology* 57:84–90.

Salzinger, K., and S. Pisoni. 1961. Some parameters of the conditioning of verbal affect responses in schizophrenic subjects. *Journal of Abnormal and Social Psychology* 63:511–516.

Sarnoff, I., and S. M. Corwin. 1959. Castration anxiety and the fear of death. *Journal of Personality* 27:374–385.

Schjelderup, H. 1955. Lasting effects of psychoanalytic treatment. *Psychiatry* 18:103–133.

Schmidt, F. 1992. What do data really mean? Research findings, meta-analysis, and cumulative knowledge in psychology. *American Psychologist* 47:1173–1181.

Schwartz, B. J. 1956. An empirical test of two Freudian hypotheses concerning castration anxiety. *Journal of Personality* 24:318–327.

Scodel, A. 1957. Heterosexual somatic preference and fantasy dependence. *Journal of Consulting Psychology* 21:371–374.

Searle, J. 1990. Author's response. *The Behavioral and Brain Sciences* 13:4:632–642.

Searle, J. 1992. *The Rediscovery of the Mind.* Cambridge, Mass.: MIT Press.

Sears, R. R., and G. W. Wise. 1950. Relation of cup-feeding in infancy to thumbsucking and the oral drive. *American Journal of Orthopsychiatry* 20:123–138.

Sharma, V. P. 1977. *Application of a Percept-Genetic Test in a Clinical Setting.* Lund, Sweden: University of Lund.

Siegel, H. 1988. *Relativism Refuted: A Critique of Contemporary Epistemological Relativism.* Boston: Reidel.

References

Silverman, L. 1976. Psychoanalytic theory: "The reports of my death are greatly exaggerated." *American Psychology* 31:621–637.

Silverman, L. 1982. A comment on two subliminal psychodynamic activation studies. *Journal of Abnormal Psychology* 91:126–130.

Silverman, L. 1985a. Comments on three recent subliminal psychodynamic activation experiments. *Journal of Abnormal Psychology* 94:640–643.

Silverman, L. 1985b. Rejoinder to Oliver and Burkham and to Porterfield. *Journal of Abnormal Psychology* 94:647–648.

Silverman, L., S. Frank, and P. Dachinger. 1974. Psychoanalytic reinterpretation of the effectiveness of systematic desensitization: Experimental data bearing on the role of merging fantasies. *Journal of Abnormal Psychology* 83:313–318.

Silverman, L., H. Klinger, L. Lustbader, J. Farrell, and A. Martin. 1972. The effect of subliminal drive stimulation on the speech of stutterers. *Journal of Nervous and Mental Disease* 155:14–21.

Silverman, L., J. Kwawer, C. Wolitzky, and M. Coron. 1973. An experimental study of aspects of the psychoanalytic theory of male homosexuality. *Journal of Abnormality.* 82:178–188.

Silverman, L., D. Ross, J, Adler, and D. Lustig. 1978. Simple research paradigm for demonstrating psychodynamic activation: Effects of Oedipal stimuli on dart-throwing accuracy in college males. *Journal of Abnormal Psychology* 87:341–357.

Silverman, L., and J. Weinberger. 1985. Mommy and I are one: Implications for psychotherapy. *American Psychologist* 40:1296–1308.

Sloane, R., F. Staples, A. Cristol, N. Yorkston, and K. Whipple. 1975. *Psychotherapy versus Behavior Therapy.* Cambridge, Mass.: Harvard University Press.

Smith, M., and G. Glass. 1977. Meta-analysis of psychotherapy outcome studies. *American Psychologist* 32:752–760.

Smith, M., G. Glass, and T. Miller. 1980. *The Benefits of Psychotherapy.* Baltimore: Johns Hopkins University Press.

Snyder, S. 1975. *Madness and the Brain.* New York: McGraw-Hill.

Sober, E. 1990. Let's razor Ockham's razor. *Philosophy* 27:73–93.

Stagner, R. 1931. The reintegration of pleasant and unpleasant experiences. *American Journal of Psychology* 43:463–468.

Stalker, D., and C. Glymour (editors). 1985. *Examining Holistic Medicine.* Buffalo, N.Y.: Prometheus.

Stephens, W. N. 1961. A cross-cultural study of menstrual taboos. *Genetic Psychology Monographs* 64:385–416.

References

Strean, H. 1984. The patient who would not tell his name. *Psychoanalytic Quarterly.* 53:410–420.

Suppes, P. 1970. *A Probalistic Theory of Causality.* Amsterdam: North Holland.

Svartberg, M., and T. Stiles. 1991. Comparative effects of short-term psychodynamic psychotherapy: A meta-analysis. *Journal of Consulting and Clinical Psychology.* 59:704–714.

Taylor, C. 1979. Interpretation and the sciences of man. In *Interpretive Social Science: A Reader,* edited by P. Rabinow and W. Sullivan. Berkeley: University of California Press.

Taylor, C. 1985. Peaceful coexistence in psychology. In Charles Taylor, *Philosophical Papers, I.* New York: Cambridge University Press.

Tjeltveit, A. 1986. The ethics of value conversion in psychotherapy: Appropriate and inappropriate therapist influence on client values. *Clinical Psychology Review* 6:515–537.

Ullmann, L., and Krasner, L. 1969. *Psychological Approach to Abnormal Behavior.* Englewood Cliffs, N.J.: Prentice-Hall.

Varga, M. 1973. An experimental study of aspects of the psychoanalytic study of elation, unpublished doctoral dissertation, New York University, New York.

Van Fraassen, B. 1980. *The Scientific Image.* Oxford: Oxford University Press.

Van Fraassen, B. 1989. *Laws and Symmetry.* Oxford: Oxford University Press.

Von Wright, G. H. 1971. *Explanation and Understanding.* Ithaca, N.Y.: Cornell University Press.

Wallenstein, R. 1986. Psychoanalysis as a science: A response to the new challenges. *Psychoanalytic Quarterly* 55:414–451.

Watson, C. 1965. A test of the relationship between repressed homosexuality and paranoid mechanisms. *Journal Clinical Psychology* 21:380–384.

Weinberger, J., and L. Silverman. 1987. Subliminal psychodynamic activation: A method for studying psychoanalytic dynamic propositions. In *Perspectives in Personality: Theory, Measurement and Interpersonal Dynamics,* Vol. 2, edited by R. Hogan and W. Jones. Greenwich, Conn.: Jai Press.

Weiss, J., H. Sampson, and the Mount Zion Psychotherapy Research Group. 1986. *The Psychoanalytic Process: Theory, Clinical Observations and Empirical Research.* New York: Guilford Press.

Weiss, L. 1972. Perceived effectiveness of psychotherapy: A Function of suggestion? *Journal of Consulting and Clinical Psychology* 39:156–159.

Westerlundh, B. 1976. *Aggression, Anxiety and Defence.* Lund, Sweden: Gleerups.

References

White, R. 1956. *The Abnormal Personality.* New York: Ronald Press.

Whiting, J. W. M., and I. L. Child. 1953. *Child Training and Personality.* New Haven, Conn.: Yale University Press.

Wilkes, K. 1990. Analyzing Freud. *Philosophical Quarterly* 40:241–254.

Wilson, G. T. 1985. Limitations of meta-analysis in the evaluation of psychological therapy. *Clinical Psychology Review* 5:35–47.

Wollheim, R. 1993. *The Mind and Its Depths.* Cambridge, Mass.: Harvard University Press.

Wolowitz, H. 1965. Attraction and aversion to power: A psychoanalytic conflict theory of homosexuality in male paranoids. *Journal of Abnormal Psychology* 70:360–370.

Wolpe, J. 1977. Inadequate behavior analysis: The Achilles heel of outcome research in behavior therapy. *Journal of Behavior Therapy and Experimental Psychiatry* 8:1–3.

Woolfolk, R. 1992. Hermeneutics, social constructionism and other items of intellectual fashion: Intimations for clinical science. *Behavior Therapy* 23:213–224.

Yarrow, L.J. 1954. The relationship between nutritive sucking experiences in infancy and non-nutritive sucking in childhood. *Journal of Genetic Psychology* 84:149–162.

Zamansky, H. 1958. An investigation of the psychoanalytic theory of paranoid delusions. *Journal of Personality* 26:410–425.

Zeichner, A. 1955. Psychosexual identification in paranoid schizophrenia. *Journal of Projective Techniques* 19:67–77.

Name Index

317

Name Index

Subject Index

.